FIRST WORLD WAR – STILL NO END IN SIGHT

First World War – Still No End in Sight

Frank Furedi

B L O O M S B U R Y
LONDON • NEW DELHI • NEW YORK • SYDNEY

First published in Great Britain 2014

Copyright © Frank Furedi, 2014

The moral right of the author has been asserted

A Continuum book

Bloomsbury Publishing Plc
50 Bedford Square
London WC1B 3DP

ISBN 978 1 4411 251 01

10 9 8 7 6 5 4 3 2 1

Typeset by Fakenham Prepress Solutions, Fakenham, Norfolk NR21 8NN

Printed and bound in Great Britain by CPI Group (UK) Ltd, Croydon CR0 4YY

www.bloomsbury.com

Contents

Preface

Writing about the First World War often turns into a search for beginnings. Something occurred in 1914 that makes it very challenging to grasp the century to come. This difficulty does not simply pertain to understanding what led up to the war or what were its causes, but also to the broader existential issues confronting European and, to a lesser extent, American society. Now and again great literature helps us to make an imaginative leap into that fast-vanishing world of Kings, Emperors, Tsars, pioneering trade unionists and complacent Edwardian middle classes.

Joseph Roth's *Radzetzky March* takes us on a journey that begins from the secure world of Emperor Franz Joseph and moves on to the terrain that will soon see the collapse of the Austro-Hungarian Empire. The book conveys an atmosphere where an irresistible force ruptures people's links with the security of their taken-for-granted assumptions. The main characters in Roth's novel, the Trotta family, are 'homesick' for the old Kaiser. For reasons that are not entirely clear, they have lost their place in the world and are existentially homeless. Soon they, along with hundreds of thousands of other homeless minds, will find themselves lurching towards the battlefields of the Great War. For some this war served as a distraction, for a minority it offered the promise of a home, others regarded it as an opportunity to fight for a just cause. Surprisingly there were very few cynics who questioned the call to arms and even less who actively opposed it.

The First World War disappointed all who looked for answers in the battle-fields of Europe. Instead of providing answers, it also threw up problems that continue to serve as a source of conflict – military, ideological, cultural – to the present time. *First World War – Still no End in Sight* attempts to explore the changing ideological and cultural forms through which the issues raised during the Great War have continue to haunt public life. It concludes that the unresolved tensions within society during the 1914–18 era have undergone a series of mutations and are expressed through the Culture Wars of the twenty-first century.

There were many ideological casualties along the road that led from the heady summer of 1914 to the present day. Indeed, as this historical sociology of the battle for ideas explains, there are very few ideologies left standing. And though the ideal of democracy just about survived, it is in serious need of intellectual attention. This book is written in the hope that this ideal can be cultivated and given greater moral depth so that the century-long war can finally come to an end.

I never met my Grandfather, who unwillingly served in the Hungarian army on the Italian front and who was delighted when illness led to his early return to civilian life in early 1916. He must have known that this war never ended when he was taken away in 1944 and forced into a slave-labour battalion. When he froze to death somewhere near the Hungarian-Ukrainian border the Second World War was about to come to its final phase of armed conflict. But the war of ideas continued and especially those of us with strong cultural connections to the eastern part of Europe never quite believe that what began in 1914 will ever be over. Of course it will as long as there are those who are willing to step up to affirm and develop the legacy of humanism and the Enlightenment.

Faversham
15 August 2013

Introduction: The war without end

This book is about a war that is still going on. The cause of World War One still remains a topic of controversy. Disputes about the source of this conflict are not confined to pointing the finger of blame at a particular party such as the Prussian military caste or French generals seeking revenge for the humiliation suffered in the war of 1870 and the loss of Alsace-Lorraine to Bismarck. Disputes also centre on the role of other factors such as the arms race, nationalism, imperialism or domestic social pressures. No doubt all these forces had a significant influence on the unfolding series of events that to led this most unexpected and unusual war. One unique feature of this conflict was the widespread enthusiasm with which the public greeted its outbreak. That so many ordinary Europeans identified with their nation's war drive was shaped by the *zeitgeist* of the time. European societies were permeated by the vague sensibility of a life bereft of direction and purpose. A longing for meaning by millions of people estranged from the world they inhabited led many to regard the war as a medium through which their life could be affirmed. The cause they embraced was that of a 'way of life', which is why German propaganda referred to it as a 'war of cultures'.

Writing about meaning is a tricky if not a dangerous enterprise. Since the search for it appears to possess a general and eternal quality, there is a risk that its exploration collapses into a banal discussion about the human condition in isolation from the influences through which it is experienced. But something was in the air on the day in June 1914 when Archduke Franz Ferdinand was assassinated in Sarajevo. The cultural and emotional climate was one that was hospitable to a display of fervent passion. The historian A. J. P. Taylor wrote how even 'the traditional standards of art and culture were being broken down, as if artists unconsciously anticipated the destruction of the Great War'. He observed that 'men's nerves were on edge'.[1]

Throughout Europe the language of public life had become steadily more intemperate and displays of a loss of conventional restraint more common. In England, domestic tensions had, by the summer of 1914, led some political figures to endorse violence as a legitimate instrument for resolving political problems. Responding to the unsettled domestic scene confronting him,

Winston Churchill asserted that 'bloodshed no doubt is lamentable' but 'there are worse things than bloodshed, even on an extensive scale'.[2] In the twenty-first century such a casual attitude towards death, especially 'on an extensive scale', appears almost incomprehensible, but a century ago many regarded war as a legitimate means for resolving domestic tensions. One study of the cultural climate of those times observed that the language used by Churchill and others 'suggests that the antagonists had reached the point at which they desired battle almost for the sake of the battle, as a release of feelings that could find no resolution'.[3]

The relationship between the outbreak of the Great War and the existential conflict experienced by Western society was mediated through the dissonance of culture and the sensibility that there ought to be a way of life to defend and uphold. At the time this sensibility was often expressed through the idiom of nationalism. But as one commentator on the background of the Great War explained, 'nationalism had penetrated all spheres of human pursuits'. It blended in with other diffuse currents of sentiment that idealized a way of life. It provided the frame through which the aspiration for affirming an exclusive way of life could be experienced with psychological depth.[4]

There is a large corpus of literature that dwells on the role of nationalism prior, during and after the Great War. However what's often overlooked was that insofar as nationalism played a significant role, it was as the medium through which a cultural solution to the search for meaning could gain definition. In his fascinating study *The Anti-Enlightenment Tradition*, Zeev Sternheel argues that intellectual and cultural reaction against the Enlightenment led to 'some form of nationalism'.[5] But nationalism was not the only medium through which the rejection of rationalism, materialism or of liberal democracy could be expressed and, as we shall see, the cultural revolt against modernity and capitalism has assumed a variety of different forms during the past century. Today, hostility to materialism or consumer culture or rationalism is stridently communicated by post-modernist intellectuals, consumer rights campaigners, anti-capitalists, environmentalists or conservative activists. That these disparate groups, with little in common, voiced similar sentiments indicates that the anti-modernist sentiments can come in different shapes and sizes.

The emphasis that is frequently attached to the role of nationalism is influenced by a retrospective, after-the-event imagination that is dominated by its destructive role in the decades following the Great War. At the time, the intensity of popular support for the war caught even governments by surprise.

That it also captured the imagination of the most unlikely group of people – the intellectuals – was also unexpected.

Battle of ideas

There are several interrelated questions that motivate the writing of this book. They all pertain to a remarkable development, which is that so many of the political and philosophical ideas that used to inspire advocates of capitalism as well its bitter opponents have appeared to lose salience in the twenty-first century. Since the onset of the global recession, arguments supporting capitalism and the free markets have lost much of their force. But the erosion of the intellectual influence of market economics has not been paralleled by the ascendancy of alternative models. The question of 'why there is an absence of alternatives' immediately raises supplementary queries about what happened to the principles and ideals associated with socialism, welfare-statism, communism or even old-fashioned Keynesianism.

Nor is the loss of intellectual or cultural influence of fundamental principles associated with modernity confined to the domain of politics and economics. The philosophical and cultural assumptions of the Enlightenment – the idea of progress, rationality, human autonomy – enjoy far less valuation than a century ago. In intellectual circles the Enlightenment has been dubbed as a misguided 'project' and its allegedly 'naïve assumptions' are frequently treated with derision.

This study began as an exploration of three crucial events that continue to shape the way we think about the world. These are the Second World War, the Cold War and the Culture Wars. It was hoped that through focusing on these historical episodes it would be possible to develop an argument that I had raised in an embryonic form in my previous work. To put the argument in its baldest form, it seems that each of these wars had a significant impact on the fate of the key movements of modern times. The Second World War fatally undermined the intellectual and political credibility of the Right. In turn, the Cold War fundamentally discredited many of the ideas and practices associated with the Left. Finally, the Culture Wars fought out in the last quarter of the twentieth century weakened the key ideas associated with modernity and thereby called into question most forms of prevailing authority.

In the course of exploring the political battlefields on which these three wars were fought it became evident that, though significant in their own right, they constituted key moments in a drama that actually began in 1914. There are those who would take the origins of this drama back into the nineteenth century. Some have gone back as far as Luther or German reunification as the beginning of the beginning.[6] Others locate the origins of the rise of fascism and Nazism in the nineteenth century in irrationalist reaction to the Enlightenment.[7] There are no doubt a variety of ways of conceptualizing historical continuities. But from the standpoint of today, what's interesting about World War One is that it represents a key moment of transition between the old and the new. That is why it seems as if the real historical twentieth century began after the end of World War One.[8]

When the Great War began, the political categories of Left and Right had far less significance than they would have in the decades to come. Although European societies had experienced significant social upheavals and social democracy and the labour movement had emerged as a major force in the late nineteenth century, the politicization of the masses and their ideological affiliations were still at a stage of emergence. At its outbreak, attitudes towards the war were not polarized along now-familiar ideological lines. With the exception of small groups of pacifists and internationalist socialists, most political movements supported their government's call to arms – albeit with different degree of enthusiasm. Some of the most enthusiastic supporters of the war were motivated by a cultural disposition to react against what they took to be the meaningless or soulless world of capitalist modernity. During the war anti-modernist militants reacted against the growth of social tensions and class conflict and expressed themselves through a synthesis of nationalist and anti-democratic ideology. Others moved in the opposite direction and their rejection of capitalist society gained clarity through the ideologies of the Left.

As we shall see, although the ideologies that crystallized during the course of World War One seemed to acquire a life of their own and shape the conflicts of the twentieth century, they were never entirely autonomous from the cultural tensions that provided the initial impetus for the revolt against the old order. Today, a century later, the old ideologies are conspicuously feeble but cultural conflicts over norms, values, identities, lifestyles are flourishing. The aim of the chapters to follow is to explore the question of why some of the conflicts that influenced the cultural sensibility of 1914 continue to challenge twenty-first-century society.

The spirit of the age

Stefan Zweig, the world-renowned Austrian novelist and playwright and well-known pacifist, lived to see two world wars. When the Great War broke out in 1914, he – along with almost all European intellectuals – supported his nation's war effort. Later, with a hint of embarrassment, he recalled the sense of excitement and celebration that the news of the impending conflict provoked amongst people. 'And to be truthful, I must acknowledge that there was a majestic, rapturous, and even seductive something in this first outbreak of the people from which one could escape only with difficulty', he recalled.[9] The mood of excitement that swept Zweig off his feet was fuelled by the powerful impulse to forge a sense of belonging in a world where growing numbers of people, especially the young, had become estranged from their community. Capitalist society succeeded in rationalizing everyday life to the point that the domain of values seemed to be dominated by economic calculation alone. Finding a language for expressing the human spirit preoccupied the thought of groups of increasingly influential artists and intellectuals. Not all were touched by this mood of estrangement, but it was widely noted that material security coexisted with spiritual and moral confusion. This dissonance between material and moral encouraged a cultural reaction against the rationalizing imperative of modernity, particularly among the youth. To many young people it seemed as if bourgeois society 'had lost its spirit'.[10]

Capitalist society was relatively successful in offering a measure of economic security to a substantial section of society but could do little to provide people with purpose. Robert Musil's great novel *The Man Without Qualities* captured the tension between the façade of bourgeois convention and its aimless inner and moral life. Set in Vienna on the eve of the Great War, it captures the spirit of an age that deprives people of the capacity to endow their experience with purpose or direction. In this moment of moral confusion the drive towards war provided many estranged individuals with the promise that there was something more to life than the banality of their apparently pointless existence. The American political theorist Francis Fukuyama reminds us that, back in 1914, 'many European publics simply wanted war because they were fed up with the dullness and lack of community in civilian life'.[11] At least in part, the unexpected popular enthusiasm for the war can be interpreted as a 'rebellion' against what was experienced as the stultifying and alienating conventions of middle-class Europe.[12] Though such revolts would recur after the devastating experience of the Great War – for example, that of the 1960s counter-culture – they would cease to assume such an explicit militaristic form.

In the end Zweig succeeded in breaking away from the militaristic culture that dominated his own nation as well as the rest of Europe. His pacifist convictions and self-conscious anti-nationalist identification with Europe would go against the grain of political developments in the decades to come. By the time the Second World War broke out, Zweig must have felt that the world that he had known and loved before 1914 was lost. Forced out of Europe by the threat of Nazi power, he ended up as an immigrant in Brazil, where he and his wife took their own lives on 22 February 1942. His suicide note was not simply a statement about himself but about a world that had vanished. He wrote of the disappearance of the 'world of my own language' and of 'my spiritual home'. He indicated that there may well be a 'dawn after the long night' but he was too 'impatient' to carry on with life.[13] His premonition that a very long night lay ahead intimately meshed with his belief that the Great War had shattered once and for all the pre-existing 'Golden Age of Security'.

The Golden Age of Security referred to the more than four decades of prosperous peace in pre-1914 Europe. During the years leading up to the Great War, the Golden Age of Security had become the target of criticism by young people and intellectuals disenchanted by its spiritual emptiness. However, by the outbreak of the Second World War many would look upon these decades wistfully as an 'age of innocence' and they served as a focus for nostalgia.

In his disturbing Foreword to his remarkable novel *The Magic Mountain*, the German author Thomas Mann characterizes the outbreak of the Great War as a seminal moment 'with whose beginning so many things began, whose beginnings, it seems have not yet ceased'.[14] The beginnings that Mann intuited also marked the ending of a world that the cultural historian Modris Eksteins has reluctantly characterized as one dominated by a bourgeois outlook.[15] More specifically, the values, norms, certainties or taken-for-granted assumptions through which the cultural and political elites understood their place in the world appeared to lose its vitality and meaning. The experience of the century to come indicates that what has been lost has been neither regained nor replaced. Jacques Barzun wrote in his magisterial review of the history of Western cultural life that the Great War was unlike any of its eighteenth- or nineteenth-century predecessors because those 'did not threaten civilization or close an era'.[16]

Many of those who lived through the Great War knew that this conflict had created more problems than it solved. 'It was not long after the Great War that far-seeing observers predicted the likelihood of another and it became plain that western civilization had brought itself into a condition from which full recovery was unlikely', observed Barzun.[17] It was evident to many that the 'War to End All Wars' had not only eclipsed all others with its scale of destruction but marked the beginning of ominous conflicts to come.

Numerous historians have rightly drawn attention to a chain of events that leads directly from the First to the Second World War. Others have posited the Cold War as the Third or Final Act in the drama. However the conflicts and issues left unresolved by the Great War were not settled with the fall of the Berlin Wall. Why? Because World War One was not simply a struggle over territory or ideology. It also served as a catalyst for eroding the prevailing system of meaning and helped intensify disputes over norms and values. That is why the beginning of what is currently often termed as the Culture War can also be situated at some time around August 1914. At that time culture became politicized through the construction of patriotic narratives that linked a nation's geopolitical ambitions to a way of life.

Today patriotism enjoys little cultural valuation in Western societies. It is frequently ridiculed as an outdated sentiment that periodically takes possession of the easily manipulated urban crowds. In contrast to 1914, very few self-respecting intellectuals would be caught waving their national flag. Instead of the flag, competing groups flaunt their identity and instead of celebrating their way of life, they acclaim their lifestyle.

Writing in the 1920s, the French man of letters Julian Benda sought to explain why intellectuals throughout Europe became spineless apologists for crude nationalism and the war effort. He came to the conclusion that it was through the mobilization of the resources of culture that patriotism gained clarity and force. He observed perceptively that 'patriotism today is the assertion of one form of mind against other forms of mind'. He stated that national tensions were often represented as conflicts among rival cultures: 'every nation now hugs itself and sets itself up against all other nations as superior in language, art, literature, philosophy, civilization, "culture".'[18] This insight is confirmed by other studies of this subject. 'Widespread support for the war among the learned was grounded on a general European understanding that the conflict was ultimately a "war of cultures"', notes one study of this subject.[19]

A war of cultures may be conducted between societies and nations as claimed by Samuel Huntington, the author of *Clashes of Civilisation*.[20] However, as is evident in the twenty-first century, cultural conflicts can also exacerbate domestic disputes and divide groups within the same community. The contestation of cultural authority has been a recurrent theme, but invariably it assumes new and different forms. The durability of this conflict was well expressed by the historian Henry May in his study of this subject. Writing in 1959 on the eve of the emergence of the 1960s counter-culture, the historian Henry May argues that some time around the years 1912–17 the United States experienced a cultural revolution. The subtitle of his book *The End of American Innocence* is *A Study of the First Years of our Time, 1912–1917*.[21] What this subtitle succeeds in capturing is a significant historical turning point when divisive cultural conflicts would often unsettle Western societies.

Why wars?

Wars permeate the political culture of the past century. Time and again the major global conflicts serve as a point of reference in the calculation of policy-makers. They are not just perceived as the key milestones of the twentieth century but also of the twenty-first. Allusions to the wars of the past continue be made by policy-makers and commentators attempting to clarify the issues at stake in the series of conflicts that has broken out in the wake of the destruction of the World Trade Center.

Wars have an impact on how people think and during the past century its threat had a palpable bearing on political and intellectual life in Western societies. This was the case particularly between 1930 and 1960. Raymond Aron, in his 1955 Cold War classic *The Opium of the Intellectuals*, alluded to this point when he stated that:

> One cannot live through the Thirty Years' War or the Peloponnesian War or, least of all the two world wars of 1914 and 1939, without asking oneself about their causes and consequences. One seeks, in a slightly disingenuous way to give them a meaning – not in the positive sense of establishing the main facts in order to understand what in fact happened, but a meaning that will provide an excuse for all the accumulated horrors.[22]

Wars also call into question previously accepted meanings of concepts that guide public life. And that legacy has retained its significance to this time.

The conflicts explored in this book are, in part, a consequence of the unresolved issues and questions unleashed through the experience of the First

World War. Until the horrors of World War Two overwhelmed the historical imagination, the conflict of 1914–18 was frequently referred to as the Great War. We shall frequently use this appellation through this book in order to highlight its distinct role as the point of departure for a chain of events that continue to influence the way we interpret our world.

Our historical memory of the Great War has as its focus the millions of wasted lives lost in the muddy trenches of European battlefields. The focus of this study is not on the military dimensions of the Great War but on its impact on the way we think about cultural and political life. Those mobilized into military service, as well as their peers and families at home, reacted in a variety of different ways to the war. Some could not let go of the sense of exhilaration and camaraderie that they experienced in the midst of fighting. Others were traumatized and devastated by the brutality and inhumanity of the conflict. These different responses coexisted with a diffuse sensibility of cultural disenchantment with the promise of European and Western civilization. This mood of disappointment with the legacy of the past exposed the prevailing political order to the scrutiny of millions.

The political upheavals precipitated by this conflict called into question the norms and values associated with the ideals of freedom and democracy. Indeed, for a time during the interwar years it looked as if liberal democracy would be overwhelmed by the authoritarian temper of those times. As we argue, despite the passage of a century the disturbing questions raised during the Great War are still in search of a satisfactory answer.

The Great War was both preceded and followed by what the Hungarian sociologist Karl Mannheim has called a crisis of valuation. Mannheim's concept of a crisis of valuation refers to the decomposition of a normative consensus about the principles that guide communities. At times this crisis was obscured by periods of artificial unity forged through war and social conflicts and through the mass mobilization achieved by radical ideological movements. However, since the Cold War, the disappearance of a normative consensus has been difficult to ignore. Questions that could be ignored in the past can no longer be evaded. That's one compelling reason for writing this book.

Notes

1   Taylor (1966) p.20.
2   Cited in Hynes (1991) p.3.

3 Hynes (1991) p.3.
4 Neumann (1946) p.28.
5 Sternhell (2010) p.25.
6 The argument that Luther was Hitler's spiritual ancestor is put forward by Wiener (1945).
7 Sternhell (2010) p.407.
8 As argued by Strenhell (2010) p.15.
9 Zweig (1953) p.223.
10 Neumann (1946) p.34.
11 Fukuyama (1992) p.331.
12 See pp.331–2.
13 Zweig (1953) p.437.
14 Mann (2005) p.xxxv.
15 Eksteins (1989) p.185.
16 Barzun (2000) p.683.
17 Barzun (2000) p.712.
18 Benda (1959) p.14.
19 Pietila (2011) p.100.
20 See discussion on Huntington's views on http://www.pewtrusts.org/news_room_detail.aspx?id=24374
21 May (1959).
22 Aron (1957) p.192.

1

The Great War – the beginning of beginning

It is widely argued that ideas and ideologies have made a significant contribution to the outbreak of modern wars. At various moments nationalism, imperialism, communism, fascism and even liberalism have been portrayed as significant influences on the conduct of ideologically driven wars. That ideologies and ideas may play a significant role in the conduct of warfare is beyond doubt. But what is also significant is that wars do not leave the ideas that promoted the outbreak of military conflict untouched. The very experience of a war, its impact on the military and civilian population and on the national psyche, influences and sometimes alters the way societies think about the fundamental issues confronting them. Shifts in the global balance of power sometimes strengthen and sometimes erode the legitimacy and workings of national institutions. The dramatic displacement of the prevailing institutional equilibrium forces society to question existing traditions and assumptions. The exhaustion of the dominant cultural norms can have a significant impact on the way that people think and interpret their place in the world. How the Great War and the conflicts it bred changed the way we think is the principal subject of this book.

The economic costs of this war were so enormous that it would take decades before financial stability would be regained. All the major participants bore a heavy burden of financial debt which significantly undermined the political stability of European nations. The victorious powers demanded punitive reparations from their opponents, thus fuelling bitter resentment amongst the defeated. The Versailles Treaty created a world of disputed borders and which fanned the flames of resentment and revenge. The question it raised was 'not if but when' the next global conflict would erupt. Marshal Foch of France reportedly reacted to the Versailles Treaty by exclaiming: 'This is not peace. It is an armistice for twenty years.'[1]

Marshal Foch was on the right track, though peace took far longer than twenty years to achieve. The German political theorist Sigmund Neumann characterized the period between 1914 and 1946 as a second Thirty Years' War.[2] As a refugee from Nazi Germany he was desperately hoping that the Second World War would lead to a durable peace. His appellation of the second Thirty Years' War proved to be an optimistic one. The ease with which the hopes for peace were engulfed by the Cold War indicated that war – albeit in a different form – had become integral to the workings of modern societies.

It is generally acknowledged that the First World War represents 'the great dividing line of European society and politics'.[3] By the time that exhaustion on the battlefield led to the signing of the armistice on 11 November 1918 the pre-war social and political order that prevailed in Europe had all but disintegrated. The overthrow of Czarism in Russia and the abdication of Kaiser Wilhelm II were the most dramatic manifestations of the end of the old political order. This was a war that directly caused the collapse of the four great empires – the Ottoman, Austrian, German, Russian – that played important roles in global affairs in the nineteenth century. 'All changed, changed utterly', wrote the poet W. B. Yeats in reference to the 1916 Easter Rebellion. And all changed utterly throughout the West as well. Moreover, as I note elsewhere, it also unleashed a chain of events that led to the unravelling and fall of Western empires in Africa and Asia.[4]

The old empires and political orders were not the only casualties of the Great War. Arguably this conflict called into question many of the most fundamental assumptions and ideals of nineteenth-century Western societies. Until the outbreak of this war, belief in values such as national and racial superiority, the right of higher civilizations to dominate their inferiors, the civilizing mission of Christianity and of imperialism and the legitimacy of territorial expansion exercised great influence in Western cultural life. Such sentiments were widespread not only in autocratic societies such as Russia but also in more liberal nations such as Britain, France and the United States. As one observer noted, these sentiments 'played no small role in causing the Great War'.[5] Although some these ideals survived the war, they lost much of their intellectual appeal and cultural force. That the West lost confidence in itself was a direct consequences of the war. As Francis Fukuyama remarked, the 'First World War was a critical event in the undermining of Europe's self-confidence'.[6] Or as Jacques Barzun observed, 'the blow that hurled the modern world on its course of self-destruction was the Great War of 1914–18'.[7]

As one prescient review of the changing fortunes of political ideas in the twentieth century stated, 'the First World War put into question every single institutional arrangement and every single political idea' on which the pre-war age rested.[8] However, the war did not simply inflict serious damage on such political ideals but also on the cultural attitudes that underpinned them. Arguably one of the durable legacies of the Great War was the consolidation of cultural pessimism that was to dominate much of public life in the twentieth century. Such sentiments were widespread even among the people of the victor nations. This was a war that failed to generate a feel-good factor even within the victor nations. The scepticism and cynicism provoked by the conduct of the conflict undermined enthusiasm for militaristic glory and imperial adventure. In Britain, 'militarism was now vilified because it was assumed it would prove an inefficient instrument at best'.[9] The historian Werner Kaegi argued that the mass slaughter of 'dedicated persons' during the Great War had a significant and direct impact on Western culture. 'On the battlefields of 1914–1918 the freest of the free died in countless numbers; it was the mass slaughter of the self-sacrificing elites, of the creative talents.' According to Kaegi, this was 'no less destructive of culture than the bombs of the Second World War; it opened the realm of silence in which the usurpers of 1933 could speak and act.'[10]

The realm of silence in the post-World War One period to which Kaegi alluded can be understood as an expression of a sense of loss – existential and cultural – that overwhelmed the elites of European societies. This was a silence of the shocked, whose values and worldview had been dramatically overturned by events. Though the decade leading up to the outbreak of the Great War saw the emergence of influential currents of thought that questioned capitalist rationality and modernity, this was still, on balance, a relatively optimistic era – one that that possessed great faith in human progress. Although sections of the cultural elites expressed a *fin-de-siècle* mood of estrangement from the modern world, the wider public tended to be immune from such influences. When Max Nordau published his moralistic bestseller *Degeneration* in 1895, he could still count on his readers to share his disdain for the recent vogue of *fin-de-siècle* pessimism. He could affirm with confidence the conviction that 'the great majority of the middle and lower classes is naturally not *fin-de-siècle*'.[11]

Two decades later the fashionable pessimism of avant-garde *fin-de-siècle* Europe gave way to malaise that was far more profound. When the British Foreign Secretary, Sir Edward Grey stated on the eve of the Great War that the 'lamps are going out all over Europe, we shall not see them lit again in our time', he had little idea just how long darkness would last. Richard Overy characterized the decades following the Great War as 'The Morbid Age', one where intellectual and cultural life appeared to be haunted by expectation of a new Dark Age and an end to Western civilization.[12] This war had more than the usual unsettling outcomes associated with a military conflict. It called into question the self-belief of the political and cultural elites of Western societies.

The crisis of self-belief of the ruling classes

Accounts of the legacy of the Great War emphasize its inability to overcome the geopolitical conflicts of interest that led to the unravelling of the global system in 1914. Such studies also draw attention to the failure of the post-war settlement to restore political stability. In light of subsequent catastrophic events, the seemingly permanent character of post-war instability of the 1920s and 1930s is associated with the eruption of political violence and the growth of extremist movements throughout the continent. The ascendancy of so-called totalitarian movements and regimes in Russia, Germany and Italy during the interwar period is frequently represented as the direct consequence of the unsettled conditions created by First World War. The Holocaust, the Gulag and the Second World War are regularly portrayed as the logical outcomes of the catastrophic legacy of the Great War. That is why the American strategist and Cold War diplomat George Kennan could say, in 1979, that this war was the 'greatest seminal catastrophe' of the twentieth century.[13]

The Great War set in motion a chain of events which has been described as the Age of Catastrophe. Political polarization in the interwar period tends to be interpreted through the prism of ideological struggles between the Left and the Right. However the dramatic upsurge of radical polarization obscured an equally important development, which was the erosion of the norms and values that supported the taken-for-granted practices that defined life before the war. 'Political polarization, which was to be the hallmark of the interwar era everywhere, confirmed the disappearance of a normality everyone craved but no one knew how to affect', remarked Eksteins.[14] The normality that was sought was not merely political and should not be seen as pertaining merely to the weakening of moderate, pragmatic and centrist public culture. As one American historian pointed out, 'the First World War had a dissolvent effect upon conventional belief and behaviour'.[15]

One of the most momentous and durable legacies of the Great War was that it disrupted and disorganized the prevailing web of meaning through which

Western societies made sense of their world. Suddenly the key values and ideals into which the early twentieth-century elites were socialized appeared to be emptied of meaning. In historical moments when people are confused about their beliefs, they also become disoriented about who they are and where they stand in relation to others. The psychiatrist Patrick Bracken writes about the 'dread brought on by a struggle with meaning'. In circumstances when the 'meaningfulness of our lives is called into question', people become painfully aware that they lack the moral and intellectual resources to give direction to their lives.[16] 'Europe was exhausted, not just physically, but also morally', writes a study of the 'crisis of confidence among European elites after the war'.[17]

One response to this existential crisis was to lament the sense of loss of the old order. But even those who possessed a strong conservative impulse understood that there was no obvious road back to the past. Another, and culturally more influential reaction was to leave the past behind and embrace the novelty of the new. For many intellectuals and artists the end of the war marked the beginning of a new cultural Year Zero. The sensibility of epochal rupture dominated the modernist intellectual and artistic imagination. The contrast between the old and the modern became a recurring theme of the literature produced by Virginia Woolf and individuals associated with the Bloomsbury Set. This moment was represented as a beginning of the new, the different – the modern.

The impulse to innovate often became overwhelmed by a sense of anomie and meaninglessness that drew artists and intellectuals towards the destructive side of the human experience. One contemporary critic of modernism wrote that 'musicians and painters, as well as novelists and poets, found themselves obsessed with the problem of the machine age, the decay of culture, the confusion of moralities, and the loss of confidence in human nature and progress'.[18] Such sentiments extended beyond the circle of artists and intellectuals and even influenced those who sought meaning through public life. Arguably what gave interwar political radicalism such energy and force was the conviction that a break with the past was both possible and necessary.

Coinciding with all the drama of the post-war revolutions, the mobilizations of the radical left and the far right and the retreat of parliamentary democracy in continental Europe was an all-prevailing crisis of self-belief that afflicted the ruling classes of these societies. This erosion of ruling-class confidence was fuelled by the recognition that the values and beliefs that had underpinned its view of the world had lost much of their meaning in the post-war epoch. The destructive consequences of the Great War – estimates of total deaths range from 9 to 16 million – highlighted the precarious status of the civilizational claims of Europe. It is worth noting that prior to this experience 'war and civilization had not been regarded as incompatible'.[19] However by 1916 the 'glory and romance had gone out of the war', argues Taylor.[20] The experience of pointless destruction on an industrial scale significantly diminished the moral status of ideals – duty, honour, valour, military prowess, sacrifice – associated with the worldview of Europe's political elites.

Disenchantment with traditional bourgeois values was widespread and, according to one of its defenders, 'novelists, humourists and low comedians helped to bring it into contempt'. The poet and literary critic Michael Roberts described the corrosion of traditional norms in Britain in the following terms:

> Because some old loyalties were false, the idea of loyalty itself was discredited: and attacks on the British Empire which began as generous movements on behalf of subject peoples merged in a general subversiveness that included everything from the English Public Schools to marriage, parenthood, and family life.[21]

Frequently the post-war years were labelled as an 'age of disillusionment'. Although rarely elaborated, the term disillusionment referred to the loss of illusions in the norms and values of the pre-war order. The appellation illusion served to communicate the sentiment that the values associated with the pre-war outlook were at best a product of self-deception, at worse of cynicism and dishonesty. Once this system of values lost meaning, everything from democracy to the sanctity of marriage could be interpreted as illusory. Over the decades to come, the rejection of such apparently illusory or false norms would gain significant cultural support. By the twenty-first century many of these values and norms were rejected on more fundamental grounds – not so much because they were illusions, but because they were deemed to be repressive and wrong.

The crisis of bourgeois self-belief acquired a peculiarly intense sensibility in relation to cultural values that were directly related to the conduct of war. Although modern values have always exited in an uncomfortable relationship with the code of militarism, it wasn't until the unfolding tragedy of trench warfare was fully digested in the immediate post-war years that pacifist attitudes gained significant cultural authority. Europe's quiet disenchantment with militarism had profound implications for the way its public regarded foreign policy and its overseas empires. As Thornton noted in relation to Britain:

In a deeply pacifist age, whose adults had returned from a four years' war with a certain scepticism as to the manner in which it had been conducted, Empire and militarism were now as ever equated. But it was not an equation that commanded the unwilling respect of former times.[22]

The anger that some directed at the powerful coterie of advocates of militarism often led to suspicion directed at the claims of all 'superiors'. In the eyes of an unapologetic defender of the Empire, like Winston Churchill, such sentiments smacked of cowardice and defeatism. However, even the most incorrigible defender of the traditional way of life intuitively grasped that something important had been lost and that the authority of the old hierarchy could not be restored.

Looking back a century after the outbreak of World War One it is possible to identify that loss as that of **existential certainty**. Values and ideals which endowed existence with direction and meaning now stood exposed to inter-rogation and scrutiny. 'The virtues of loyalty, hard work, perseverance and patriotism were brought to bear in the systematic and pointless slaughter of other men, thereby discrediting the entire bourgeois world which had created these values', observed Fukuyama.[23] It is important to note that the exhaustion of pre-war ideals did not merely affect those pertaining to the conduct of military warfare. Many core principles associated with modernity, such as the benevolent influence of rationality and of progress, were now queried by intel-lectuals and public figures experiencing a crisis of belief.

In retrospect it is difficult to be absolutely certain about the depth of this crisis of belief in the interwar era. Certainly American society was far less haunted by it than those on the other side of the Atlantic. Constant literary references to well-known anti-war literature such as Erich Maria Remarque's *All Quiet on the Western Front* or Ernest Hemingway's *A Farewell To Arms* suggests that such remarkable books were the exception. It is likely that war-weariness was far more prevalent than a principled commitment to pacifism. Within wider public opinion pacifist sentiments coexisted with other, more pragmatic attitudes. Pacifism and anti-militarism may have gained respectability, but it was still only one cultural current competing with others and not a hegemonic force. Even anxieties directed towards the capacity of the war machine to harness the innovations of industrial progress for such destructive ends did not lead to the widespread rejection of the benefits of modernity. Indeed, in the 1920s, a faith in progress, sustained by the belief that science and technology would support the advance and well-being of society, continued to inspire mainstream public opinion. But such optimistic sentiments had a far more muted existence in artistic and intellectual circles. Even during the relatively prosperous Roaring Twenties, cultural pessimism and anti-modernist themes exercised a significant influence in intellectual and cultural life.

At this historical conjuncture, the sense of loss was most forcefully and eloquently expressed by artists and imaginative writers. They were part of what Gertrude Stein characterized as the 'Lost Generation' of artists and intellectuals, whose works expressed the hopelessness and despair of the interwar years. It is likely that many of these artists self-consciously cultivated the sensibility of estrangement and loss. Artistic pessimism and rejection of prevailing values had become mandatory in the cultural circles of Paris and other leading cities. Artists such as Paul Valéry, D. H. Lawrence, Ernest Hemingway, Franz Kafka, James Joyce, T. S. Eliot and Ezra Pound voiced in different ways a rejection of modern civilization. As Hemingway, a veteran of the Italian campaign, wrote in his 1929 novel *A Farewell to Arms*, 'abstract words such as glory, honor, courage, or hallow were obscene besides the concrete names of villages, the numbers of roads, the names of rivers, the numbers of regiments and the dates'.

For many interwar poets and writers the language of duty and honour appeared insincere and irrelevant. The French novelist Roland Dorgelès declared after the war that 'there are grand words that don't sound the same today as in 1914'.[24] The dissonance between traditional language and the post-war experience encouraged some to search for new forms of expressions. Others simply opted for deconstructing a language from which they felt estranged. Roberts observed that the 'fashion' was 'not to construct but to demolish; the popular activity was debunking, the favourite epithet was "bogus"'.[25] In retrospect it is possible to interpret this debunking of language as an activity pursued by individuals who were otherwise lost for words. The search for a new language, like the 'craving for newness', can be decoded as symptomatic of a spiritual crisis that afflicted all sections of society.[26]

Even beyond artistic circles the exhaustion of existential certainty in the interwar period called into question the manner in which capitalist modernity represented the relationship between the present and the future. The power of destruction unleashed during the Great War, with its unexpected and uncontrollable trajectory, and the failure of the intellectual legacy of modernity to make sense of this tragedy undermined society's faith in future progress. Despite the rhetoric that this was a 'War to end all Wars', it was widely understood that four years of slaughter did not resolve any of the problems that caused the conflict in the first place. Premonition of the war to come in future coexisted with fears of uncertainty about the capacity of society to absorb internal conflicts. Suddenly, the taken-for-granted assumptions about civilization, progress and the nature of change lost their capacity to illuminate human experience. The prominent English historian H. A. L. Fisher acknowledged in 1934 that he could no longer discern in history the 'plot', the 'rhythm and 'predetermined pattern' that appeared so obvious to observers in the past. 'I can see only one emergency following upon another as wave follows upon wave', he stated.[27]

Fisher's inability to find meaning in history expressed his generation's psychic distance from the past. The cultural historian Paul Fussell claims that after the First World War it is difficult if not impossible to imagine the future as the continuation of the past: 'the Great War was perhaps the last to be conceived as taking place within a seamless, purposeful "history" involving a coherent stream of time running from past to future'.[28] Many social commentators experienced the interwar era as fundamentally different to their pre-war way of life. As noted previously, the past was depicted as an alien territory and the ideals and beliefs associated with it were frequently described as illusions. Reminiscing about the happy *belle époque* of pre-war Europe, the novelist H. G. Wells reminded his readers that the 'spectacular catastrophe' of the Great War had shattered such illusions.[29] Graham Wallas echoed this point when he wrote that 'one only needs to compare the disillusioned realism of our present war and post-war pictures and poems with the nineteenth-century war pictures at Versailles and Berlin, and the war poems of Campbell, and Berenger, and Tennyson, to realise how far we now are from exaggerating human rationality'.[30]

Overy argues that the 'juxtaposition of illusions of pre-war progress with post-war disaster' was a contrast that 'became a literary trope which survived even the experience of a second war'.[31] Overy cautions his readers from 'believing that there was more promise in the pre-war world than in the new'.[32] He is right to question the elaborate historical contrast drawn between a pre-1914 golden age and the post-war hell. However, the very fact that people felt that their present and their future was so detached from the past indicates that a sense of terminus had captured their imagination and internal life. The sense of continuity that many communities could take for granted at the turn of the twentieth century had become a major casualty of the war.

The unravelling of a consciousness of continuity had a profound influence on the way that Europe's cultural and political elites viewed their place in the world. Their identity and self-belief in a mission was inextricably linked to the idealization of progress and of civilizational advance. The barbarism of the Great War, followed by political upheavals and economic dislocation under-mined an ethos based on the presumption of progress. The American historian William McNeill argued that 'World War I had called earlier generations' faith in progress into question', which in turn disposed society to perceive many of its experiences through the prism of decline. 'Especially from the point of view of the educated upper classes, it often seemed that instead of progress of civili-sation, its decline was taking place around them – what with the "revolt of the masses" at home and the "natives" growing restlessness in empires overseas', he wrote.[33]

The loss of existential certainty possessed an important psychological dimension. What the British political sociologist Graham Wallas characterized in 1920 as the 'disillusioned realism' of his time expressed a loss of faith in humanity's capacity to reason. From his perspective the Great War and its destructive aftermath served as proof that rationality and progress were ideas that stood discredited.[34] He asserted that

> [...] the assumption that men are automatically guided by 'enlightened self-interest' has been discredited by the facts of the war and the peace, the success of an anti-parliamentary and anti-intellectualist revolution in Russia, the British election of 1918, the French election of 1919, the confusion of politics in America, the breakdown of political machinery in Central Europe, and the general unhappiness which has resulted from four years of the most intense and heroic effort that the human race has ever made.[35]

Wallas, too, was playing the game of exaggerating the contrast between the naivety of an illusion-prone pre-war era and his own time. The idea that humanity is 'automatically guided by "enlightened self-interest"' is a caricature drawn by those who wished to draw attention to the cultural and intellectual revolution against a rationalist understanding of society.

Disillusionment with rationality was paralleled with an outburst of interest in what Virginia Woolf described in a 1919 essay as the 'dark places of psychology'.[36] A palpable shift towards introspection was coupled with a tendency to interpret everyday life through the prism of irrationality and the instinctive. Explorations of the dark places of psychology invariably adopted a tone of despair towards regaining what had been lost. From this perspective it was regression rather than progress that corresponded to the spirit of the times. The French poet and philosopher Paul Valéry voiced the loss of existential security in the following terms:

> We think of what has disappeared, we are almost destroyed by what has been destroyed; we do not know what will be born, and we fear the future, not without reason. We hope vaguely, we dread precisely; our fears are infinitely more precise than our hopes; we confess that the charm of life is behind us, but doubt and disorder are in front of us and with us.[37]

Valéry's evocation of a mood of anxiety and disorientation was connected to the exhaustion of belief. 'The Mind has indeed been cruelly wounded: its complaint is heard in the hearts of intellectual men: it passes a mournful judgment on itself', he observed, before concluding 'it doubts itself profoundly'.[38]

Valéry's musing about loss of self-belief was far more than a personal statement. Numerous commentators wondered out loud whether civilization could neutralize the corrosive powers that were exposed through the conduct of the war. During the 1920s and 1930s the mood, at least among the intelligentsia, fluctuated between deep pessimism and the conviction that everything was absurd. 'People are coming to believe that everything is breaking down: there is nothing that can't be questioned: nothing that is real stands the test', exclaimed the German philosopher Karl Jaspers in 1931.[39]

At first sight it is puzzling why European intellectual and political life was so drawn towards such a morbid interpretation of life. Indeed, this is a question that engages the attention of Richard Overy in his study of *The Morbid Age* in Britain. His diagnosis of a disjuncture between domestic malaise and its culture of crisis and reality suggests that there was an element of cultivated over-reaction on the part of interwar doom-mongers. 'The constant theme of civilization in crisis, if repeated often enough and in different contexts, develops an explanatory power that does not have to take account of any existing disjuncture between historical reality and the language of threat', concludes Overy.[40]

It is possible that the constant allusions to a crisis of civilization were promoted by a rhetorical strategy that harnessed the symbolic significance of the Great War to gain the attention of the public. However, that Europe was gripped by a crisis of confidence about the threats it faced and lacked a system of meaning through which they could be interpreted is not in doubt.

How a society engages with uncertainty and threats is influenced by the way that cultural norms and values interpret them. Uncertainty and threats are mediated through taken-for-granted meanings about the nature of social reality and one's place in the world. In an important essay about the relationship of meaning and anxiety, the sociologist C. Wright Mills has argued that people's consciousness of being threatened is mediated through their system of values. C. Wright Mills claimed that whether or not people feel well or insecure is influenced by their relationship with the prevailing sense of meaning. So 'when people cherish some set of values and do not feel any threat to them, they experience *well-being*'; in contrast, 'when they cherish values but *do* feel them to be threatened, they experience a crisis'. 'And if all their values seem involved they feel the total threat of panic', adds Mills. Mills also projected a scenario that captures an important dimension of the interwar experience. 'Suppose, finally they are unaware of any cherished values, but still are very much aware of a threat', he states, before concluding, 'that is the experience of *uneasiness*, of anxiety, which, if it is total enough, becomes a deadly unspecified malaise'.[41] From this perspective it is possible to interpret the 'crisis of civilisation rhetoric' as an attempt to give definition to a threat without a name.

Overy was on the right track when he asserted that 'in explaining the regular and extensive mobilisation of general metaphors of decline and fall that characterized the inter-war years it is evident that more than the general anxieties generated by the Great War and the slump were at work'.[42] That something more had to do with the way in which the pre-war system of meaning lost its relevance for the post-war generations. What Mills characterized as a 'deadly unspecified malaise' was literally experienced as a form of cultural annihilation. In its most extreme manifestation the loss of a web of meaning disposed society towards a morbid orientation towards death.

A War of Culture

Both explicitly and also implicitly, the Great War intruded on the terrain of culture. This was most explicitly addressed by Germany, where advocates of war argued about the need to defend *Kultur* and thereby also free Europe. In 1902 Kaiser Wilhelm II called for the 'world supremacy' of the German mind. Twelve years later, many leading intellectuals of Germany appeared to respond to this call and used their considerable knowledge and prestige to promote this cultural crusade on the battlefields of Europe. A significant proportion of German scholars regarded 'the war of 1914 as an ideological war, which would assure the victory of the German "ideas of 1914" over the Western "ideas of 1789".'[43]

The Manifesto of the Ninety-Three German Intellectuals, issued on 4 October 1914, showed the willingness of some of this nation's leading thinkers to assume responsibility for the promotion of war propaganda. The Manifesto begins with the words: 'as representatives of German Science and Art, we hereby protest to the civilized world against the lies and calumnies with which our enemies are endeavouring to stain the honour of Germany in her hard struggle for existence – in a struggle that has been forced on her.' This unwavering defence of 'Germany's honour' insists that Germany bears no responsibility for causing the war. It insists that 'neither the people, the Government, nor the "Kaiser" wanted war'. While protesting the innocence of the German nation, the ninety-three intellectuals accuse their enemy of war crimes. 'But in the east, the earth is saturated with the blood of women and children unmercifully butchered by the wild Russian troops, and in the west, dumdum bullets mutilate the breasts of our soldiers', it states.[44]

One aim of this manifesto was to provide an intellectual defence of militarism and to reconcile it with a defence of civilization. The reputation of the best of German culture and civilization was mobilized to assist the war aims of this nation. Its final words actually appeal to the tradition of the German Enlightenment. It states:

> Have faith in us! Believe, that we shall carry on this war to the end as a civilized nation, to whom the legacy of a Goethe, a Beethoven, and a Kant, is just as sacred as its own hearths and homes.

That the reputation of one of the leading figures of the liberal Enlightenment, Immanuel Kant, the author of the idea of perpetual peace, could be called upon to justify German militarism exposed the ease with which intellectuals made the leap from a battle of ideas and culture to the embrace of the ethos of militarism.

The German sociologist Max Weber, who remains one of the most influential figures in Western social theory, was in no doubt that promoting his nation's superior culture was a cause well worth fighting for. 'It would be shameful if we lacked the courage to ensure that neither Russian barbarism nor French grandiloquence ruled the world', he asserted, 'that is why this war is being fought'.[45]

Nor was the intellectual reconciliation with militarism confined to Germany. Emile Durkheim, the French sociologist and one of the towering figures of his discipline, embraced his nation's cause with a relish that matched that of Weber. Durkheim was deeply involved in the production of French war propaganda. His pamphlets sought to discredit not just German militarism but also its culture. He attributed German war atrocities to the 'morbid nature' of the German public mentality. He claimed that there was 'something abnormal and harmful' about German idealism, which made it 'a threat to humanity as a whole'.[46]

A. J. P. Taylor pointed out the significance of the mobilization of 'intellectual abilities' to win the propaganda war, which was also a battle of ideals. He wrote that while Thomas Mann 'demonstrated the superiority of German culture', H. G. Wells 'discovered that this was a war to end all wars'. Meanwhile, 'historians proved, to their own satisfaction, the war-guilt of the enemy and the innocence of their own country', while 'poets composed hymns of hate'.[47] There were very, very few honourable exceptions to this trend. 'To those of us who still retain an irreconcilable animus against war, it has been a bitter experience to see the unanimity with which the American intellectuals have thrown their support to the use of war technique in the crisis in which America found herself', wrote Randolph Bourne, the radical essayist. In his powerful essay, 'The War and the Intellectuals', Bourne castigated American intellectuals for their willing complicity with the promotion of war propaganda. What really disturbed Bourne was the realization that intellectuals were actually in the forefront in the advocacy of war. 'They are now complacently asserting that it was they who effectively willed it, against the hesitation and dim perceptions of the American democratic masses', argued Bourne, before concluding: 'a war made deliberately by the intellectuals'.[48]

Barzun wrote: 'from the earliest days of the struggle each belligerent also carried on an internal war of ideas'.[49] The historian Alan Kramer asserted that the 'enemy was not merely the enemy army, but the enemy nation and the culture through which it defined itself'.[50] Although geopolitical calculations dominated the drive to war, conflicts between competing norms and values became crystallized during the course of the struggle. As Eksteins reminds us:

> At the same time that tensions were developing between states in this turn-of-the-century world, fundamental conflicts were surfacing in virtually all areas of human endeavour and behaviour: in the arts, in fashion, in sexual mores, between generations, in politics.[51]

Compared to national conflicts such as that between Germany and France and ideological struggles such as between communism and fascism, such cultural conflicts appeared relatively insignificant. That is because cultural conflicts are not always expressed with a capital C. Cultural aspiration is often communicated through a language that obscures it. In the interwar era cultural conflicts were often associated with national characteristics and rivalries.

Conflicts about different 'ways of life', which informed propaganda during the war, continued and intensified during the interwar period. Celebrations of national character and culture provided a resource for mobilizing public opinion. One perceptive observer of the 1920s stated that 'patriotism today is the assertion of one form of mind against another form of mind'. He added that national rivalries were often experienced as conflicts between cultures: 'Every nation now hugs itself and sets up against all other nations as superior in language, art, literature, philosophy, civilization, "culture".'[52]

Consciousness of decline

The most dramatic symptom of interwar cultural malaise was the eruption of doubt about the status and authority of Western civilization. It is important to recall that until that point 'a belief in the eventual Europeanization of the world, in the sense of European dominance of the world and global acceptance of Europe's civilization as a model' was a rarely contested assumption of the pre-war age.[53]

'Gnawing uncertainty' on the part of Europeans about their central place in the world was one unexpected outcome of the Great War.[54] Civilizational decline was expressed in a variety of forms – spiritual, racial, cultural and natural. Oswald Spengler's *Decline of the West* outlined many of these sentiments and quickly became a point of reference for discussions in the interwar era. Spengler had forcefully captured the prevailing sense of terminus through a historical theory that posited the past as a story of the rise and fall of civilizations. According to this interpretation of history, 'the future of the West is not a limitless tending upwards and onwards for all time' but one that is 'strictly limited and defined as to form and duration'.[55]

One of the most evocative themes raised during this moment of loss of confidence about the authority of the West was the apprehension of racial decline. The sudden transformation of the previous celebration of white racial superiority into an intense anxiety about racial survival is a direct legacy of the Great War. In the eyes of some commentators the Great War had struck a fatal blow to the assumption of Western racial superiority. In its most extreme form, the First World War was reinterpreted as a civil war between white nations. Anxieties regarding the breakdown of white solidarity featured prominently in racist literature of the interwar period. Those who were drawn towards associating World War One with the theme of racial survival decried the fact that not only were white armies slaughtering each other but also that they were using African and Asian soldiers on the battlefields. They feared that the dissolving of racial boundaries would show colonial soldiers that Europeans were ordinary mortals. That in turn would have the effect of nullifying the pretensions of white racial superiority.

At the time, many Western observers feared that the First World War would soon be followed by a conflict between races. The deployment of African and Asian troops by European powers was interpreted as a fatal error that would dissolve racial boundaries. Criticism was directed at the French when they used African soldiers during the occupation of the Ruhr in 1920. In Britain, even left-wing and liberal periodicals castigated the French for 'thrusting her black savages' into the 'heart of Germany'.[56]

The preoccupation with Western decline led to the emergence of a new genre of racially obsessed alarmist literature. Sir Leo Chiozza Money's *The Peril of the White,* published in 1925, expressed such obsessions in an unrestrained form. This former protégé of Prime Minister Lloyd George was intent on raising the alarm about the danger that 'whites in Europe and elsewhere are set upon race suicide and internecine war'.[57] Race suicide was also a theme embraced by Spengler. He decried that the 'unassailable privileges of the white races have been thrown away, squandered and betrayed' and warned that the 'exploited world is beginning to take its revenge on its lords'.[58]

Whatever the objective reality behind the theme of racial decline, it is important to note that the association of the Great War with the unravelling of the West retains influence over the interpretations of the interwar years to this day. One American study published in the 1990s recalled that 'Europe's prestige was ruined by the First World War, a suicidal war of an intensity and scale never before seen'. It concluded that 'the notion of the moral superiority of the West was finished in Asia after that'.[59] This conclusion was also drawn by the French sociologist Jean Baudrillard, who wrote that the Great War 'ended the supremacy of Europe and the colonial era'.[60]

During the interwar decades the Great War was often perceived as a catalyst for the emergence of a new cycle of anti-white and anti-Western revolts and conflicts. Alarmist stories that predicted a future where conflicts would be conducted along racial lines were widely circulated in the immediate post-war period.[61] Indeed the emergence of a new field of study, that of race relations, was closely connected to the attempt to prevent a global 'clash of colour'. The global dimensions of this problem were explained by an editorial in 1923 in the *Journal of Applied Sociology* in the following terms:

> The Europeanization of the world has lost its momentum. The World War augmented the spirit of nationalism in nearly all countries with the result that India, Turkey, Egypt, the Philippines, the South American republics, as well as China and Japan, are asking, if not demanding, autonomy regarding changes in their cultures and traditions.[62]

The concerns raised by this editorial were often conveyed in a language that was characteristically diffuse and vague. But the one point through which such apprehensions gained clarity was their linkage to the Great War.

Time and again warnings about Western decline and of racial conflicts to come stressed the significance of World War One as the catalyst for the rise of the new peril of a global struggle for survival. Such alarmist prognosis went hand-in-hand with warnings of Western decline. In the 1920s and 1930s, the Great War often served as the symbol of moral exhaustion and Western decline. In numerous accounts this event was associated with a historic blow against Western moral authority. That such sentiments were so widely transmitted throughout the West can only be explained as the outcome of the crisis of self-belief that afflicted it.

The corrosive disorientation of the Western official mind caused by the Great War had a uniquely powerful impact on the outlook of Christian thinkers and particularly on missionaries, who experienced the spiritual crisis in a particularly intense form. A mood of disillusionment and despair towards Western civilization's claim of moral authority was widespread in missionary circles. In his study of the reaction of Protestant missionaries to the post-World War One era, Brian Stanley wrote of the 'gradual disintegration of Christian confidence in Western cultural values'. One manifestation of this crisis of confidence was the shift in the way that many missionaries assessed their own culture relative to those of the colonial people. For many of them, 'aspects of tribal society began to appeared less "dark" and indeed preferable to the secular modernity of the West'.[63] Missionary organizations felt acutely concerned about the status of the moral authority of Western churches. Such anxieties were fuelled by the perception that the Great War had gravely diminished the prestige of the missionary enterprise.

Interwar missionary literature captured the consciousness of decline in a strikingly dramatic form. Given the nature of missionary activity with its evangelizing ambition, it is understandable why this institution was so intensely preoccupied with its moral authority. Although the themes of anti-Western reactions and racial grievances were the dominant issues in missionary statements about East-West relations, it is likely that this narrative was directly shaped by the inner crisis of Western belief that acquired an exceptionally powerful force within the Christian churches.

Constant references to the irreparable damage caused to white prestige by the Great War by missionaries notwithstanding, it is unlikely that there was a causal relationship between this global conflict and the 'clash of colour'. No doubt the war set in motion a chain of events that would destabilize the colonial system and lead to a revolution in race relations.[64] However, in this context it is much more useful to perceive the war as an experience through which the Western imagination sublimated its anxieties about the future. From this vantage point the Great War can be interpreted as both the source of conflicts to come and as a catalyst that brought to the surface the existential crisis facing early twentieth-century Western societies. Missionaries were uniquely confronted with the crisis, which in the interwar era they interpreted through the prism of the moral wasteland created by the Great War.

The moral and spiritual disorientation of Western societies was frequently communicated through the narrative of racial decline. Basil Matthews, an influential liberal commentator on the missionary movement, offered a synthesis of racial and moral concerns to express this point. His 1924 book, *The Clash of Colour* expressly represented the war as the means through which Western moral authority disintegrated.

Based on a series of lectures delivered in Belfast and sponsored by the Presbyterian Church of Ireland, *The Clash of Colour* relied on the symbolic significance of the destructive forces set in motion by the Great War to argue for a shift in attitude by the white races towards racial relations. Throughout the lectures the war symbolizes the point of no return to the comfortable assumptions of the nineteenth-century imperial imagination. Matthews's focus is the 'worldwide upheavals, nationalistic earthquakes and racial tidal waves' that are apparently sweeping all over the globe. This diagnosis is based on the conviction that the authority of the West, which rested on flimsy foundations, has now been exposed to the scrutiny of colonial people and found wanting. According to this analysis the Great War was a 'stupendous white civil war' which led to the erosion of the 'white man's hypnotic authority'. This authority 'crashed in the moral ruin' of the Great War and is unlikely to be revived in the future.[65]

Matthews's use of the term 'hypnotic authority' is integral to an analysis that is uncomfortable with the pretensions of Western civilization. When he writes how African and Asian soldiers became exposed to the dark side of Western civilization during the war and became 'disillusioned' with what they saw, he appears to be nodding in agreement.[66] His conclusion is that after the 'moral debacle of world war', the 'old authority of the white man in the sense of its automatic acceptance by the other races as inevitable and enduring has ended'.[67] Matthews contends that rather than following the futile course of attempting to restore this authority, the West should abandon its attempt to dominate the African and Asian races. This statement is cast in the form of a warning: 'if the white man resists "the rising tide of colour", the breakers of that tide will surge and pound upon the dykes till they crumble and collapse.' Citing H. G. Wells's warning that the world faces a 'race between education and catastrophe', Matthews warns that unless racial harmony is achieved, global war is inevitable.[68]

Matthews's book – which went through twenty-two impressions between the years 1924 and 1930 – exercised great influence in Anglo-American missionary circles. His views were echoed by the leading missionary intellectual Joseph Oldham, who, in his *Christianity and the Race Problem*, argued for a liberal orientation towards race relations.[69] Because of their vocation and peculiar sensitivity to moral and cultural influences that might undermine the Christian message, missionaries took a leading role in international deliberations on race relations. However the preoccupation with Western decline and its destabilizing influence on race relations was by no means confined to missionary circles.

The association of the Great War with an impending global racial conflict was shared by a significant section of intellectuals and cultural elites. This interpretation of the future informed contributions to a conference of American academics on 'Public Opinion and World Peace' in December 1921. The apprehension they voiced was that the war had 'laid bare the skeletons in the closet of western civilization'.[70] Anxieties about the loss of authority of the white race seamlessly converged with wider preoccupations regarding cultural and moral decline. This intellectual climate was well captured by the American sociologist Louis Wirth, who drew attention to the 'extensive literature which speaks of the "end", the "decline", the "crisis", the "decay", or the "death" of Western civilization'.[71]

The constant coupling of a civilization in crisis with the First World War endowed this relationship with the status of a truth. What mattered was not the specific details surrounding the global position of the West. Western domination of the world remained intact and was only challenged on the margins of their empires. Concern about decline had an anticipatory quality. The anticipation of decline and loss of moral authority were as much fuelled by the crisis of belief of the ruling classes as by questions raised about white domination. As far as race relations were concerned, the importance of the Great War was to consolidate and give shape to pre-existing doubts about Western superiority. Such concerns as well as fears about decline expressed the underlying doubts and confusions that the elites had about their way of life. The war opened a can of metaphorical worms and, as we shall see, the ontological insecurity of the Western elites became integral to their way of life.

From the vantage point of military history, the Great War can be interpreted through the battlefield narrative of winners and losers. However the devastating impact of the conflict on the self-consciousness and authority of the different national elites meant that all of them felt that something important had been lost. The German sociologist Max Weber, in his remarkable 1918 lecture 'Politics as a Vocation', sought to grapple with a new world where authoritative leadership was conspicuous by its absence. The future he outlined sounded like the unfolding of a Greek tragedy. 'Not summer's bloom lies ahead of us, but rather a polar night of icy darkness and hardness, no matter which group may triumph externally now', lamented Weber.[72] The clarity with which he projected a future without hope expressed the mood of existential insecurity and inner anxieties of Europe's elites.

The historian Eric Hobsbawm contends that the outbreak of World War One 'marked the breakdown of the (western) civilization of the 19th century'. Integral to this civilization were ideals and values associated with capitalist economics, liberal politics, bourgeois in its social and cultural outlook, 'glorying in the advance of science, knowledge and education material and moral progress; and profoundly convinced of the centrality of Europe'.[73] What underpinned the loss of authority of the specific ideals associated with Western civilization was the existential insecurity of an elite that had lost its way.

Lost for words, or the search for a new language

It was not only modernist writers who became conscious of the difficulty they had in expressing themselves through the old language. The political elites of Europe were sensitive to the fact that terms like capitalism, imperialism, liberalism or progress had lost considerable legitimacy. The Great War and the problems it threw up forced society to rethink and rework its political and social ideals and language. Words that communicated a sense of pride and served as a focus for the constitution of elite identity suddenly became a source of embarrassment.

Take the example of the term imperialism. At the insistence of US President Woodrow Wilson, the 1919 Paris Peace Conference accepted the principle of national self-determination. Although the affirmation of this principle had as its main aim the re-drawing of the map of Europe and of the Ottoman Empire, it also implicitly called into question the legitimacy of the West's overseas colonies. Consequently the acceptance of the principle of self-determination at Versailles in 1919 directly undermined the moral authority of colonialism and imperialism. The mandate system established by the newly established League of Nations implied that the subordinate status of colonial people would be temporary. As one study contends, by accepting the provisional character of mandates 'the liberal imperialists had, in effect, made the first public admission that empire in and of itself was no longer a legitimate political form'.[74]

Until the interwar era, the moral claims made on behalf of Empire and Imperialism were rarely contested in the West. School textbooks, policy documents even religious sermons promoted the belief that the expansion of Western powers to the four corners of the earth represented a significant contribution to human civilization. Indeed, until the late 1920s, individual members of the Anglo-American ruling classes would often associate themselves with the Imperial Ideal. Far from being a source of disquiet, imperialism and its tradition provided inspiration and pride to the ruling elites. At times even individuals who perceived themselves to be progressive stood up for Empire. Indeed, as late as 1949, the future British Labour Prime Minister Harold Wilson could assert that 'no party can or should claim for itself the exclusive use of the title Imperialist, in the best sense of the word'.[75] For a few individuals like Wilson, imperialism 'in the best sense of the word' still meant something important. But by this time most Anglo-American public figures were not prepared to openly endorse this term.

The First World War more or less destroyed the imperial ideal. Lenin's condemnation of imperialism as the force most responsible for the drive to war resonated with significant sections of public opinion. The thoroughgoing discrediting of this ideal meant that even organizations devoted to the cause of defending the European overseas empires were searching for a new vocabulary for expressing their case. 'In the period after the First World War Imperialism began to be on the defensive and it became fashionable in the Round Table and in the Raleigh Club to speak of Commonwealth rather than Empire', notes a study of this period.[76]

In the 1920s the word imperialist could still be used to connote a respectable standpoint or identity. The *Economist* referred to the geographer and diplomat Sir Halford Mackinder as 'a representative British Imperialist'. But this periodi-cal's positive or at least neutral reference is to the imperialism of the past, and the article concludes with the reminder that the 'prestige' of the Imperialist school represented by Sir Halford is 'on the wane'.[77] Indeed, by the 1930s it was evident to all that those who still believed in imperialism had lost the argument. A policy document, 'A British Policy for World Peace and Prosperity' circulated in April 1938 in Whitehall stated that 'the Empire is suffering from malaise and, even apart from its material requirements, it needs today a re-definition of purpose'.[78]

The project of redefining the purpose of imperialism turned into half-hearted attempts to develop a narrative of imperial virtue. It was in this vein that in 1940, the Secretary of State for the Colonies, Malcolm MacDonald declared that the 'great purpose of British Imperialism' was 'the freedom of all of His Majesty's subjects wherever they lived'. MacDonald was aware that this argument constituted a bit of a stretch and conceded that imperialism may have had 'other motives in the past'.[79] By this point in time, the unease about the imperial ideal had crystallized into a moral crisis of imperialism. Numerous letters to *The Times* decried the 'perverted meaning that has been fastened upon "imperialism"'. Sir Frederick Sykes of the Royal Empire Society called for a campaign to educate the British public about the ideals of the Empire.[80] An editorial took up this point a few weeks later:

Many distinguished correspondents have lately protested in these columns against the fashion of using as a term of disparagement the word 'imperialism', charged as it is with magnificent traditions and a present content of hope for the emancipation of mankind.

The editorial blamed the misuse of this word on Marxists who propagate idea that imperialism is the 'primary cause of war' and represents exploitation of 'backward peoples'. It insisted that 'all history cries out against this base interpretation of human motives'.[81] Attempts to limit the damage caused by the unanswerable questions raised in the aftermath of World War One proved futile. In the end, the attempt to rehabilitate the imperial ideal was abandoned and replaced by the tactic of pretending that it never existed. 'The main feature of British Imperialism, in fact, is that it does not exist', argued an editorial in the *Economist* in October 1942.[82] In subsequent decades a word that had been used with pride by members of the British Establishment would be redefined as a meaningless polemical slogan used by mean-spirited radicals to have a go at the West. As one opponent of this 'pseudo-concept' argued, imperialism 'is a word for the illiterates of social science, the callow and the shallow who attempt to solve problems without mastering a technique'.[83]

At the outset of the Great War the status of Western empires was solid and rarely questioned. Paradoxically, a war that in part sought to defend or expand such empires significantly contributed to their subsequent decline. The moral authority of imperialism was a direct casualty of this conflict. As the historian Hans Kohn asserted in the early 1930s, 'the cultural mission of the West as a basis of its dominance is no longer recognised in the East, and even in the West it is called in question by an increasing number of people'.[84]

But as we shall see, imperialism was not the only ideal that was shattered by the Great War. The Great War – the manner in which it was fought, its unexpected lengthy duration, the scale of destruction it brought – directly undermined belief in the Western way of life. In the years that followed Armistice it was the radicalization of political life and the destabilization of the international balance of power that absorbed most of the attention of political leaders and commentators alike. But arguably a development that was no less significant had been put in motion – this was the exhaustion of the normative foundation of all forms of authority.

Throughout the Great War, governments needed to mobilize the public and, to realize this objective, promised to provide social reforms and opportunities for greater participation after the termination of hostilities. The upheavals of the war shook up the old routines and, as the historian Hans Kohn remarked, 'roused the desire for a thorough-going change'. Demands for a 'recasting of the social order' could not be ignored and it was generally accepted that the relation between government and people would have to be constituted on a new foundation.[85] The existing vocabulary of politics lacked the words and concepts through which a new balance between authority and popular consent could be expressed. In effect the Great War and the events that followed created a demand for new concepts and political categories. Concepts like liberalism, capitalism or democracy stood in need of justification. As we shall see in the next chapter, instead of elaborating the old concept to meet the new conditions, many Europeans sought answers in the new ideologies that emerged out of the war.

The loss of confidence in these classical concepts of liberal democracy was integral to what was in effect the moral collapse of the old order. Lord Eustace Perry wrote in 1934 that there was 'no natural idea in which we any longer believe'. He added that 'we have lost the easy self-confidence which distinguished our Victorian grandfathers'.[86] This was a point at which the British establishment experienced the humiliation of serving as the object of ridicule for its own intellectuals. The image of Colonel Blimp would not be easy to shake off. Across the Channel in France, the situation was no better. 'The 1930s have conventionally been depicted as an era of almost unparalleled squalor in modern French history', wrote the cultural historian Stuart Hughes.[87]

In their important discussion of how the concept of dictatorship changed during the 'stormy periods that preceded and followed World War I', Peter Baehr and Melvin Richter raise the pivotal question of 'when, why, and how do certain concepts cease to be inescapable parts of the political vocabulary, and drop out of discourse'.[88] An equally important theme is the quest to recover meanings that were lost when ideals cease to motivate.

As the Great War drew to a close, modern societies became aware of a problem that endures to this day – what Fukuyama has characterized as the 'intellectual crisis of Western rationalism'.[89] In the interwar period the perceptions of this crisis were understandably overwhelmed by threats posed by Stalinism and fascism. But there was a less perceptible – though far more durable – threat at work. Disillusionment and estrangement with Western rationality was symptomatic of the loss of normative foundation for authority.

This was a loss that affected every dimension of human experience. As one observer commented on the zeitgeist of his time:

> The belief that endurance, diligence, honesty and unselfishness were virtues independent of their consequences had weakened as religious faith decayed; and the growing sense of insecurity that came from the fear of war and unemployment combined with the prevailing philosophies of the age to give many people a profound feeling that life had no values or significance at all.[90]

In decades to come, such confusions about beliefs would invite scepticism and counter-beliefs which would eventually crystallize into what is sometimes characterized as the Culture Wars.

Modris Eksteins's fascinating study of the cultural and aesthetic impact of the Great War highlighted its disruptive, indeed destructive effect on the prevailing system of meaning. But it did not merely represent a significant turning point in Western culture; it also called into question the prevailing system of values without offering any plausible alternatives. 'Old authority and traditional values no longer had credibility', yet 'no new authority and no new values had emerged in their stead' asserts Eksteins.[91] The Great War called into question everything and solved nothing.

The early modern Wars of Religion lasted for decades but in the end they were resolved through a peace treaty between the states. Thus the Thirty Years' War had a definite ending which was ratified by a Peace of Westphalia. The Treaty of Versailles provided only the pretence of peace, in part because this was not just a war for territory but one that divided people on ideological and – significantly – on cultural lines. Moreover, all the questions that invested hope in the war for an answer were still in search of a convincing reply.

Notes

1   Cited in Tucker & Roberts (2005) p.426.
2   Neumann (1946) p.8.
3   See Carsten (1988) p.1.
4   Furedi (1994) p.80.
5   Fukuyama (1989) p.3.
6   Fukuyama (1992) p.4.
7   Barzun (2000) p.683.
8   Muller (2013) p.16.

9   Thornton (1979) p.303.
10 Kaegi (1968) p.222.
11 Nordau (1913) p.2.
12 See Overy (2009).
13 Cited in Horne (2010a) p.19.
14 Eksteins (1989) p.255.
15 See http://www.nytimes.com/books/first/h/himmelfarb-cultures.html
16 Bracken (2002) pp.14, 207.
17 Muller (2013) p.24.
18 Roberts (1941) p.50.
19 Taylor (1966) p.32.
20 Taylor (1966) p.32.
21 Roberts (1941) p.46.
22 Thornton (1959) p.303.
23 Fukuyama (1992) p.4.
24 Cited in Eksteins (1989) p.218.
25 Roberts (1941) p.49.
26 Eksteins (1989) p.257.
27 Cited in Eksteins (1989) p.291.
28 Fussell (1975) p.21.
29 Cited in Overy (2009) p.11.
30 Wallas (1929) p.21.
31 Overy (2009) p.11.
32 Overy (2009) p.11.
33 McNeill (1970) p.20.
34 Wallas (1929) p.21.
35 Wallas.(1929) p.114.
36 Cited in Sontag (1971) p.209.
37 Valéry (1927) p.1.
38 Valéry (1927) p.54.
39 Cited in Kohn (1966) p.259.
40 Overy (2009) p.384.
41 Mills (1959) p.11.
42 Overy (2009) p.48.
43 Kohn (1964) p.306.
44 This manifesto is republished on http://wwi.lib.byu.edu/index.php/Manifesto_of_the_Ninety-Three_German_Intellectuals
45 Cited in Mommsen (1984) p.208.
46 Cited in Fournier (2013) p.682.
47 Taylor (1966) p.30.
48 This essay is reproduced on http://www.randolphbourne.columbia.edu/war_and_the_intellectuals.pdf
49 Barzun (2000) p.706.
50 Kramer (2007) p.31.

51   Eksteins(1989) p.xv.
52   Benda (1959) p.14.
53   Müller (2013) pp.12–13.
54   Horne (2010) p.xxi.
55   Spengler (1926) pp.38–9.
56   Fryer (1984) pp.319–20.
57   Money (1925) pp.88–9.
58   Mazower (1999) p.112.
59   Pfaff (1993) p.144.
60   Baudrillard (2003) p.11.
61   For a discussion of these fears, see Furedi (1998) Chapter 2.
62   See 'Notes', *Journal of Applied Sociology,* vol.7, no.6, 1923, p.291.
63   Stanley (1990) pp.135, 168.
64   For a discussion of this trend, see Furedi (1998).
65   Matthews (1930) pp. 27, 28.
66   Matthews (1930) p.28.
67   Matthews (1930) p.30.
68   Matthews (1930) pp.161, 163.
69   See Oldham (1924).
70   Cited in Turner (1923) pp.29–30.
71   Wirth (1960) p.xiii.
72   Weber (1919) p.128.
73   Hobsbawm (2004) p.6.
74   Mayall (1990) p.47.
75   Cited in the *Daily Express*; 21 October 1949.
76   Symonds (1991) p.94.
77   'Imperialism and Cosmopolitanism', *Economist*; 21 November 1925.
78   Public Record Office (PRO) CRO 1/54/11: 'A British Policy for World Peace and Prosperity', p.11.
79   See *The Times*; 17 February 1940, p.8
80   See 'Letters', *The Times*; 4 April 1940.
81   'Editorial' *The Times*; 22 April 1940.
82   'Leader', *Economist*; 17 October 1942.
83   Hancock (1950) p.9.
84   Kohn (1932) p.63.
85   Kohn (1929) pp. 1–2.
86   Cited in Rich (1989) p.65
87   Hughes (1969) p.15.
88   Baehr, P. and Richter, M. (2004) p.25.
89   Fukuyama (1992) p.11.
90   Roberts (1941) p.39.
91   Eksteins (1989) p.256.

2

Interwar intellectual crisis of the West

It is 24 September 1938 and the Germans have invaded Czechoslovakia. In desperation the British and French Governments opt for appeasing Hitler. But despite the soon-to-be signing of the now-infamous Munich agreement, only the self-deluded can really believe Chamberlain's proclamation that he had secured 'peace for our time'. The conflict that erupted in 1914 is about to turn into a new phase of unprecedented global violence and struggle. Sitting at a café table, Mathieu, the central character in Jean-Paul Sartre's novel *Reprieve*, reflects on the past two decades and its desperate attempt to maintain the illusion of peace. But now, he sees the two decades of the interwar era 'as they had been: a finite number of days compressed between two high, hopeless walls, a period duly catalogued, with a prelude and an end, which would figure on the history manuals under the heading: Between the two wars.' As if awakened from twenty-year-long slumber, Mathieu declares that 'all the experiences of the last twenty years have been spurious' and that those apparently 'lovely days led to a dark and secret future'.[1]

The two decades following the Great War have a distinctly nightmarish quality about them. But as Mathieu indicates, this was also a new era of artistic creativity. He reminds himself that 'jazz was a beginning', and 'the cinema, which I so much enjoy, was also a beginning', as was 'surrealism' and 'communism'. In retrospect it is evident that, despite a feverish search for new beginnings, the unresolved problems thrown up by the Great War continued to haunt the interwar era.

If anything, the Great War had intensified the crisis of meaning of the Western social order. It is worth noting that, at its outset, the war was embraced by many public figures as a crusade through which a sense of community and meaning could be regained. A significant proportion of European artists and intellectuals welcomed the war with enthusiasm. As Barzun recollects, 'looking over the roster of great names in literature, painting, music, philosophy, science, and social science, one cannot think of more than half a dozen or so who did not spout all the catchphrases of abuse and vainglory'.[2] A similar reaction also characterized the international socialist movement. World War One swiftly exposed the claims of socialist internationalism as empty rhetoric. The leaders of the trade union and social democratic movements swiftly joined war cabinets and took the lead in promoting the war efforts of their respective nations.

The preeminent sociologist Max Weber was preoccupied with the problem of meaning that afflicted modern society. His ardent support for Germany's entry into the war was motivated by the hope that this event could serve as a focus for the forging of moral unity in an otherwise disoriented world. He wrote that war could help forge the 'pathos and a sentiment of community' that was missing from the disenchanted and calculating world of modern life. 'War thereby makes for an unconditionally devoted and sacrificial community among the combatants and releases an active mass compassion and love for those who are in need', he argued in 1915.[3] Weber, who at the outbreak of the war greeted his guests sporting his reserve officer's uniform, welcomed the conflict because he believed that a community of solidarity created on the battlefield could provide soldiers with the meaning and motivation comparable to the experience of religious brotherhood. He stated that a 'war does something to a warrior which, in its concrete meaning, is unique', because 'it makes him experience a conse-crated meaning of death which is characteristic only of death in war'. Unlike normal death, which in normal times has no special meaning, in war and '*only* in war, the individual can *believe* that he knows he is dying "for" something'.[4] Weber claimed that the sacralization of an individual's sacrifice of life has important implications for the community as a whole, since it gives purpose not just to death but to life.

Within a few years of his exaltation of an individual's sacrifice of life, Weber was forced to realize that the war had, if anything, intensified the problems facing his society. Indeed, by the final stages of the conflict his 'overriding concern was with the survival of the German state and nation'.[5] The promise of unity and community which attracted so many idealist artists and intellectuals to this violent conflict was soon negated by the reality of bitter divisions and domestic discord.

Despite the promise of community and national unity, the Great War could not create a world that could resolve the cultural tensions immanent in modern society. The sense of unity and of belonging proved transitory and domestic tension hardened into social discord. That sacrifice and suffering proved to be pointless encouraged a mood of bitterness that comes in the wake of the trauma of disappointment. The enthusiasm with which a significant section of public opinion responded to the outbreak of the Great War soon gave way to resignation and internal strife. Throughout Europe the authority of the old order faced questions to which it had no answers.

The survival of social order was the fulcrum around which so much of interwar political and cultural life turned. The greatest revolutionary upheaval in modern Europe occurred between 1917 and 1921. In 1917 the Tsar was overthrown and the twentieth century's first revolutionary regime was inaugurated in Russia. A strike wave led by militant trade unionists hit Britain. In 1918 the monarchies in Austro-Hungary and Germany collapsed. Workers' councils and radical militias seized control in Austria and a revolution erupted in Hungary. Workers' councils emerged in Germany and by January 1919 the strike wave had precipitated a civil war. In May 1920 France experienced its first major industrial upheaval in the post-war era. In September workers occupied factories and seized land in Italy. Three months later a mass strike broke out in Czechoslovakia. As this upsurge of left-wing radicalism gradually ran out of steam, Europe was confronted with a wave of reaction. The rise of the authoritarian and fascist movements of the right was a direct response to the insecure political environment created by the war. The French historian Francois Furet has claimed that 'Bolshevism and Fascism are the children of World War I'.[6] These movements and other political experiments can also be interpreted as reactions to a political order that had by the end of the war had become discredited.

The years following the Great War have often been described as the Era of Ideologies. The destruction and violence that afflicted the world in the decades to come are frequently associated and even blamed on the ideologies and the movements which were advocating them. As one recent account observed, the twentieth 'century was also one in which political ideas seemed to play an exceptionally important role – so much so that contemporaries connected them directly to the catastrophes and cataclysms through which they were living'.[7] Yet an emphasis on ideology and the pre-eminent role of political ideas may well obscure a far more significant development, which was the disintegration of the old order and the intellectual culture that underpinned it. Lurking behind these ideologies was the intellectual crisis of Western society – one that acquired its intensity and form through the experience of the Great War. It was the weakness or lack of legitimacy of the Western liberal order that nurtured the terrain on which anti-liberal and anti-democratic ideas could flourish.

The Great War and the subsequent trauma confronting social order had many causes. But perhaps the most important issue facing Western societies was how to maintain order – in war and peace – at a time when it required the consent of the masses. The necessity for gaining and institutionalizing popular consent influenced the calculations of governments as they prepared for the outbreak of World War One. This problem was compounded during the war years due to the upheavals caused by the conflict. As Kohn recalled, 'the masses became politically conscious, their sufferings sharpened their ability to detect cause and effect not otherwise observed in everyday life' and became far more critical of the prevailing order than before the war.[8] The question of how to endow public institutions with legitimacy became a central question facing societies in the interwar years. The coincidence of rising expectations of the public with the weakening of the old order challenged the assumptions on which the ideals of liberal democracy were based.

Today, a century after the war, it is the unprecedented scale of violent destruction and the physical dislocation that shapes our understandably negative attitude towards this event. It is likely that during the immediate post-war years people's negative verdict of the conflict was not so much a statement about what happened on the battlefield as about what happened afterwards. The nation did not become a 'Land Fit for Heroes' and in a society like Britain the 'crucial factor' at work was a 'loss of confidence in the war's promised benefits'.[9] The feeling that all the sacrifice was in vain embraced the disenchanted public of the victor and the defeated nation alike. It directly contributed to a loss of belief in the legitimacy of the institutions and ideals associated with the pre-war regimes.

The quest for legitimacy

The First World War coincided with a moment in history when governments became directly exposed to the scrutiny of public opinion and, in many cases, subject to the pressure of a mass electorate. Wars could no longer be declared, fought or won without public support. Governments understood that they could no longer simply issue diktat. Policies needed to be publicly justified and required the support or at least the acquiescence of the people. The intellectual crisis of Western rationalism coincided with a moment when the consent of the public had become essential for the maintenance of order.

In his influential essay on the domestic causes of World War One, the historian Arno Mayer argued that it is precisely in periods of heightened social tension that calculations about the maintenance of order become intertwined with the conduct of foreign affairs.[10] Pointing to the high levels of internal strife that dominated the period leading up to the Great War, Mayer claimed that at this point in time geopolitical tensions coincided with domestic conflict. He observed that this 'symbiotic growth of domestic and international tensions' occurred at a time when in the West 'government policies, including foreign policies, were shaped in the crucible of organized party, pressure, and interest politics'.[11] In other words, foreign policy and diplomacy, which had hitherto been more or less insulated from domestic pressure, now became increasingly exposed to the influences emanating from mass politics and public opinion. Consequently political conflicts and debates about the future course of society influenced not only foreign policy but also military affairs. Wars could no longer be conducted without gaining a measure of public endorsement. When domestic issues become entangled with foreign ones, wars can become a medium through which political objectives were conducted.

'War is merely the continuation of politics by other means', argued the pre-eminent German military theorist Carl von Clausewitz. In Clausewitz's sociology of war, domestic pressures are meshed with foreign ones. According to his perspective, war is as much about domestic politics as a response to interstate relations. Mayer points out that Clausewitz 'invariably opts for the comprehensive concept of politics which subsumes diplomacy thus leaving open the possibility that recourse to war can be not only influenced but, in some instance, even determined by internal political considerations'.[12] The emergence of so-called 'war parties' in European societies during the early years of the twentieth century indicates that political rivalries were directly refracted through conflicting attitudes to military affairs.

With the ascendancy of public opinion and a mass electorate, the relations between states 'ceased to be the private preserve of an encapsulated elite'. Pointing to the arms race leading up to World War One, Mayer contends that it is likely that the 50 per cent increase in military spending during the five pre-war years 'may not have been exclusively a function of mounting inter-national distrust, insecurity, and hostility'.[13] He asserted that the expansion of military spending was influenced by nationalist politicians who were playing the patriotic card to 'maintain the domestic status quo'. The immediate pre-war era was one where the 'European nations experienced more than routine political and social disturbance'.[14]

Even relatively stable Britain was not immune to the outbreak of domestic tension that swept the Continent. The Curragh incident in March 1914 indicated that at least a section of the military were prepared to defy the British Parliament. Ulster had become a *cause célèbre* for conservatives and nationalists. At the same time, employers and the Establishment felt threatened by the growing power of the Labour Movement and the influence of militant syndicalists. The Triple Alliance of railwaymen, miners and transport workers threatened a general strike in the autumn of 1914. The polarization of public life placed great strain on Britain's political institutions. 'Indeed historians have wondered whether if external war had not come in 1914 England might not have been caught up in civil strife, with fatal damage to her time-honoured parliamentary system', wrote Mayer.[15]

The pattern that prevailed in England was also evident on the Continent. Political struggles between left and right and labour and capital in France and Italy encouraged political polarization and the strengthening of radical parties of all shades of opinion. In Germany too, political and social tensions had intensified in the pre-war years. Russia faced a prolonged period of industrial strife during the first half of 1917 and the Austro-Hungarian Empire faced a nationalist unrest. Only vestiges of the traditional order – monarchy, aristocratic hierarchy, customary deference – survived the upheavals of this period. At the time, the divisions within the social democratic movement leading to a split between its moderate and revolutionary wing seemed to be the first institutional victim of World War One. But the main casualty of the unravelling of European order was the politics of consensus and compromise represented by liberalism. Throughout Europe liberalism was on the defensive and clearly in retreat.

That the First World War failed to resolve the international tensions that preceded it has been widely noted. What is far less appreciated is that it also failed to resolve the domestic political issues that confronted European societies in the pre-war years. On the contrary, one of the most significant legacies of the Great War was that it radicalized public life and called into question the legitimacy of political categories and ideas that emerged with modernity. As we argue in this book, the ensuing battle of ideas continues into the twenty-first century.

During the years 1914–1918, the political tensions that preceded the war acquired new forms and an intensity that that caught policy-makers unaware. In particular, the metamorphosis of normal domestic conflict into ideological wars represented a significant departure from the pre-war era. 'While the ascendancy of the nation-state was a long-term trend, the explosion of an ideological conflict that would reshape national politics and the European balance of power in the interwar period was altogether more unexpected', asserts a recent review of World War One.[16] The language of the new ideologies often expressed a call to arms through such concepts as class war, war for survival, race and national war. These ideologies contained the implication of conflicts which were to be fought for objectives that were irreconcilable and therefore not susceptible to diplomatic or pragmatic resolution.

The ascendancy of ideologies and the concomitant hardening of political conflict was a direct outcome of the corrosive effect of the war on the legitimacy of Europe's political order. This legacy was the consequence of a war that was from the outset a deeply politicized conflict. Experience of twentieth-century wars indicates that once they become fought for political ends, wars risk acquiring their own inner dynamic. In contrast, wars that are mainly diplomatic and possess a specific external intent 'neither involve nor require the overthrow of the enemy's regime' and the 'fabric of legitimacy, both international and national, tends to weather hostilities intact'.[17]

Politicized from the outset, the conduct of the Great War was not simply subject to geopolitical realities. The exigencies of regime survival, the maintenance of order and a way of life interwove with nationalist ambitions that ultimately led to the tearing of the fabric of legitimacy that helped maintain inter-state conventions and national institutions.

In effect, the problem of order that predated the war had, by 1919, turned into a crisis of legitimacy of the old order. At this crucial conjuncture the ruling elites were confronted with the double challenge of not only gaining public consent but also of winning it in circumstances where their own authority was seriously compromised. As Jan Werner Muller pointed out:

> Once traditional conceptions of legitimacy, as well as the principles of dynastic descent had become widely discredited – as they had been after the first world war at the latest – the justifications for political rule had to become different.[18]

The point that Muller emphasizes is that, after 1919, the necessity for public justification needed to be 'both more extensive and more explicit'. Moreover it was not simply societies where the political order was subject to the influence of a mass democratic electorate that were required to justify their action and policies. Muller wrote that such considerations operated even in the 'case when legitimacy was supposed to be grounded in the personal charisma of a leader, or rely on a functioning state bureaucracy capable of delivering what citizens desired'. He adds that the 'new pressure for public justification was especially evident with right-wing regimes which precisely sought to rule in the name of tradition, as well as the royal dictatorships which flourished in interwar Europe', since neither tradition nor the monarchical principle possessed legitimacy on its own. Such ideals had to be 'articulated and actively promoted'.[19]

Even Adolf Hitler could not ignore the necessity for claiming to express the aspiration of the German public. On numerous occasions he favourably contrasted the principle of 'old Germanic democracy' with the majoritarianism of modern democracy. Hitler defined his old Germanic democracy as one which 'knows only an authority which proceeds downwards from the top and a responsibility which proceeds upwards from the bottom'.[20]

The justification for political rule had to be different to ones discredited by experience of the Great War. Politicians and movements associated with the pre-war order found it difficult to find a language with which to validate themselves. The old regime stood morally and politically compromised. That this moment represented the final demise of the monarchical principle of rule based on tradition was unsurprising. But none of the principles of government of the pre-war era were spared. Liberal constitutionalism and parliamentary democracy also had to justify themselves.

That legitimation through the gaining of public consent had become a far more pressing issue than in previous times did not mean that democracy as such became a powerful political force. The political elites understood that they needed to demonstrate that their rule was validated by public opinion, but since they were wary of its disruptive effect they were more concerned managing it than in providing greater scope for participation. Democracy was seen instrumentally as a source of validation rather than as an institution of public participation. Indeed, in the minds of numerous observers, the gaining of legitimacy was seen as inconsistent with the workings of a mass democracy.

Weber's demons

The problem of order faced by the European elites before 1914 paled into insignificance compared to the upheavals of the post-war years. Western societies faced not only the task of economic reconstruction and the recasting of inter-state relations but also the challenge of responding to the 'massification' of public life by establishing new constitutional and institutional arrangements. The collapse of the old order was most apparent in societies facing the threat of revolutions. But the erosion of authority was not confined to a handful of societies. The crisis of legitimacy transcended national borders and forced political elites throughout the West to rethink their relationship with their public. At this conjuncture the main narrative through which these elites experienced and interpreted the problem of order was that of the threat posed by the rise of the masses.

Through the construction of a narrative about a highly volatile, self-serving but easily manipulated 'mass', elite theorists sublimated their anxiety about the loss of their authority through devaluing the moral status of the public. The public now constituted a problem rather than a solution. The masses were deemed far too unpredictable and irrational to serve as a reliable partner in the maintenance of constitutional democracy. The Enlightenment ideal of an active, responsible and above all rational citizen was now habitually castigated as an illusion exposed by the behaviour of the masses before, during and in the years following the Great War. A study of the modern history of crowds and masses points out that after World War One 'there was a critical revision of modern mass democracy' by political theorists and policy-makers. This was a point at which Europeans 'critically re-examined the idea of democratic citizenship, which traditionally was based on the rational capacity of participation and decision on the part of the citizen'.[21] Public opinion was increasingly represented as a threat to stability, order and good government.

The containment and control the behaviour of the masses emerged as one of the principal issues facing the political elites of the interwar era. Governments had to be seen to act with the consent of the public –yet by their very existence the masses threatened the prevailing order. This was a paradox confronting Max Weber, Europe's most influential sociologist. His writings on the problem of legitimating authority were an attempt to both explain and resolve this paradox.[22]

Weber's concern with legitimate order and the process of legitimation – that is, how order is rendered valid – represented an attempt to engage with this fundamental question. Put simply, the term legitimation crisis is based on the insight that mere appeals to self-interest are unlikely to provide social or political stability. 'An order which is adhered to from motives of pure expediency is generally much less stable than one upheld on a purely customary basis through the fact that the corresponding behaviour has become habitual', claims Weber. He adds that even habit turns out to be 'much less stable' than an order which 'enjoys the prestige of being considered binding', that is, where 'belief in legitimacy' is achieved.[23] What Weber feared was that the instrumental orientation of modern liberal society could not generate values that the public could accept as binding and in such circumstances its capacity to legitimate institutions of authority would be weakened. The absence of foundational norms for liberal politics and institutions rendered their legitimacy problematic. At a time when the influence of traditional and religious sources of authority had become exhausted, the constitution of legitimacy represented the principal political issue facing the post-war world.

Weber believed that the crisis of legitimacy constituted a formidable threat to the future of Germany.[24] He had little doubt that the post-World War One German state lacked the legitimacy needed for authority and for a political class to act authoritatively.[25] At this conjuncture some German conservatives called for return to old national traditions. But Weber was far too sensitive to the workings of society to look for an escape into the past. In 1917 he observed that the problems confronting his society 'cannot be solved by distilling the "German spirit" from works of the past, however great their value may have been'.[26] What was required was a form of authority that could claim a bond and an association with the public of post-war mass society. One way or another the legitimation of German state required a measure of public assent.

Weber diagnosed the malaise that afflicted Germany as one that had its origins in the refusal – or inability – of the bourgeois class to confront the question of leadership. One of the unique features of Weber's response to the post-World War One crisis of legitimacy was that he pointed the finger of blame at the failure of the political elite to exercise responsible leadership. Unlike his contemporary elite theorists, Weber regarded the masses and the propertied with equal contempt. Writing about threats facing post-war Germany, he wondered whether 'the emotional effect of the blind fury of the masses will activate the equally emotional and senseless cowardice of the bourgeoisie'.[27] His lack of faith in the German bourgeoisie played an important part in his analysis.

Weber took the view that only exceptionally able, charismatic leaders were in a position to enjoy the legitimacy necessary for authoritative governing. Towards the end of the First World War he criticised those who blamed Germany's misfortune on either 'autocracy' or on a conspiracy of 'international democracy'. As far as he was concerned, what Germany lacked was 'leadership of the state by a politician', by which he meant leaders who were motivated by a calling to serve Germany and were prepared to struggle to realize their objectives.[28]

Weber's emphasis on calling and vocation bears the legacy of the influence of Machiavelli. In not entirely dissimilar circumstances, Machiavelli was preoccupied by the quality of leadership in his sixteenth-century Italy. In response to this problem he placed emphasis on public spirit and service and concluded that the strength of the state was proportional to its significance.[29] Weber placed greater faith in the moral integrity of a leader than in the creative potential of the democratic process.

Weber, who regarded mass political life with suspicion, found it difficult to elaborate a concept of authority that rested on democratic consent. As far as he was concerned, the mass had a 'largely negative significance'.[30] His negative evaluation of the masses intensified in response to the revolutionary upheavals of 1918–1919. A this point, Weber became so anxious about the threat from below that his own views acquired a distinctly anti-parliamentarian dimension.[31] While avoiding the cruder forms of interwar anti-mass prejudice, Weber clearly disdained the collective. Despite his previous liberal political leaning, he adopted a distinctly elitist and authoritarian tone.

As the German historian Wolfgang Mommsen notes, Weber reacted to the growth of mass democracy with concern. He was worried about the displacement of liberal parties controlled by 'eminent leaders' by mass political parties such as that of the social democrats. He felt that, given the peculiar weakness of the German bourgeoisie, it would be difficult, if not impossible, to construct institutions of modern liberal constitutionalism.[32] As far as he was concerned, parliament had 'lost its character as a political arena for independent personalities and became a place where partisan struggles worked themselves out before the court of public opinion'.[33] Accordingly, insulating the German state and its institutions from public pressure became an important theme in Weber's political writings.

Weber was preoccupied with the question of gaining the obedience of the public to the dictates of the state. His concern with the question of legitimation sensitized him to the need for ensuring that leaders enjoyed the mandate of public opinion. He opted for a solution that relied on the election of a leader through direct popular consent. For Weber, a plebiscite – direct election of Germany's leaders – appeared as the vehicle for ensuring that they possessed legitimate presidential authority. In his 1919 article 'The Reich President' he proposed a constitutional arrangement that had as its focus a powerful president, who was directly elected by plebiscite and who even possessed the power to dissolve parliament. In part this proposal was based on his belief that such a plebiscitary president could become a publicly acknowledged leader, whose authority could be justified on grounds that such leader enjoyed public acclamation.

Weber insisted that nothing should come in between the people and the president whose leadership 'rests on the will of the whole people without inter-mediaries'. Only through being able to claim the support of millions could a leader enjoy the authority required to make difficult decisions. Weber directly counterposed the legitimacy gained through the support of the masses to reliance on formal law. 'Only a President who has millions of votes behind him can have the authority to introduce socialization, which legal paragraphs alone can do absolutely nothing to achieve.'[34] Weber insisted that what was needed was a powerful but elected leader. He went so far as to suggest: 'let the social democrats remember that the much discussed "dictatorship" of the masses does indeed require the "dictator", chosen by them, to whom they subject themselves just as he retains their confidence.'[35] Weber claimed that no other form of political arrangement 'could ever bring into the administration that unity without which the reconstruction of our economy, on whatever foundation is impossible'. Weber was conscious of the need to restrain the power of the elected dictator and argued that such a person should see the "noose and gallows" before his eye if he ruled autocratically – 'but the Reich Presidency must be set firmly on its democratic feet.'[36] This was a formula that relied on the institution of direct democratic election to legitimate the authority of a strong ruler.

For Weber, democracy served as an instrument of impression management. It served as the most suitable institution for legitimating and cultivating charismatic leaders. The role of the public was relegated to the act of accla-mation. What he characterized as the 'Caesarist transformation of leadership selection' represented an attempt to harness the power of a referendum to the project of cultivating an authoritative leader. As Mommsen observes, Weber 'approved of it, even at the cost of rationality and objectivity in the formation of public opinion', since he believed that this was the only way to 'bring about rule by independent and genuinely qualified leaders'.[37] Drawing on his understanding of the taming of the *demos* in ancient Athens, Weber stated that 'mass democracy' had 'always bought its successes since Pericles' time with major concessions to the Caesarist principle of leadership selection beginning at the times of Pericles'.[38]

For Weber, Pericles personified the Caesarist political leader with an honourable calling. Such leaders combined integrity with charismatic leadership. Weber's commitment for cultivating charismatic leaders who possessed intellectual integrity stands in sharp contrast to his indifference to the wider public's level political culture. In his famous 1918 lecture 'Politics as a Vocation', Weber stated that although plebiscitarian leadership leads to the 'soullessness' of their following and their 'intellectual proletarianization', this is 'simply the price paid for guidance by leaders'.[39] He looked to the force of charismatic authority either exercised by an individual leader or through the ascendancy of a new spiritual aristocracy in a half-hearted attempt to create a focus for the obedience of the public.

Weber regarded mass opinion as a volatile, self-serving and ultimately destructive force that had to be indulged so that its influence could be used to consolidate the authority of the ruler. He believed that public pressure diminished the rationality of governing institutions and the administration of justice to a point where its regressive influence was potentially greater than that of 'the "star chamber" proceedings of 'an absolute ruler'. Weber was convinced that 'under the conditions of mass democracy, public opinion is communal conduct born of irrational "sentiments"' and that it lacked any independence since 'normally it is staged or directed by party leaders and the press'.[40]

Webers's writings on the problem of legitimacy represent an important intellectual legacy that scholars can draw on today. Sadly he left this problem unresolved. His project of cultivating charismatic leaders whose personal authority could inspire a renewal of public life exposed his own desperate attempt to find a prophet or a saviour. That he sought salvation in *Fuhrerdemokratie* or leader democracy indicated that Weber did not believe that that a public life of debate, competition and representation could prevail over the threat posed by the allegedly irrational masses. Nor did he have much faith in the power of ideas and arguments to enlighten or educate the public. His one-dimensional reliance on the Leader bears testimony to a failure of ideas. This was not a personal affliction, for Weber, like most of his peers, could not transcend the crisis of the West.

In the short run Weber's emphasis on the key role of the charismatic leader would prove to be prescient. But tragically it turned out that Europe was to be blessed with charismatic leaders of a very different kind. Weber died in 1920 and of course would have been appalled by the rise of the charismatic dictators. But because of his intuitive grasp of the problem of authority he would not have been totally surprised by the terrible events that would soon overwhelm Europe.

Democracy without democrats

When on 2 April 1917 President Woodrow Wilson asked a joint session of Congress to declare war on Germany, he justified his demand through appealing to the values of liberty and democracy. 'The world must be made safe for democracy', he asserted, before reminding the assembled representatives of the American people that 'peace must be planted upon the tested foundations of political liberty'.[41] Tragically, within a short period of time 'Wilsonian idealism' would become an object of cynicism and scorn. Instead of 'making the world safe for democracy', the war destabilized domestic political life and exposed liberal constitutionalism to hostile scrutiny. Contrary to the hopes expressed by Wilson in April 1917, one of the most significant casualties of the Great War was the ideal of democracy.

After the senseless slaughter of millions on the battlefields of Europe and the political chaos and violence that followed the termination of the war, supporters of liberal democracy were forced on defensive. In many parts of Europe, parliaments appeared as ineffectual talking shops whose indecisive behaviour was brought into relief by the energy and force of the new radical movements which took their politics to the street. With exception of the United States, the ruling classes of the post-war order were conscious of their loss of legitimacy. Frequently the decline of relations of deference was attributed to the emergence of a public that had yet to be tamed. The weakening of the system of state authority was experienced as the outcome of the impossible pressures placed on it by the unrestrained demands of the newly empowered masses. The problem of order was directly associated with the volatility, immaturity and irrationality of the masses. Too much freedom and democracy and too high a regard for public opinion was held responsible for the post-war erosion of authority.

The association of democracy with ineffectual government and political chaos provided a political terrain where authoritarian values could flourish. Although the term authoritarian came into usage in the late nineteenth century, it was only in the years following the Great War that it acquired a widespread positive connotation. Whatever the emphasis its supporters placed on this term, it communicated an affirmation of the necessity for the restoration of authority. According to the *Oxford English Dictionary*, in the nineteenth century an authoritarian was 'one who supports the principle of authority'. One 1879 definition defined an authoritarian as 'favouring imposed order over freedom'.[42] By the interwar period this definition mutated into one where authoritarian was interpreted as the upholder of authority. This interpretation retained its influence into the 1940s. One significant sociological contribution on the subject complained that 'too often, "authority" has been confused with "authoritarian" which is merely a particular type of authority'.[43]

For a significant section of the political and cultural elites, making the world safe for authority seemed far more important than securing the integrity of democratic institutions. On reviewing the post-war deliberations on the subject, it is difficult not to be struck by the casual manner with which democracy was dismissed as a dangerous illusion. Thomas Mann's wartime essay, 'Reflections of a Nonpolitical Man', published in 1918 described democracy as 'foreign and poisonous to the Germanic character'. The essay was not simply an attack on democracy but also a celebration of authoritarianism. He exclaimed that the 'much decried "authoritarian state" is and remains the one that is proper and becoming to the German people, and the one they basically want'.[44]

Mann himself would eventually repudiate the sentiments expressed in this essay, but during the interwar decades suspicion towards democracy, popular sovereignty and public opinion influenced mainstream views throughout the Western world. 'Of all the developments in the Age of Catastrophe, survivors from the Nineteenth century were perhaps most shocked by the collapse of the values and institutions of the liberal civilization whose progress they had taken for granted', concluded Hobsbawm in his discussion of the interwar era. The collapse of liberal democracy had a physical and intellectual dimension. The interwar era saw the overthrow or dissolution of representative electoral regimes throughout the world. In Europe constitutional governments gave way to authoritarian ones and with the exception of Britain, Ireland, Sweden and

Switzerland, democratic political institutions could not endure the upheavals of these decades.

The rise of authoritarian regimes was paralleled by a loss of faith in democracy, or, more specifically, in popular sovereignty. Even in democracies the model of the rational and responsible citizen gave way to the suspicion that the masses lacked the moral and intellectual resources necessary to make wise judgements. Such sentiments were most systematically expressed by ideologues of the far right and the fascists. Their hostility to popular sovereignty and liberal constitutionalism was unwavering. Mussolini declared in 1923 that to 'speak of the sovereign people is to utter a tragic jest'.[45] Nor did he have much time for liberalism. He asserted that 'Fascism is not afraid to declare itself illiberal or anti-liberal' and added that 'it has already passed and, if necessary, will again pass, without the slightest hesitation, over the more or less decomposed body of the Goddess of Liberty'.[46]

Advocates of authoritarian order represented liberal democracy as an outdated fantasy that could not survive for long. 'I am convinced that within twenty years, if there is not some retrograde movement in political evolution, there will be no legislative assemblies left in Europe', stated the Portuguese dictator Antonio Salazar in 1934.[47] The far right did not have a monopoly over such pessimistic prognosis of the future of liberal democracy. Many leftist and liberal thinkers regarded the success of right-wing and fascist movement as proof that the public could not make democracy work. The success of authoritarianism was interpreted as evidence that there was a demand for it from the masses. Consequently the masses were characterized as unreliable and irrational canon-fodder for authoritarian movements. In this narrative of the irresponsible public, the irrational masses served as a convenient scapegoat for the weakness and incoherence of liberal democratic institutions. In 1921, a prominent British sociologist, Morris Ginsberg, warned that 'the laziness, indifference, and apathy of the masses is probably the obverse side, so to speak, of their longing for leadership'.[48] Ginsberg insisted that this longing for authority by the masses encouraged the rise of power-hungry leaders. He explained that 'the apathy of the masses and their longing for leadership is accompanied by an insatiable thirst for power on the part of the leaders'.[49]

If, as Ginsberg asserted, the longing of the masses for strong authoritarian leaders had such a significant impact on public life, then the prospects for democracy were indeed dire. This conclusion was drawn even by many disappointed liberals, who regarded the rise of interwar dictators as the negation of their hope. In his 1933 essay 'The Democratization of Culture', renowned sociologist Karl Mannheim asserted that it was democracy itself which created the terrain for the flourishing of totalitarian movements:

> Dictatorships can arise only in democracies; they are made possible by the greater fluidity introduced into political life by democracy. Dictatorship is not the antithesis of democracy; it represents one of the possible ways in which a democratic society may try to solve its problems.[50]

Mannheim's pessimistic account of democracy was widely influential in the mainstream of Western intellectual and public life. The sense of disappointment and demoralization with the failures of liberal democracy was often coupled with a condemnation of the masses.

The German legal philosopher Karl Loewenstein blamed democracy for paving the way for fascism in the following terms:

> The rise of the semi-military and revolutionary movements of the Black-shirts and the Brown-shirts was made possible by the protection of, and under the cover of, the liberal and democratic institutions of Italy and Germany. Democratic magnanimity was suicidal for both. Democracy sharpened the dagger by which it was stabbed in the back. The National Socialist party was admittedly antiparliamentarian. Hatred of the Western parliamentary system was the most attractive plank of its political platform, as racism was the sociological incentive for the masses. Nevertheless, by the generous and lenient Weimar republic, Hitlerism was allowed to use democracy for the avowed and explicit purpose of destroying democracy.[51]

This depiction of the rise of fascism conveyed the implication that, as against the powerful influence of racism, a constitutional democracy was helpless. In characterizing racism as the 'most attractive plank' of fascism, Loewenstein indirectly condemned the masses for their inclination to embrace bigotry and prejudice. This view of the unreliable masses persists into the twenty-first century and influences the way that public debate and governance is managed.

Disappointment with liberal democracy was widely expressed even in the United States – the nation which was least afflicted by the post-war problem of order and the intellectual crisis. During the 1920s and 1930s American academic periodicals and magazines oriented towards a highbrow readership regularly ran articles that expressed scepticism about the viability of liberal democracy. Sceptics would often point to the examples of Stalinist Russia and Nazi Germany as efficient and authoritative alternatives to their own floundering liberal democracies. Walter Shepard, President of the American Political Science Association acknowledged that 'we have been impressed, more than we care to admit, with the practical failure of democratic government in Europe'. Pointing to the 'spread of fascism and the success of the communist experiment in Russia' and the 'breakdown of the capitalistic system and the prolonged economic depression', he suggested that Americans had become a 'nation of political skeptics'.[52] The conclusion he drew was to call into question the viability of liberal democracy. 'Is it not evident that the theory of popular sovereignty, the central idea of democratic ideology, cannot stand up under an objective critical analysis and must be frankly abandoned?', he asked.[53]

Shepard's rejection of the 'theory of popular sovereignty' was underpinned by the conviction that only authoritarian solutions could fix the problems facing 1930s America. As one contributor to *The American Political Science Review* indicated, 'most thinkers admit that some changes must be made if democracy is to survive, and one solution which seems to be gaining more adherents than the others is that some elements of fascist organization and authority must be carried over into democratic liberalism'.[54] Such views even influenced individuals who identified with the liberal wing of the Democratic Party. Even some New Dealers were awestruck by Mussolini's Italy.[55]

One Harvard academic, William Elliott, noted in 1926 that liberal democracy was in retreat. He commented: 'Italy and Russia have cast the die', and 'Spain and the Balkans have followed their lead, while Germany and Central Europe waver on the verge'.[56] Although he retained a belief in constitutional government, Elliott had little faith in the capacity of the people to manage their affairs. One of the lessons that he drew from his experience of the 1920s was the need to subject representative democracy to the influence of the expert: 'The necessity of more independent expert administration and advice is obvious'.[57] Elliott, a future counsellor to several American Presidents and a member of Roosevelt's 'brain-trust', could find only technical solutions to the problem of legitimacy experienced by interwar liberal democracy.

The war that millions fought to make the world safe for democracy helped create a world where this political idea lost much of its capacity to inspire and motivate people. Specifically, democracy as a form of popular sover-eignty lacked a significant body of intellectual and cultural support in the interwar era. During this period of political upheaval democracy was not simply threatened by its totalitarian enemies but also by its own intellectual crisis. One of the indirect consequences of the Great War was to change the way that democracy was seen and experienced. And at least for a couple of decades it appeared to many that democracy was losing the battle. Even in the late twentieth century this wounding of democracy by the Great War would continue to have an impact on the thinking of policy-makers and officials. A widely discussed report published in 2000 on the theme 'What's Troubling the Trilateral Democracies' made a 'happy contrast' between the fate of democracy after the end of World War One and World War Two. 'In sharp contrast to the period after World War 1, no serious intellectual or ideological challenge to democracy has emerged', it stated.[58]

Liberalism without liberals

The fate of political democracy was paralleled by a general erosion of influence of liberal values. The loss of legitimacy of the pre-war order intersected with the very apparent decline of free- market capitalism. After the Great War capitalism looked very different to the pre-war model of a dynamic system of production driven by free competition. It was difficult to celebrate a system of production that appeared inherently unstable and prone to economic malaise. Though economic chaos was followed by episodes of prosperity, the interwar period experienced unprecedented economic upheaval and uncertainty. The Wall Street Crash of 1929 was a global catastrophe and the Great Depression that followed intensified the belief that it was only a matter of time before capitalism collapsed. The economic woes of the capitalist world stood in sharp contrast to the apparent success of the Soviet Union. An outwardly depression-free Soviet Union served to reinforce the impression that economic crisis was a disease of capitalism.

The failure of liberal capitalism to retain the credibility it enjoyed during the nineteenth century was not entirely due to the severe economic problems that afflicted the interwar Western world. Capitalism itself appeared to be abandoning its rhetorical commitment to free competition and the free market. Although the claims made in support of *laissez-faire* capitalism rarely corre- sponded to reality, they appeared plausible in the nineteenth-century context of the limited state.

Since its inception, capitalism has always coexisted with a measure of state intervention, organized competition and monopolization of market relations. During the Great War these trends were intensified as a result of the necessity for mobilizing society's resources. State intervention in economic life was systematic and the market was subordinated to the exigency of fighting a total war. The merging of the state with economic life was frequently characterized as an expression of organized capitalism. This new development was also heralded by both its supporters and opponents as the end of the era of classical free-market capitalism.

Freedom from the state – a key theme of liberal political theory – was called into question by the fundamental and seemingly irreversible changes to the capitalist system. At times it seemed that the only issue up for debate was the form that state intervention should assume. Corporatism was favoured by conservative Christian and fascist movements. Keynesian economics flourished in Western democracies, though it was also well received in Nazi Germany. The state-managed and directed Soviet economy was seized upon as a model by left-wing and centrist intellectuals. In the United States, the New Deal was the medium through which organized capitalism was institutionalized in the land of the free. The belief that state intervention and public works programmes were the most effective institutions for overcoming the depression and the scourge of mass unemployment was held by both left- and right-wing movements. Numerous leftist public figures such as the former Belgian socialist leader Henri de Man or the ex-British Labour Party Minister Oswald Mosley became attracted to the corporatist economic policies of fascism.

The dramatic loss of credibility of ideas associated with free-market capitalism is illustrated by the fact that both during the Great War and in the decades that followed, the merging of the state and economic life was rarely contested. On the contrary, the principles of organized capitalism or state capitalism or the command economy were frequently represented as essential for assuring the security and welfare of society. By the mid-1930s the constant expansion of the state was treated as a fact of life. In Britain, Sydney and Beatrice Webb, notwithstanding their deeply held anti-Marxist sentiments, became ardent supporters of the Soviet system after a visit in 1932. The Soviet bureaucracy, they asserted, was the 'unavoidable apparatus of any highly developed industrial community'.[59]

Capitalism was not only diagnosed as sick, it was often described as a system whose very survival was at issue. Even the advocates and beneficiaries of capitalism often gave the impression that they too believed that the collapse of this system was imminent. In 'the 1930s the underlying assumptions and the language used suggested a system that would have to change or die, even among businessmen who were its chief beneficiaries', wrote Overy.[60] The mood of pessimism regarding the future of capitalism even affected the US. In 1940 the American Federal Trade Commission warned that 'the capitalist system of free initiative is quite capable of dying and dragging down with it the system of democratic government'. It cautioned that that monopoly constituted the 'death of capitalism and the genesis of authoritarian government'.[61]

The experience of the Great War and its legacy of economic dislocation had a profound impact on the way that Western society thought about liberalism and capitalism. 'The thirties had been a miserable time', recalled the American economist John Kenneth Galbraith. He noted that 'many had lost confidence in the economic system, many more had come to assume that it could endure only as the result of more of the government intervention that had been the hallmark of the New Deal'.[62] One of the direct consequences of the shift towards government intervention was to severely damage the credibility of economic liberalism.

During the 1930s those who still retained faith in liberal capitalism were lost for words. They inherited 'conceptual apparatuses that many saw as ambiguous or obsolete'. When a group of liberals met in Paris in 1937 to form an international network to save their doctrine from extinction, the first diffi-culty they faced was how to define themselves. As an important study of this network wrote, the term Liberalism had been discredited with its association with the 'Manchester doctrine' of *laissez-faire*. At this meeting of the 'Colloque Lippmann', often referred to as the founding moment of neo-liberalism, the participants 'shared a commitment to attempt to save liberalism by changing it, even as the ideology seemed to be ineluctably entering the later stages of self-inflicted decline'.[63]

Those in attendance 'could no longer consider themselves "liberals" because the use of that title would identify them with the very philosophy they were attempting to overcome'. At the meeting, terms like 'liberalism', 'neoliberalism', 'individualism', 'laissez-faire' and 'liberalism of the left' 'were all variously raised and rejected'.[64] This was an important moment when the movement oriented towards the rescuing of the liberal tradition was forced to confront the corrosion of its own public identity. In subsequent decades those who identified with this tradition would attempt to 'develop additional allegiances around the terms "classical liberalism", "libertarianism" and "conservatism"'. But 'The failure of the participants in the "Colloque Lippmann" at this moment to name themselves generated a problem that would plague the movement in later years, as in the absence of a shared reference its members increasingly identified themselves with divergent labels and focused intensively on the differences their respective choices entailed'.[65]

In his insightful review of this event, Burgin wrote that the participants of the conference were remarkably vague about their beliefs. They realized that nineteenth-century liberalism and ideas associated with *laissez-faire* 'had proved itself unsustainable as an abstract framework for ordering of social interaction'. They were committed to the 'rehabilitation of the market mechanism and to the advocacy of a social structure that preserved' – with limitations – 'a general framework for free discussion and exchange' and they 'were committed to the idea of a "revised", "progressive", "constructive", "new" liberalism without having yet identified precisely what the revisions entailed'.[66] Burgin noted that the Colloque Lippmann had 'difficulties identifying constructive "revisions" that did not violate the philosophy they were attempting to save'.[67] Arguably, in all but name they had given up on liberalism. The participants 'shared a belief that the principles of traditional liberalism had proved unsustainable, and perhaps more important, that they did not present a viable option to those in position of academic or political power'.[68]

The illiberal moment

The difficulty that interwar liberals faced in finding a name was but one expression of the disintegration of the old intellectual universe. In retrospect it is evident that the Great War did not spare any of the political movements from having to legitimate themselves through a new language. But as we noted previously, liberal democracy and the outlook associated with Western rationalism suffered a severe setback as a result of the war. In his magnificent study of the shifting contours of early twentieth-century American culture, Henry May showed that the 'most obvious aspect of the change brought by the war was the complete disintegration of the old order, the set of ideas which had dominated the American mind so effectively from the mid-nineteenth century until 1912'.[69]

May claims that after the war belief in progress seemed 'shattered' and it was hard to find a convincing or intellectually respectable spokesman for the prewar faith'.[70] Pre-war advocates of progress found it difficult to promote their beliefs in the interwar years. H. G. Wells, the author of *The Modern Utopia* (1905) and one of the most renowned proponents of social progress, died a demoralized and disillusioned man, warning of the 'ever swifter whirlpool of disaster in which man is spinning'.[71] The trajectory followed by Wells was followed by a significant body of intellectuals and artists. As May remarked, 'before the war, most of the literary rebels had believed in progress as strongly as their opponents', but 'after the war, typical attitudes of writers ranged from Eliot's religious conservatism to Jeffers' naturalistic despair'.[72]

The displacement of a belief in progress by a sensibility oriented towards crisis was in part an understandable reaction to the unexpected violence and destruction wrought by the war and the precarious future facing the post-conflict world. More specifically, Western society's estrangement from the idea of progress was also attributable to the intellectual crisis facing Western society. Western society was at a crossroad. The pre-war intellectual world could no longer offer the signposts and meaning necessary to engage with the future. At the same time the ideas that were thrown up in the interwar era did not offer a credible alternative. Obviously interwar societies could not simply abandon the intellectual legacy of modernity. But with a few exceptions – technocrats in the Soviet Union or Italian Futurists – they could not enthusiastically endorse it.

Outwardly it seemed as if the intellectual crisis of the West was a direct consequence of the challenge posed to Enlightenment, liberal and democratic thinking by the influence of the Soviet Union and of the fascist movements. However it is more useful to conceptualize this crisis as logically prior to the rise of these new radical movements. It was the failure to defend and give meaning to ideas of progress, rationality, scientific knowledge, capitalism and democracy that provided the terrain on which new radical movements could thrive. Writing in 1937, the pre-eminent American sociologist Talcott Parsons compared his era to the seismic intellectual revolution unleashed by the Reformation. He wrote that 'a revolution of such magnitude in the prevailing interpretations of human society is hardly to be found occurring within the short space of a generation unless one goes back to about the sixteenth century'.[73]

However there was one important difference between the changes brought by the Reformation and by the Great War. The Reformation may have led to the outbreak of a protracted period of religious war and strife. But it also led to elaboration of new ideas and values, which had the effect of providing society with a system of meaning and helped foster a climate that was hospitable to modernity. In contrast, interwar society was uncomfortable with itself and with its achievement. Aldous Huxley, grandson of the progressive scientist

Thomas Huxley, personified this trend. His anti-utopian fiction *Brave New World* (1932) outlined a future where the world was technically advanced and acted in accordance with the ethos of technical rationality but was emptied of its humanity.

With the advantage of hindsight it is possible to conclude that it was the intellectual exhaustion of Western liberal democracies rather than the attraction of new radical alternatives that accounts for the success of fascist and Stalinist movements in the interwar period. The historian E. H. Carr was conscious of the difficulty that liberal democracies had in motivating the public: 'The attraction of Bolshevism, Fascism and National Socialism lay not in their obscure, elastic and sometimes incoherent doctrines, but in the fact that they professedly had something new to offer and did not invite their followers to worship a political ideal enshrined in the past'.[74] The contrast that Carr drew between the appeal of the new and the loss of relevance of the old were not simply an outcome of political confusion but also of an unsettled cultural imagination. With the passing of time these tensions would harden and acquire a significant role in modern public life. As we shall see in the next chapter, the gravest symptom of the intellectual crisis of the West was the apparently irresistible triumph of new radical ideologies.

Notes

1   Sartre (1973) p.86.
2   Barzun (2000) p.700.
3   Weber (1915a) p.335.
4   Weber (1915a) p.335.
5   Lassman & Speirs (2008) p.xviii.
6   Furet (1999) p.19.
7   Muller (2013) p.1.
8   Kohn (1929) p.1.
9   Ceadel (1994) p.227.
10 He argues that the 'interconnection of domestic politics and foreign policy is exceptionally intense under prerevolutionary conditions'. Mayer (1967) p.287.
11 Mayer (1967) p.287.
12 Mayer (1969) p.292.
13 Mayer (1967) p.288.
14 Mayer (1967) p.288.
15 Mayer (1967) p.289.
16 Horne (2010a) p.xx.

17   Mayer (1969) p.294.
18   Muller (2011) p.588.
19   Muller (2011) p.588.
20   Cited in Krieger (1977) p.255.
21   Frezza (2007) p.128.
22   See Furedi (2013).
23   Weber (1978) p.31.
24   For a discussion of this problem in interwar Europe and Weber's relation to it, see Furedi (2013) Chapters 14 and 15.
25   Weber (1917) pp.107–23.
26   Weber (1917) p.123.
27   Weber (1978) p.1461.
28   Weber (1918) pp.159–63. For Weber, authentic political leaders were ones who 'live *for* politics' rather than those who 'live *from* politics'. See Weber (1918) p.190.
29   See the discussion in Chapter 1, Part IV in Allen (1964). The relationship between Weber and Machiavelli remains relatively unexplored. It is worth noting that both of them drew on the experience of Rome in their attempt to elaborate a concept of leadership.
30   Beetham (1985) p.112.
31   Mommsen (1984) pp.184, 340.
32   See Eliaeson (2000) p.135.
33   Mommsen (1984) p.185.
34   Weber, M. (1986) (originally 1919) 'The Reich President', *Social Reserarch*, vol.53, no.1. p.129.
35   Weber (1986) p.129.
36   Weber (1986) p.129.
37   Mommsen (1984) p.186.
38   Cited in Mommsen (1984) p.187.
39   See 'Politics as a Vocation' in Gerth & Wright Mills (1978) p.113.
40   See section titled 'Bureaucracy' in Gerth & Wright Mills (1958) p.221.
41   Wilson's speech is reproduced in http://historymatters.gmu.edu/d/4943/
42   http://www.oed.com.chain.kent.ac.uk/Entry/13344>; accessed 13 January 2011. Earlier version first published in *New English Dictionary*, 1885.
43   Wolpert (1950) p.680.
44   Excerpts from this essay are reproduced http://germanhistorydocs.ghi-dc.org/pdf/eng/821_Thomas%20Mann_Reflections_160.pdf
45   Cited by Stewart (1928) p.852.
46   Cited by Stewart (1928) p.852
47   Salazar is cited in Muller (2003) p.110.
48   Ginsberg (1964) p.138.
49   Ginsberg (1964) p.139.
50   Cited in Borch (2012) p.175.
51   Loewenstein (1935) p.580.
52   Shepard (1935) pp.9–10.
53   Shepard (1935) p.8.

54   Wilson (1937) p.14.
55   Muller (2013) p.104.
56   Elliott (1926) pp.163–4.
57   Elliott (1926) p.185.
58   Pharr & Putnam (2000) p.7.
59   Webb & Webb (1937) p.805.
60   Overy (2009) p.91.
61   Cited in Richards (1987) p.90.
62   Galbraith (1977) p.xv.
63   Burgin (2012) p.72.
64   Burgin (2012) pp.72–3.
65   Burgin (2012) p.73.
66   Burgin (2012) p.73.
67   Burgin (2012) p.73.
68   Burgin (2012) p.75.
69   May (1992) p.393.
70   May (1992) p.394.
71   Fay (1947) p.246.
72   May (1992) p.395.
73   Parsons (1968a) p.5.
74   Carr (1944) p.xv.

3

The spectre of ideologies

Karl Dietrich Bracher, in his study *Age of Ideologies*, asserted that the First World War destroyed liberalism. He claimed that 'not liberal democracy but a radical anti-liberalism and "illiberalism" occupied the extended field of political ideologies'.[1] The reaction to liberalism that Bracher outlined is often interpreted as the outcome of the radicalization of mass politics during the final phase of the war and the decades that followed the conflict. The very term Age of Ideologies conveys the widely held belief that, partly as a reaction to the war, new powerful political passions had captured the imagination of people. The idea that the Great War seamlessly crossed over into ideological conflict is frequently argued in history text-books. As a currently available school text argues:

> The world created after the Great War was one of economic depression and political instability. People were looking for radical solutions to these radical problems, and many began to believe that the answer could be found in ideology.[2]

This post-war search for answers implied a loss of faith in the status quo and, more specifically, in the liberal worldview that justified it. That there is an important connection between the Great War and the subsequent ideological conflicts that dominated public life in large parts of the interwar world is not in doubt. However the question of how the experience of war influenced the political thinking of people and why public life became polarized along such radically ideological lines is still a topic of debate

The relationship between the Great War and the Age of Ideologies that followed is still a subject of controversy. The Israeli political scientist Zeev Sternhell contends that there exists a significant continuity between the ascendancy of ideologies in 1920s and 1930s and pre-war movements hostile to Enlightenment and liberal values. According to this thesis, fascism developed in France and Italy 'long before the First World War'. Sternhell does not entirely dismiss the significance of the Great War for creating the conditions where radical anti-liberal ideologies could thrive. He argues:

> Let me emphasize here that I do not underestimate the importance of the Great War – by no means. The war undoubtedly produced favorable conditions which allowed ideologies which had been maturing for many years to become a political force, but it did not produce these ideologies. It provided the intellectual revolt, after a long period of incubation, with the opportunity and means to become a political force. But the basis of the rise of fascism is not to be found in the post-1918 crises but in the struggle against ideological modernity, which means against the French and Kantian tradition of the Enlightenment.[3]

Sternhell claims that a long tradition of anti-democratic thought that challenged the 'moral basis of democracy' had gained momentum as a result of the war and by the interwar period 'finally become a mass phenomenon'.[4]

Sternhell's analysis is flawed in one important respect. The basis for fascism and other radical movements did not lie in the pre-1914 past but in the conditions of the post-1918 era. Specifically, the disorganization of political life and the emergence of a mass public that was alienated from the system of authority encouraged the growth of radical oppositional movements. What distinguished these movements was not their doctrine, but their explicit and systematic orientation towards mass mobilization. These movements did not simply grow from modest pre-World War One beginnings to become a mass phenomenon. Their very attempt to voice the aspiration of the masses gave them a distinct post-World War One voice.

Sternhell is right to situate the origins of the anti-modernist and anti-liberal ideas that flourished in the 1920s and 1930s far back in the nineteenth century. But the war did not simply intensify or radicalize pre-existing political and intellectual trends. Through its corrosive impact on the prevailing system of authority it also transformed the socio-cultural and political landscape. Moreover it created a new constituency of people whose lives were uprooted, who became estranged from the old sources of meaning and who were open to radical solutions and ideas. The exhaustion of bourgeois self-belief that we noted earlier was mirrored by a palpable sense of existential insecurity among the people of Europe.

Liberal democracy concedes its irrelevance

The precondition for the emergence of the Age of Ideologies was the internal crisis of the old bourgeois order and its liberal institutions. Its defensive and alarmist reaction to the exigencies of mass society indicated that it lacked the intellectual and institutional flexibility and resilience to react to and manage the challenge it faced. The most poignant feature of this crisis was that even individuals who had identified themselves with liberalism ceased to retain their outlook with conviction. Increasingly liberals regarded their values as precious possessions that had to be protected from the ungrateful masses.

It is worth noting that liberalism had always possessed an elitist dimension. As one study of *Aristocratic Liberalism* recalled, many of the leading theorists of nineteenth-century liberalism were anxious about the rise of the lower classes.[5] Even relatively radical liberals tended to portray the lower classes as an unreliable mass that could be easily corrupted or let astray by unscrupulous demagogues. In 1919, the soon-to-be-Marxist political theorist Harold Laski warned that 'few things have been more easy than for an able and energetic government, which was willing to pay the price, to bribe a whole people into slavery'.[6]

During the decades following the war, liberal thinkers more or less gave up on the possibility of influencing the masses. Their account of mass society and the irrationality of its people often comes across as an apology for their failure to compete with movements of the radical left and right. If indeed the masses were as fickle and as easily seduced by the propaganda of nationalistic, authoritarian and militant leaders, then liberalism could blame its failures on circumstances beyond its control. John Dewey, one of the most important American liberal thinkers of the twentieth century, sought to account for the crisis of his creed by offering an analysis of a mass society that was inhospitable to the workings of a rational democracy.

Although Dewey avoided the explicit contempt that the elite theories of his time directed towards the masses, he still characterized the emotional life of the American public as 'undiscriminating, lacking in individuality and in direction by intellectual life'. His diagnosis was that 'our pronounced trait is mass suggestibility'.[7] Dewey claimed that this problem was compounded by the failure to replace the old and irrelevant political vocabulary of the past with a new grammar of meaning. He believed that this predicament was particularly difficult for liberals. 'The lack of secure objects of allegiance, without which individuals are lost, is especially striking in the case of the liberal', he wrote. He elaborated on the quandary facing interwar liberalism in the following terms:

> The liberalism of the past was characterized by the possession of a definite intellectual creed and programme; that was its distinction from conservative parties which needed no formulated outlook beyond the defence of things as they are. In contrast, liberals operated on the basis of a thought-out social philosophy, a theory of politics sufficiently definite and coherent to be easily translated into a programme of politics to be pursued. Liberalism to-day is hardly more than a temper of mind, vaguely called forward-looking, but quite uncertain as to where to look and what to look forward to.[8]

The failure of liberalism to adjust to new circumstances and provide a political outlook appropriate for the challenges facing the interwar world meant that it could exercise only a minimal influence over public life.

It was widely recognized that liberalism was comfortable with public opinion as long as it was mainly composed of the middle classes and influenced by them. However, once public opinion expanded to include a much wider section of society, liberals became pessimistic about their capacity to deal with this development. One American student of interwar public opinion noted that 'middle class opinion' could not compete for authority with its radical counter-parts. He stated that middle-class opinion was 'given unhealable wounds by the new revolutionary movements that use techniques of mass communication to establish or to stabilize their own power'.[9]

The problem exercising Dewey was the inability of liberalism to provide a normative foundation for democratic public life. Without such a foundation liberalism could not motivate and gain the loyalty of a significant section of mass society. Dewey argued that nationalist and militaristic movements had an advantage over democratic ones. They could could harness the imagination of the masses and marginalize the influence of liberal democracy. 'The most militaristic of nations secures the loyalty of its subjects not by physical force but through the power of ideas and emotions', he stated. Dewey warned that in the absence of everyday bonds and peaceful focus for community life, human emotions will be 'mobilized in the service of a war that will supply its temporary stimulation'.[10] The enthusiasm with which millions of people greeted the outbreak of the First World War haunted liberals like Dewey, who regarded the emotional power of militant nationalism as a force that democracy would struggle to control.

Although the association of the Great War with the mass enthusiasm of the public has been contested by historians in recent decades, at the time this view was rarely questioned by commentators.[11] The Great War was seen as a watershed in the development of public opinion. From this point onwards, public opinion is increasingly represented as a powerful and irrational force that threatens the integrity of democratic institutions. Paul Palmer, in his path-breaking essay 'Public Opinion in Political Theory', underlines the significance of the experience of the Great War for the way its relation to democracy is perceived. He insisted that the

> [...] experience of the World War intensified the tendency to emphasize the non-rational forces involved in the formation and manipulation of public opinion, and it promoted a deep and wide-spread scepticism as to the validity of democratic theory in general and the competence of public opinion in particular.[12]

Pessimistic accounts of public opinion were not confined to the Anglo-American world. German writers on the subject, such Wilhelm Bauer, drew attention to the manipulation of a non-rational and emotional opinion by official propaganda, especially by Germany's enemies.[13] In turn, liberal democratic commentators such as Walter Lippmann argued that public opinion was a dangerous and potentially destructive force that had to be controlled.

Although the 1920s and 1930s were often characterized as the Age of Ideologies, advocates of liberal democracy tended to represent the threat they faced in psychological and cultural terms. In this way liberalism sought to displace its difficulty in competing with its political foes by blaming the masses for their irrational behaviour. Its critique of mass society absolved liberalism from its failure to deal with its illiberal and anti-democratic opponents. Supporters of liberalism argued that the threat a democratic society faced was not the ideas but the manipulative techniques of their opponents. This argument was most coherently expounded by Karl Loewenstein, who sought to de-legitimize the ideological claims of fascism by insisting that it was 'not an ideology, but only a political technique'.[14]

Loewenstein, who was a German émigré living in the United States, reacted to apparently irresistible expansion of fascism by calling on democrats to use militant – that is, authoritarian and repressive – methods against their opponents. Loewenstein's call to fight fire with fire was based on what for liberals was a disturbing discovery, which was that democracies seemed helpless when confronted with the emotional appeal of fascism. This acknowledgement of the inability of liberalism to compete with fascism was explained as due to the irresistible power of irrational emotionalism. This force was portrayed as one that would always prevail over the appeal of reason and rationality. The problem lay not with liberal doctrine but with the unfair advantage enjoyed by its opponents. The masses also stood condemned for not appreciating the rational methods of liberal democracy.

Loewenstein noted that 'perhaps the time has come when it is no longer wise to close one's eyes to the fact that liberal democracy, suitable, in the last analysis, only for the political aristocrats among the nations, is beginning to lose the day to the awakened masses'.[15] In this revealing comment he gets to the nub of liberalism's dilemma – how to manage and restrain the 'awakened masses'. His solution was to confine democracy within the circle of a small group of elites who were insulated from the pressure of public opinion. The distinction he drew between rational and emotional forms of governance dictated that decision-making should be freed from the burden of gaining popular consent. He sought to 'clarify the vital difference between constitutional and emotional methods of government' by pointing to the example of England. He stated:

> The solution of the recent political crisis in England by the cabinet and the Commons was sought through rational means. To have left the issue to the verdict of the people would have been resorting to emotional methods, although general elections are manifestly a perfectly legitimate device of constitutional government.[16]

The argument that the 'verdict of the people' could only be influenced by 'emotional methods' served as a justification for the practice of a very illiberal form of liberalism. It all but conceded the point that the ideas of liberalism could no longer capture the popular imagination.

Loewenstein was far more explicit than most of his co-thinkers about the inability of liberal ideals to motivate the masses. He warned that not even the ideal of liberty could inspire people to fight for their freedom:

> One method of overcoming fascist emotionalism would certainly be that of offsetting or outdoing it by similar emotional devices. Clearly, the democratic state cannot embark on this venture. Democracy is utterly incapable of meeting an emotional attack by an emotional counterattack [...] The emotional past of early liberalism and democracy cannot be revived. Nowadays, people do not want to die for liberty.[17]

For Loewenstein the long-term challenge of liberalism was to develop techniques that could alter mass behaviour to match the effectiveness of its political enemies.

> In order definitely to overcome the danger of Europe's going wholly fascist, it would be necessary to remove the causes, that is, to change the mental structure of this age of the masses and of rationalized emotion. No human effort can force such a course upon history. Emotional government in one form or another must have its way until mastered by new psycho-technical methods which regularize the fluctuations between rationalism and mysticism.[18]

But the world could not wait until the mental structure of the masses was altered and Loewenstein believed that there was no choice but for 'militant democracy' to energetically repress its political enemies.

The model that Loewenstein proposed was the autocratic emergency regime adopted by Western democracies during World War One. He argued that:

> Democracies withstood the ordeal of the World War much better than did autocratic states – by adopting autocratic methods. Few seriously objected to the temporary suspension of constitutional principles for the sake of national self defense. During war, observes Leon Blum, legality takes a vacation. Once more, democracy is at war, although an underground war on the inner front. Constitutional scruples can no longer restrain from restrictions on democratic fundamentals, for the sake of ultimately preserving these very fundamentals.[19]

This call to adopt the autocratic methods of its autocratic enemies indicated that he regarded the use of anti-democratic methods to defend 'democratic fundamentals' as the only effective antidote to the threat of fascism.

Loewenstein's pessimistic account of the state of liberalism and his call for adopting authoritarian measures to hold the line against political rivals echoed sentiments that were widely shared by interwar defenders of constitutional democracy. After the Second World War the institutionalization of militant democracy was pursued in many parts of Western Europe. Its principles became enshrined in the Basic Law of West Germany.

The rise of ideologies – the second Thirty Years' War

What Loewenstein characterized as the 'awakened masses' was actually a public whose experience has taught them to call into question the legitimacy of the old order. This was a public that no longer routinely deferred to the pre-war system of authority and one that was open to new ways of making sense of its place in the world. Suspicion if not outright fear of the people inhibited liberalism from engaging with the masses. Its hesitation and self-paralysis provided an opportunity for alternative ideologies to thrive. It was liberalism's indecisive behaviour and gradual retreat from public life that provided an opening for the growth of political movements in search of a mass constituency.

World War One created conditions whereby new ideologically motivated movements could gain a mass constituency. But the rise of these movements should also be seen as a response to a demand for answers to questions which the old elites refused to countenance. The crystallization of new ideologies occurred in the context where Western societies were uniquely disposed to politically experiment. As Muller argued, 'Europeans were partly forced to experiment because both tradition and the dynastic legitimacy had ceased to provide principle for public order, but new ones had hardly become entrenched'.[20] In this moment of transition, political experimentation acquired its own inner momentum. The loss of legitimacy and the absence of consensus freed ideas from their conventional restraints and the interwar battle of ideas often appeared to assume the form of a continuation of war by political means. Michael Freeden in his analysis of these 'intense ideational battles' stated that

> [...] those conflicts did not evolve around civilization and its discontents, but around civilization and its annihilators. Fascism, communism and what was variably called democracy or liberalism locked horns in a pattern far more symmetrical than was recognized by the latter's adherents in the allegedly free world: all were promoters of non-negotiable principles that sought the status of universal truths, and all became hardened in that battle of the absolutes.[21]

The hardening ideological positions were not simply the result of the inner logic of competing ideas. They emerged in conditions when society was both intensely polarized and insecure. The weakening of institutions of consensus meant that the polarization of opinion could develop relatively unimpeded.

This tendency towards polarization was further reinforced by the unsettling effects of the economic crisis.

It was the Great War that created conditions that were hospitable for political experimentation. The collapse of the Tsarist Regime and the victory of the 1917 Revolution was at the time rightly understood as a direct consequence of the war. The end of the Great War was regarded by many as a prelude for conflicts to come. Ideologists of the time often appealed to the unresolved problems raised by the war to justify their doctrines and solutions. John Strachey, who left the Labour Party to support communist and other radical causes, wrote in his *The Coming Struggle For Power* that since 1914 the survival of civilization was at risk. 'In 1914 we allowed ourselves to believe that Armageddon had been an "unfortunate accident"', he stated in his call to avoid the next war through a workers' revolution.[22]

During the 1930s the term Thirty Years' War was coined to warn that a new war of revenge might be launched by the previously defeated powers. This theme of revenge was coupled with the radicalization of ideologically driven movements to illustrate the continuity between the conflicts of the 1914–45 period. The concept of a 'second Thirty Years' War' was elaborated by the political scientist Sigmund Neumann in his book *The Future in Perspective*. Published in 1946, this study attempted to locate the origins of the war in the struggle of nineteenth-century liberal democracy to readjust to the demands of twentieth-century mass society.[23]

In his writings Neumann was sensitive to the changing sociological dimension of war as it acquired an increasingly ideological form. His discussion of the 'international civil war' emphasizes the significance of its mass base and, by implication, of the tension between a democratic order and the masses. According to Neumann, ideological dictatorships are able to 'capitalize on the failures of rational and democratic leadership and on its inability to satisfy and integrate large segments of society'.[24] Neumann's analysis of the failure of liberal leadership to connect with the masses carries forward the themes advanced in the interwar years. His most interesting contribution is the way that he attaches significance to the increasingly civil or ideological tensions contained within twentieth-century wars.

While the First World War was occasionally described as a European civil or fratricidal war, it was a conflict that was basically fought by nations. However, as the questions left unresolved by the 1918 Armistice continued to serve as the focus of conflict, its character as a civil war became increasingly evident.

Unlike the First, the 'Second World War was not only a war of nations'. As one study of the historical contrast between the Great War and the global conflict that followed noted, 'the resistance to the Nazis took place within a set of civil wars, more or less officially declared between the locals who supported the Nazis and those who opposed them'.[25] The convergence of domestic ideological conflicts with geopolitical ones in the Second World War was a legacy of the Age of Ideologies. However, as the civil war fought in post-revolutionary Russia indicates, such conflicts emerged at the very outset of the so-called new Thirty Years' War. Indeed, one of the interesting features of the Great War was that it already contained within itself a tendency to transform an externally focused conflict into a domestic one.

It is something of a platitude to note that after the Great War it was evident to most thinking people that there could be no return to the *status quo ante*. The new reality facing people in the post-war world was not simply one where old borders were redrawn, new nations created, old regimes were overthrown and the certainties of domestic life were shattered. The war had also exacerbated the problem of legitimacy that afflicted all domains of human experience. In many parts of the world new constitutions were cobbled together and questions were raised about the real source of sovereignty. First and foremost came the 'theoretical problem of what the "foundation" or "source" of the system was', states a review of the debate around the new German constitution.[26]

Constitutional debates invariably assumed a political and increasingly cultural form. But these debates were influenced by competing attitudes towards the cultural and moral dimensions of life. Arguments about the values that underpinned the new constitutions raised questions about the significance of the traditions of the past, of religion, of the role of rationality and emotions and of the status of the rule of law. There were numerous points of conflict between ideologies that expressed themselves through the vocabulary of left and right. But such conflict also intersected with profound cultural differences in attitude towards the ideals of Enlightenment modernity. Hostility to liberalism was not simply a political expression of right-wing conservatism but a cultural rejection of its values. Carl Schmitt, the German reactionary philosopher, regarded liberal values with contempt. He denounced 'modern mass democracy' as a charade.[27] Instead his 'political theology' sought to invent a form of justification that did not have to justify itself in rational terms.

Although Schmitt is known as a political philosopher closely associated with the German Nazi movement, his contempt for parliamentarism, elections, individual conscience and other basic liberal values was frequently expressed by public figures associated with mainstream opinion in Western democracies. Even in the United States many leading opinion-makers believed that unless their government became more centralized and unified and emulated some of the authoritarian techniques of Mussolini's Italy, Hitler's Germany or Stalin's Russia, their society would be overwhelmed by the economic crisis.[28]

Ideology of the state

When Isaiah Berlin described the twentieth century as 'the most terrible century in history' he knew that his readers would know that he was referring to the cycle of conflict that began with the Great War, which in turn spawned the threat of totalitarian movements and states, a new global war and finally the precarious stalemate of the Cold War. From the vantage of today the Great War looks relatively humane compared to the unrestrained political passions that were released by this conflict. The pursuit of ideological objectives by movements frequently characterized as totalitarian is often perceived as the defining moment of the twentieth century. As Furet remarked, communism and fascism 'permeated the twentieth century'.[29]

During the interwar years radical ideologies of the far left and far right were on the offensive. From the outset, the struggle between competing ideologies of left and right contained the implication that sooner or later the differences between them would be resolved by force. Ideological hostility between political rivals 'made the period 1914 to 1945 in particular seem like a modern version of the Thirty Years' War'.[30] In numerous accounts the ideologies of fascism and communism appear as an omnipotent force that could literarily transform otherwise normal citizens into fanatical militants.

In 1960, when the American sociologist Daniel Bell published his famous essay *The End of Ideology*, he used the word 'exhaustion' to refer to the demise of the ideas that haunted the interwar world. He reminded his readers that

[...] the two decades between 1930 and 1950 have an intensity peculiar in written history: world-wide economic depression and sharp class struggles; the rise of fascism and racial imperialism in a country that had stood at an advanced stage of human

culture: the tragic self-immolation of a revolutionary generation that had proclaimed
the finer ideals of man; destructive war of a breadth and scale hitherto unknown; the
bureaucratized murder of millions in concentration camps and death chambers.[31]

That the decades following the Great War were a period of massive change
and intense conflict is a matter of record. But the question that remains to be
answered is to what extent were the ideologies that confronted one another
across the field of battle responsible for the descent into this Age of Catastrophe?
What was it about the ideologies of the interwar years that turned them into
such formidable and powerful forces? Today, of course, neither fascism nor
Stalinism retain any significant intellectual or political appeal. So why did they
succeed in gaining such influence in the 1920s and 1930s?

There are a variety of explanations for the immediate post-war revolutionary
upsurge of the left, the right-wing reaction that followed it, the rise of authoritarian and fascist movements and the consolidation of the Stalinist Soviet Union
and Nazi Germany. However what stands out as the critical force that detonated
these political quakes was the sudden unravelling of the pre–1914 institutional
order and the system of authority through which it was legitimized. As I argue
elsewhere, the intensity of the crisis of post-World War One institutional
authority is strikingly confirmed by the dramatic ascendancy of the Leader.
It is a testimony to the exhaustion of the political imagination that so many
commentators invested their hopes in the capacity of the Leader to maintain
order. For a while at least, the Leader served as an authority substitute.[32] It
wasn't only Max Weber and other demoralized former German liberals who
sought salvation in a charismatic Leader who would tame the masses. In the
eyes of many political commentators and intellectuals, the dynamic leader
appeared as an effective alternative to the ineffective disunited parliamentary
regimes of the interwar period. In 1933 the president of Columbia University,
Nicholas Murray Butler told the freshman class that the dictatorships were
putting forward 'men of far greater intelligence, far stronger character and far
more courage than the system of elections'.[33]

By the 1930s there was a distinct absence of enthusiasm for parliamentary
democracy and particularly towards any manifestation of popular sovereignty.
Economic dislocation and collapse had also significantly undermined the
legitimacy of the capitalist system. In these conditions the failure of the old
order to manage changing political circumstances and the threat of economic
disintegration were widely interpreted as proof of liberalism's irrelevance.

Socio-economic realities were likely to have contributed more to the setbacks suffered by liberal democracy in the interwar years than the compelling power of ideologies. Not only did liberalism stand condemned as irrelevant, it was also blamed for the political and economic crisis of the times.

In this period critics of capitalism did not require a sophisticated political theory or coherent ideology to win popular support. Mass unemployment, large-scale poverty and depression provided the experiences which were readily turned into arguments against capitalism. The Soviet regime could use the distressing circumstances faced by the masses in the capitalist world as proof of its superiority. That the Stalinist regime could serve as a focus of inspiration to millions in the West can only be explained as an outcome of their desperate quest for an alternative. The appeal of the Soviet Union and the significant support enjoyed by the communist parties should not be attributed to the power of their ideas. Its anti-capitalist rhetoric possessed significant appeal to the millions of desperate people facing an insecure economic future. The international communist movement was uniquely opportunist in the way it shifted and changed its doctrine. Its influence was underwritten by a widespread mistrust and dislike of capitalism as well as the belief that the Soviet Union had managed to overcome the malaise that afflicted capitalism.

The popularity of the Soviet Union in Europe was inversely proportional to the disenchantment and hostility towards the capitalist system. That is why in the 1930s a significant constituency of intellectuals and political commentators came to regard the Soviet Union as a model to be emulated. The popularity of Stalinist ideology was fuelled by widespread hostility to what was perceived as a crisis-ridden capitalist order. Its appeal was all the more startling given the poverty of the ideas promoted by the Stalinist regime. It is worth noting that the interwar years were a relatively barren one for the development of Marxist theory. The ideology of the communist movement was shallow and pragmatic. Soviet Marxism had a dogmatic and platitudinous quality. In the interwar era the official communist movement produced very few Marxist theoreticians of note. With the exception of George Lukacs, Ernst Bloch and Antonio Gramsci the Stalinist movement was bereft of intellectual heavyweights

At a time when capitalism stood exposed as a destructive and exploitative system that doomed society to a future of helplessness, it was inevitable that this system of production would provoke hostility and a mass despair. Even those disposed towards moderation regarded capitalism as a potentially dangerous beast that had to be tamed. At this conjuncture movements committed to opposing capitalism and promising a future of economic security were able to make significant headway. While the Stalinist left emphasized the question of class and the fascist right that of nation and race and appealed to different constituencies, they both looked to the state as the solution to the interwar crisis.

Fascist ideology was, if anything, even more incoherent than that of Stalinism. Its extravagant language and use of national mythology sought to harness people's emotional needs for security towards consolidating mass support around the leader. Although Mussolini stated that 'I am fascism', by the summer of 1921 he understood that he needed a doctrine to endow his movement with a measure of doctrinal coherence.[34] The absence of such a doctrine did not stand in the way of the movement's progress. The success of Mussolini and other fascist leaders was based on their ability to respond to the demand for order, offer a focus of unity and provide a measure of economic security. In this way they were able strengthen the relationship between mass society and the new activist state.

Mussolini, like other populist dictators, was a beneficiary of the anti-capitalist moment. The demand for order – economic and political – created a condition where the public's hopes could readily be channelled through the state. In retrospect the Age of Ideologies can be seen as the desperate moment when the idea of the state gained the reputation as the saviour of society. The movements of the left and right appealed to different constituencies, offered distinct explanations of the problems facing their society and proposed different visions of the future, but they were at one in the central role they assigned to the state.

By the 1930s socialists, communists and fascists alike had come to embrace counter-crisis state-led economic policies that were strikingly similar to one another. In 1931, the leading economist of the German trade union federation (ADGB), Wladmir Woytinsky elaborated a programme of public works, commonly known as the Woytinsky-Tarnow-Baade (WTB) Plan. He demanded that socialists abandon their illusions in the 'mystical power of the market' and stimulate the economy through adopting a proto-Keynesian strategy. As the Weimar Republic was about to totally disintegrate, Woytinsky warned that unless the socialists embraced his plan their ideological opponents would take the initiative and campaign for state-sponsored work creation schemes.

Woytinsky understood that it wasn't ideology but the imperative of containing the anarchy of market forces that necessitated state intervention and the institution of a comprehensive system of public works in Germany. He warned his fellow social democrats:

> The flood of unemployment is rising, [and] the people are at the end of their patience. The workers, holding us responsible for their misery, are deserting the party to join the Communists and Nazis. We are losing ground. There is no time to waste. Something must be done before it is too late. Our plan has nothing to do with any particular value theory. Any party can execute it. And it will be executed. The only question is whether we take the initiative or leave it to our enemies.[35]

His words 'any party can execute it' proved to be prophetic. As one study of the interwar German labour movement recorded, the WTB plan was eventually implemented, but by the Nazis. It observed that 'paradoxically, Hitler's work creation programme, begun after he assumed power, contained some of the basic principles of those of the WTB plan, except it included defence projects'.[36] As for Woytinski – after he fled to the United States he contributed to the implementation of the New Deal.

The pursuit of very similar economic policies by governments who were ideologically hostile to one another indicates that they were all influenced by the zeitgeist of state interventionism. It seemed that nothing less than the fully mobilized resources of the state could prevent a terrible situation from becoming even more desperate. The economic theory of John Maynard Keynes resonated with the zeitgeist of the 1930s as governments of all political persuasion opted for state-directed domestic stimulus packages. Keynes himself had little doubt that what was required was a strong state to implement effective anti-crisis measures. This former President of the Cambridge University Liberal Club and hailed by many as the embodiment of modern liberalism advocated a distinctly illiberal economic strategy.

In his preface to the 1936 German edition of his *General Theory*, Keynes indicated that his state interventionist economic theory was, if anything, more relevant to the conditions in Hitler's Germany than to *laissez-faire* capitalism. He wrote that

> [...] much of the following book is illustrated and expounded mainly with reference to the conditions existing in the Anglo-Saxon countries. Nevertheless the theory output as a whole, which is what the following book purports to provide, is much more easily adapted to the conditions of a totalitarian state [...] than is the theory of the production

and distribution of a given output produced under conditions of free competition and a large measure of laissez-faire.[37]

What this comment suggests is not so much sympathy or support for the German Nazi system but the conviction the mobilization of the apparatus of state along the lines pursued by newly empowered activist states constituted the solution to the global economic crisis.

Keynes's lack of ideological interest is also revealed by his positive comments on Sidney and Beatrice Webb's *Soviet Communism*. This book, which uncritically transmits Stalinist propaganda about the marvels of the Soviet Union, was highly recommended by Keynes in a contribution to the BBC's 'Books and Authors' series in June 1936. Keynes appeared delighted that the Soviet leadership had ceased to be doctrinaire and had adopted an open-ended pragmatic economic policy. 'There is little or nothing left which bears any special relation to Marx and Marxism as distinguished from other systems of socialism', he stated in reference to the Kremlin's policy. And he complimented the Stalinist regime on the grounds that 'they are engaged in the vast administrative task of making a completely new set of social and economic institutions work smoothly and successfully over a territory so extensive that it covers one-sixth of the land surface of the world'.[38]

The idea that Keynes appeared to convey was that the state-directed economic experiments in interwar industrial societies were far less an outcome of ideological pressures than they were a technical response to the failures of the market mechanism. The chain of events that followed World War One, culminating in the Depression, had weakened support for capitalism, even in the United Sates. As Ira Katznelson argued in his study of the New Deal, 'the economic collapse had vastly reduced the appeal, even the legitimacy' of the old political economy and 'had marginalized, at least for the moment, those scholars and policy advocates who resisted a robust economic role for the nation's government'.[39] The trend towards the consolidation of the big activist state transcended national borders and ideological differences.

The emergence of what at the time was frequently characterized as the totalitarian state was far less the accomplishment of radical ideologies than of the loss of legitimacy of capitalism. At the time it was widely believed that it was impossible for democracy to survive unless governments directly organized economic life. Donald Richberg, a leading official with the American National Recovery Commission, stated that the policies of the New Deal represented an 'effort to find a democratic and a truly American solution of the problem that has produced dictatorships in at least three great nations since the World War'.[40]

Ideological convergence

That totalitarian states were now seen as the harbinger of the future highlights the confusion and loss of belief in the possibility of reconciling economic security with free competition and popular sovereignty. Today, it is difficult to appreciate the depth of the reaction to the values represented by liberal democracy and free-market capitalism. At this point in time Western democratic governments seriously doubted their capacity to compete with the propaganda and appeal of totalitarian societies. Harold Lasswell, the leading figure in the new field of American political psychology, had no doubt that 'under democratic conditions' the 'long-run effect of this resort to propaganda is to undermine the basic loyalties upon which democratic institutions depend, and to prepare the way for impulsive revolt against them'. He warned that 'the liquidation of the sentimental basis of democratic government leaves the community more exposed than before to anti-democratic movements during crises, such as those connected with economic depression or military failure'.[41]

Doubts about the long-term viability of liberal capitalism and democracy was reinforced by the apparent success of state-organized economies. Overwhelmed by a profound sense of doubt, Western governments and observers failed to see the profound defects and contradictions of Soviet society. Impressed by the triumphs of totalitarian regimes, Western governments drew the conclusion that they too had to adopt some of their competitor's methods if they were to avoid falling behind. The adoption of state-organized rationalization of industry, planning and demand management by Western industrial societies was widely seen as evidence of the exhaustion of liberal capitalism. Such sentiments gained a coherent intellectual expression through the emerging theories of totalitarianism.

These theories claimed that free market private capitalism was giving way to repressive social order presided over by an omnipotent state. The examples of Italy, Germany and the Soviet Union were held up as the most developed manifestations of this new global trend. Through emphasizing technical features common to all industrial societies – fascist, Stalinist, democratic – accounts of totalitarianism had elaborated an idea that would, in the post-Second World

War era, crystallize into the theory of convergence. But in the 1930s the focus of totalitarian theories was on what they perceived as the transition from private to state capitalism. Claims about this transition were communicated through a language that stressed its inevitability. The title of Bruno Rizzi's book *The Bureaucratisation of the World* expressed this fatalistic sensibility.[42] It noted that 'in its communist (Stalinist), fascist (Mussolinian) or national socialist (Hitlerite) form, the state replaces control by private capitalism with its own control, through its functionaries'.[43]

The influential work, *The Managerial Revolution* by the American author James Burnham did much to popularize the idea of a new era of organized capitalism. Burnham stated that state intervention would lead to a 'decrease in capitalist ownership and control' – a development he represented as part of a 'general process of social transition which is taking place, a process analogous to what happened in the transition from feudal to capitalist society'. He asserted that the 'position of the capitalists as the ruling class is being undermined and, before long, will collapse'.[44] For Burnham, Soviet society constituted an advanced model of capitalism in the future.

Burnham described the process of transition which first gained definition during World War One and which continued to expand during World War Two as a 'social revolution'. His theory presented the different protagonists in World War Two as merely representing different versions of totalitarianism. Burnham believed that the liberal democratic theory was simply no match for totalitarian movements. He wrote that 'nowhere is the impotence of bourgeois ideologies more apparent than among the youth'. Pointing to the 'abject failure of voluntary enlistment in Britain' and 'indifference' of American youth to their nation's ideals, Burnham asserted that 'in truth, the *bourgeoisie* has in large measure lost confidence in its own ideologies'.[45]

Burnham's pessimistic assessment of the future of capitalism expressed a mood that even influenced the thinking of this system's most ardent supporters. Friedrich Hayek, who arguably put forward the most robust defence of classical liberalism, was intensely sensitive to its marginalization. His essay *The Road To Serfdom*, published in 1944, is permeated by a hesitant tone that is aware of the precarious status of the principal ideas associated with liberalism. Hayek writes of the prevailing 'contempt for liberalism' and notes that the belief in the inevitability of state organization and planning is ascendant. Like Burnham, Hayek posits Nazi Germany as merely a variant of totalitarianism. According to his analysis, all these totalitarian systems express the trend towards socialism.

Hayek concluded that the triumph of Nazism represented the realization of the trends towards socialism. 'It would be a mistake to believe that the specific German rather than the socialist element produced totalitarianism', he warned.[46]

The Road To Serfdom was written at a moment when the prospect for liberal capitalism appeared to be uniquely dismal, if not hopeless. Even the language of liberalism has become compromised.[47] What concerns Hayek is not who will emerge as the military victors of the Second World War but whether liberal capitalist could survive the conflict. His words are addressed to the British political elites, many of whom, he believed, were unhesitatingly embracing the politics of state planning.

Burnham and Hayek regarded the ideological movements of their time as expressions of a similar impulse. Burnham recognized that although there was 'not a formal identity' between the different ideologies, there was 'a historical bond uniting Stalinism (communism), Nazism (fascism), and New Dealism'. He characterized them all as '*managerial ideologies*' that pointed towards the direction of a managerial society.[48] During the years to come, this thesis would be developed into a theory of totalitarianism which tended to treat the different ideological movements as similar, if not the same.

The thesis of ideological convergence ignored their specific origins, practices and objectives in order to stress their role as the outcome of historical pressures and the massification of society. The coupling of Stalinism with Hitler's Germany lent totalitarianism a terrifying power which helped distract attention from liberal capitalism's failures and lack of authority. In the United States the image of Red Fascism turned into a nightmare that haunted the public in the early Cold War years. As one study concluded, 'the nightmare of "Red Fascism" terrified a generation of Americans and left its mark on the events of the cold war and its warriors'.[49] This nightmare also distracted attention from liberal capitalism's failure to recover from the wounds it suffered through the experience of the Great War.

Cultural contestation of capitalist authority

The frenetic character of interwar political experimentation should be interpreted as a response to the Great War's legacy of domestic and international disequilibrium. Although this legacy possessed different dimensions, its most significant feature was the erosion of the legitimacy of capitalist authority. In such circumstances the old order found it impossible to adjust to the demands of mass society. The lack of public consensus highlighted the weakness of liberal democracy. It also constituted an invitation to political experimentation. The brief period of revolutionary upheaval during the immediate post-war years created a demand for order, which gradually expressed itself in state-oriented ideologies.

What is frequently overlooked in studies of the interwar ideologies was their common suspicion of democracy and rejection of popular sovereignty;[50] instead they upheld the sovereignty of the state. This sentiment was most explicitly voiced by fascist ideologues. Alfred Rocco, the Italian fascist politician, argued that his movement

> [...] not only rejects one dogma of popular sovereignty and substitutes for it that of State sovereignty, but it also proclaims that the great mass of citizens is not a suitable advocate of social interests for the reason that the capacity to ignore individual private interests in favor of the higher demands of society and of history is a very rare gift and the privilege of the chosen few.[51]

But the reason why democracy was in trouble was because even many of its formal supporters found it difficult to uphold. One study of the disintegration of liberalism in Germany points out that it was as much defeated by its own paralysis as by the blows struck by its enemies. 'How was it possible for prominent intellectuals, jurists, lawyers, professors, and civil servants, who before 1933 were professed liberals, to accept, and many of them to acclaim, a despotism that repudiates in word and deed the fundamental postulates of liberalism?', asked the author of this study. His answer was that by this time liberalism had become a caricature of itself, more concerned with order than with Enlightenment values. The author, John Hallowell, argues that German liberalism refused to challenge Hitler because they 'saw nothing to fight about'. He added: 'they had no ideas, no values, for which to fight; they had no doctrine, no way of life, to defend.'[52]

But it was not only German liberals who were literarily lost for words. The First World War raised many question, but the one that appeared to be unanswerable was about the moral status of capitalism. The economist Joseph Schumpeter often sounded as if he believed that his defence of capitalism was a lost cause. In 1943 he asked: 'Can capitalism survive?' His brief answer was: 'No. I do not think it can.'[53]

From its inception, capitalism could not take itself for granted and has always faced the challenge of explicitly justifying itself against criticisms that it is unfair or outdated or exacts an unacceptable price on humanity or the planet. Since the interwar era of the twentieth century, capitalism as a social system has found it increasingly difficult to positively justify itself against its critics. The loss of cultural affirmation for capitalism and for democracy reinforced the crisis of bourgeois order and weakened the parties of centre – particularly. The subsequent political realignment strengthened the communists and the far right. When the new world war broke out it appeared as ideological from the start. That is why this war was fought not just for national survival or glory but for ideologically inspired objectives.

One important point to note is that capitalism is the first social system that through its very emergence posits the very possibility of its own alternative or counter-systems. Unlike previous societies that regard themselves as it – natural or tradition-bound – capitalism possesses a strong sense of contrast between itself and previous ways of organizing society. Consequently capitalism possesses a unique sense of historical consciousness which at times fosters an orientation towards change and an anticipation of alternatives. Its sensibility of change and variation means that capitalism not only creates ideas that justify or make sense of its existence but also critiques of itself.

However, while the absence of a coherent philosophical and social foundation for capitalism has been frequently commented upon, the parallel exhaustion of the alternative to it have not. Until the end of Second World War few observers noticed that the success of anti-capitalist ideology was not so much an outcome of its intellectual or ideological coherence but a result of the negative experience of people during the interwar global economic crisis. The Great War undermined the legitimacy of liberal capitalism, but it did not spawn an effective alternative to it.

Notes

1   Bracher (1984) pp.67–8.
2   Hallock (2012) p.68.
3   Sternhell (2008) p.281.
4   Sternhell (2008) p.281.
5   Kahan (2001) p.54.
6   Laski (1919) p.28.
7   Dewey (1941) p.26.

8   Dewey (1931) p.58.
9   Wilson (1955) p.505.
10 Dewey (1931) pp.59–60.
11 Pennell (2012) offers a more nuanced alternative for the mass enthusiasm thesis for the case of Britain.
12 Palmer (1967) p.252.
13 See Palmer (1967) p.253.
14 Loewenstein (1937) p.423.
15 Loewenstein (1937a) p.657.
16 Loewenstein (1937) p.423.
17 Loewenstein (1937) p.428.
18 Loewenstein (1937a) p.657.
19 Loewenstein (1937) p.432.
20 Muller (2013) p.50.
21 Freeden (2006) p.7.
22 Strachey (1934) p.8.
23 See Neumann (1946).
24 Neumann (1949) p.345.
25 Winter and Prost (2005) p.207.
26 Caldwell (1997) p.2.
27 See Schmitt (1988).
28 See the discussion in Katznelson (2013) pp.98–127.
29 Furet (1999) p.156.
30 Muller (2009) p.213.
31 Bell (2000) p.393.
32 See discussion in Chapter 15 in Furedi (2013).
33 Cited in Katznelson (2013) p.115.
34 See Muller (2013) p.106.
35 Cited in Berman (2006) p.114.
36 Braunthal (1978) p.65.
37 Cited in Schefold (1980) p.175.
38 Cited in Raico (1997).
39 Katznelson (2013) p.232.
40 Cited in Katznelson (2013) p.233.
41 Lasswell (1935) p.188.
42 See Rizzi (1985). This edition was originally published in 1939.
43 Rizzi(1985) p.11
44 Burnham (1941) p.106.
45 Burnham (1941) pp.4, 34, 35.
46 Hayek (1986) pp.2, 6, 7, 11.
47 Hayek (1986) p.11.
48 Burnham (1941) p.186.
49 Adler and Paterson (1970) p.1064.
50 There were of course exceptions to this trend – such as that of Council Communism and

Anarchism. But these movements existed on the margins and exercised little influence over the unfolding of events.

51   Cited in Willoughby (1930) p.139.
52   Hallowell (1946) p.107.
53   Schumpeter (1976) p.61.

4

The unexpected revival of democracy

It was as if humanity effortlessly drifted into a new world war. Most accounts of the interwar years record a series of missed opportunities to halt the drive towards a new global war. The failure of the League of Nations, the failure of disarmament, the failure to check the aggression of predatory powers or the failure of nerve of democracy are frequently held at least partially responsible for what appears as the absence of will to prevent what would be the most devastating conflict in human history. The very helplessness with which the world allowed itself to march into another destructive global conflict seemed to suggest that the Great War was not a one-off singular event. This realization has had a profound impact on the psyche of human civilization during the past century.

World War Two – not quite the last word

The speed with which one global war succeeded another had an important effect on the way that people experienced their life during and after the Second World War. For many – especially the generations that lived through the two global conflicts – it appeared as if peace and security had acquired an elusive quality and that war was likely to become an integral feature of their lives. Stefan Zweig wrote not long before his death in 1942 that he had no idea 'how many hells, how many purgatories had to be crossed' before a new peaceful world could be reached.[1] That is why when the Second World War formally drew to a close many observers regarded this historic conjuncture as merely a breathing space before geopolitical rivalries turned into a new struggle for world domination. Observers anticipated that it was only a matter of time before humanity would be confronted with the prospect of a new global conflict. Policy-makers, their experts and commentators expressed themselves through a language that indicated that they expected events in 1945 to follow the pattern that emerged in 1918. It was as if they were participating in Act Two of an unending drama. They had seen it all before. 'In a spiritual sense we are back where we were a quarter of a century ago', wrote an observer in *The Annals of the American Academy of Political and Social Science* in 1945.[2] The question of how to prevent World War Three was the issue that weighed heavily on the minds of informed public commentators and intellectuals. 'Until we establish juridical order for the world we are in grave danger of world war three with its threat of utter destruction', warned an American legal scholar in 1945.[3] The issue that preyed on people's minds was whether another global conflict could be avoided.

The Russian émigré political theorist Waldemar Gurian, a professor at Notre Dame University, regarded the future through the prism of past upheavals:

> We do not know the significance and the place in history of the second world war which ended with the unconditional surrender of Germany and Japan in 1945. We do not know if this end is a real end or only a pause. We know today that World War I ended only with an extended armistice – and even before the documents of unconditional surrender were signed, the feeling and fear spread everywhere that the series of world wars might be not over yet. All attempts to produce a general confidence in a lasting peace have until now proved vain.[4]

Gurian reminded his readers that 'at the end of World War II it must be remembered that this war was not one war, but a series of wars'. What preoccupied Gurian was not so much geopolitical as ideological rivalries. He warned that:

> The shooting war is over, but the humanitarian democratic ideology has not obtained a clear-cut triumph. We observe that old power conflicts reappear intensified by ideological and social differences, that not a brighter world full of optimism, but a world full of conflicts, fears, and insecurity – even panic – is in the making.[5]

His presentiment of alarming conflicts to come resonated with the spirit of his age.

It was as if the clock had been turned back to 1918 – except that the sheer scale of destruction to humanity during the years 1939–45 lent the war of the future a more ominous quality than the last time around. The devastation caused by nuclear weapons in Hiroshima and Nagasaki ensured that anxieties about the future world war acquired an intensely catastrophic tone. Such concerns continued to dominate global political life for decades to come. Warnings about an impending Third World War continue until the present time. Books with titles like *The Causes of World War Three* or *World War Three Is Inevitable* continued to be published into the 1980s. Articles and books on the subject proliferated in the late 1940s as the Cold War assumed a menacing form. Prophecies of a world war to come were constantly voiced during the 1950s and 1960s; they spiked in the aftermath of the Cuban Missile Crisis in the early 1960s and rose again in the early 1970s. In a more muted form they persist to this day.[6] Adam Yoshida's *A Blast of War: a Narrative History of the Third World War*, published in 2011, shows that this theme fascinates the imagination even in the post-Cold War world.

Back in 1918 it was still possible to imagine that the global conflict was an accident whose horrible consequences were both exceptional and unintended. Despite the mood of cultural pessimism, most people regarded war as something that was fought out there and would therefore only affect them indirectly. In 1945 the future threat of war appeared to have a far more pervasive and all-encompassing character. After the Holocaust, the deployment of the atomic bomb against Japan and the depth of brutality inflicted on civilian populations, it was difficult to avoid the conclusion that there were no escape routes from the war to come. What lent this conflict a particularly disconcerting attribute was its apparently pointless and irrational dynamic. As Christopher Lasch observed:

> It was not simply that this revival of barbarism on a global scale called into question naïve conceptions of historical progress and human perfectibility. The self-destructive quality of the violence associated with it appeared to undermine even the premise that ordinary selfishness normally restrains men from indulging their aggressive impulses in complete disregard of the interests of others or the fear of reprisals.[7]

The perpetration of mass murder on a grand scale seemed to suggest that atavistic forces beyond rational control had called into question the foundation of all the humanistic concepts and ideals of the modern era. That's one reason why the Second World War was not only seen as a more destructive version of the First but also as more evil.

The perception of the imminence of war gained clarity and force through the realization that, almost without warning, the world had drifted into the Nuclear Age. The atomic bomb and the realization that it was only a matter of time before even more destructive weapons would be produced fostered a climate of insecurity. In such an atmosphere an arms race was inevitable and war – or at least the preparation for it – became a permanent feature of existence. 'The tragic truth', observed William Laurence, a science correspondent for the *New York Times*, 'is that at present we really cannot be sure that the war is over.' Writing in 1946, he commented that 'twenty-five years from now, or even sooner, we may find out that what we thought was the end of the war was no more than merely another prolonged armistice, a period in which we took time out to stock up with bigger and better atomic bombs'.[8] With the arrival of the Bomb, geopolitical and ideological conflicts assumed a more ominous threatening direction.

It is evident that the appellation, the Second Thirty Years' War, fails to capture the historical process through which the tensions that gave rise the Great War became externalized through the international conflicts of the interwar era and the domestic conflicts precipitated by new powerful ideological movements. These rivalries, in turn, set in motion a barbaric global conflict that almost imperceptibly turned into a decades-long Cold War. It certainly did not feel as if the Second Thirty Years' War had ended when, in February 1946, Joseph Stalin, the leader of the Soviet Union, exclaimed that there would be no collaboration between the communist bloc and the 'the dying corrupt' capitalist world. The Supreme Court Justice William O. Douglas voiced the views of a significant section of the American political establishment when he described Stalin's intemperate words as a 'declaration of World War Three'.[9]

Many Americans felt shocked and betrayed by the realization that their nation had lost their monopoly of possessing nuclear arms. Some reacted by advocating a nuclear strike on the Soviet Union. As one study of this period observed, 'not everyone shrank from the prospect of World War III', and surveys indicated that 70 per cent of Americans opposed their Government's pledge of 'no first use' of nuclear bombs.[10]

Yet contrary to the expectations of many people living in the late 1940s, the Cold War did not turn into a hot one and the similarity between the two post-world-war eras was only superficial. As we shall see though many problems that arose during the years 1914–19 remained unresolved, it appeared that capitalism had become re-legitimized, ideologies were laid to rest and the insecurity and economic anxieties of the interwar years had been displaced by an era of unprecedented prosperity. At the time, the unexpected and at first unnoticed arrival of the Golden Age of capitalism, 1947–73, helped to steady the nerves. It provided society with the hope that a catastrophic moment in history had finally come to a close. It did, but the solutions to the issues raised during the Great War continued to elude Western society.

An ambiguous stability

Even before the Second World War ended, policy-makers looked with apprehension towards the post-war era. Post-war planners were preoccupied with the need to avoid a re-run of the troubled years that followed the Great War. Among policy-makers it was widely feared that the repetition of the political upheaval and economic breakdown that followed the end of the Great War was unavoidable. The 1914–1918 conflict and era of instability that followed it served as a point of reference for policy-makers, planners and technocrats involved in post-war reconstruction during the 1940s.

Gabriel Kolko argued that the fundamental issue confronting the leaders of Great Britain and the United States at the end of World War Two was the extent to which they could 'permit its calamitous social and economic repercussions, which had so profoundly altered a growing section of the European people's ideas and aspirations'. They understood that at this point in time 'changing the old orders became a cause that evoked the political enthusiasm and participation of far more people than at any time since at least 1918'.[11] However, contrary to expectations of a rerun of the 1918 post-war experience, Western societies proved to be far more resilient and stable than in the interwar years.

Despite a series of minor conflicts and disruptions, the evolution of the post-Second World War era contradicted the prophecy of doom-mongers. To be sure, Europe became divided into an Eastern and Western bloc. A civil war broke out in Greece, which was effectively and swiftly crushed. But there was little pressure for revolutionary and radical change in most Western societies. Even the mass communist parties of France and Italy assumed responsibility for the restoration of economic life and political order. The polarization of the labour movement between a revolutionary and a reformist wing during the interwar period acquired a muted form in 1940s post-war Europe. For its part, the Soviet Union – which emerged out of the radical upheavals precipitated by the Great War – had by 1945 turned into a *status quo* power and, as Gabriel Kolko concluded, it played an important role in the stabilization of

Europe.[12] Most of the dramatic developments occurred in Asia. The Chinese Revolution and anti-colonial struggles accelerated the disintegration of the Western empires.

The unanticipated stabilization of political life was linked to the equally surprising resilience of capitalist economies. Instead of a depression, capitalist societies experienced an unprecedented period of prosperity: the post-war boom. One study of post-war recovery has characterized this boom as 'one of the most unexpected events in western Europe's history'. The author of this study recalled:

> As the huge armies of America and the Soviet Union met amongst the endless rubble of what had been Europe's largest economy and over the corpses of a government which had mocked the long history of European civilization and culture, no matter how heroic the sentiments expressed scarcely anyone could have believed that the small, shattered nations of western Europe were on the brink of the most prosperous, peaceful and one of the most creditable periods in their history.[13]

This study, published almost half a century after the last world war, was still pondering the question of 'why was Europe's reconstruction after the Second World War so much more successful than after the First'.[14]

Writing in the first decade of the twenty-first century, Eric Hobsbawm was still not sure whether questions over Europe's successful recovery had been satisfactorily answered. 'Just how and why capitalism after the Second World War found itself, to everyone's surprise including its own, surging forward into the unprecedented and possibly anomalous Golden Age of 1947–73, is perhaps the major question which faces historians of the twentieth century', he asserted.[15] It was not only the unexpected arrival of the Golden Age of capitalism that contradicted the expectations of so many observers. 'Would there be a repetition of the wave of revolutionary upsurge that came in the aftermath of World War One' was the question that many observers implicitly answered in the affirmative. 'To be sure, the atmosphere of the immediate post-war period had seemed no less revolutionary than the years 1918 and 1919', argues one account of 1940s reconstruction political thought.[16]

One important reason why anticipation of post-war radicalization was so widespread was because capitalism had become de-legitimated and stood discredited in the eyes of millions. Capitalism was not only widely indicted for its association with the Depression and mass unemployment, it was frequently blamed for creating the chaotic conditions that led to the war. By the late 1930s there was an intellectual consensus, which influenced virtually the entire ideological spectrum, that assumed that free-market capitalism had run out of steam.

'After the catastrophic failures of capitalism between the wars, the credibility of *laissez-faire* economies and their apologists was in decline', contends a study of British society during the Second World War.[17] One striking manifestation of the de-legitimation of free-market capitalism was the near-universal embrace of planning by officials and policy-makers. Capitalism was frequently dismissed as an ineffective and outdated institution. Harold Macmillan, who went on to become a Conservative Prime Minister of Britain in the 1950s, stated during the war that 'planning is forced upon us' and 'not for idealistic reasons but because the old mechanisms which served us when markets were expanding naturally and spontaneously is no longer adequate when the tendency is in the opposite direction'.[18]

When the Second World War ended, the advocates of capitalism were conspicuous by their silence. Writing in the 1950s, the Swiss social-liberal economist Wilhelm Ropke recalled 'how poor the prospects for the market economy appeared' after the war and 'how hopeless the efforts of its advocates'.[19] On the defensive, supporters of capitalism found it difficult to refute the charge made by radical and left-wing intellectuals that it was complicit in the rise of fascism in Germany and Italy. 'Those who have nothing to say about capitalism should also be silent about Fascism', argued the German philosopher and sociologist Max Horkheimer.[20] In 1945 Edward Ross, a leading figure of American sociology, stated:

> Fascism was not begotten by capitalists or capitalistic thinkers; yet it came to be Capitalism's chief counter-offensive to Bolshevism. It says: 'Rather than endure governmental regulation or risk a "dictatorship of the proletariat," let us abolish all people-control over government. Away with political democracy and everything savoring thereof! Concentrate all power over the State in the hands of a single party which admits to its membership only those it can use.'[21]

At a time when fascism and Nazism stood exposed as a barbaric force responsible for mass murder and destruction, the mere hint of an association with this movement was sufficient to discredit capitalism. A handful of liberal thinkers, like Friedrich Hayek, tried to contest the linkage of fascism with capitalism by shifting the blame on socialism for the development of totalitarian regimes in Germany and Italy.[22] However, at the time, the attempt to cast socialism into the role of a precursor to fascism had little resonance.

Western capitalism was also losing the propaganda war to the Soviet Union. Although the ignominious Russian-German Non-Aggression Pact of August 1939 dealt a blow to the moral authority of the Soviet Union, the Stalin regime soon recovered it. The ability of the Soviet Union to defend itself against the German invasion and eventually play a critical role in the defeat of Hitler's armies was often construed as testimony to the effectiveness of its planned economy. Even the most forceful defenders of capitalism and the most hostile opponents of the Soviet Union found it difficult to confidently put a case on behalf of the free market and the values associated with it. Arthur Koestler, who became one of the most prominent anti-communist intellectuals during the 1950s, was guarded in his observations regarding the Soviet economy during the Second World War. In line with many anti-communist writers of the 1940s, his condemnation of the Soviet Union was not linked to an advocacy of free enterprise. Koestler echoed the consensus when he wrote in 1943 that the 'economic structure of Russia is historically progressive compared with private capitalist economics'.[23]

On its own, the impressive wartime record of the Soviet Union cannot account for the high regard its economy enjoyed in the West. In retrospect, it is evident that it was the collapse of confidence in capitalism during the decades following the Great War that permitted so many Western thinkers to have such an inflated assessment of the Soviet economy. The Western political and cultural elites were defensive about the legitimacy of their own way of life and tended to overestimate the power and vitality of its opponents. The historian and journalist E. H. Carr wrote about the 'moral crisis of the contemporary world' and the breakdown of the 'system of ethics that lay at the root of liberal democracy' and 'of *laissez-faire* economics'.[24] Carr's allusion to a moral crisis suggested that what was at issue was not simply a rejection of free-market economics but a way of life constructed around it.

One consequence of this crisis of confidence was the acceptance of the argument that capitalism would have to reform itself and would have to embrace planning and a more socialistic policy orientation. The Hungarian émigré sociologist Karl Mannheim, who had strong links with both British Labour Party intellectuals and Conservative Party reformers, summarized the situation in the following terms:

We are living in an age of transition from a *laissez-faire* to a planned society. The planned society which will come may take one of two shapes: it will be ruled either by a minority in terms of a dictatorship or by a new form of government which, in spite of its increased power, will still be democratically controlled.[25]

The belief that society was going through an age of transition was integral to a widely shared hope for change. This aspiration for change was enhanced by the fear of repeating the mistakes of the past. The need to avoid the repetition of taking the wrong turn of 1918 at the end of World War Two shaped the thinking of Mannnheim and his circle. The failures and betrayals of the interwar years provoked a reaction which often assumed the form of a revulsion against the past. As one British Conservative MP recalled, the Tories were identified with an England 'that had died at Dunkirk'. During negotiations between the proprietors of *The Times* and its new editor in 1941, it was agreed that 'it was the duty' of this newspaper 'to prepare for great social changes after the war'.[26]

Nevertheless, despite the moral crisis of capitalism and the widespread mood demanding change, what followed was an age that was strikingly different from that of the interwar era. One reason for this break from the past was a general reaction against the highly politicized and threatening social and cultural conflicts that engulfed the world and led to a catastrophic war. After the Second World War, the aspiration for radical change had to compete with a powerful desire for security and order. Even radicalized trade unionists looking to improve the living standards of their members adopted a surprisingly restrained tone. The mass communist parties adopted a rhetoric of restraint and order. Palmiro Togliatti, the leader of the Italian communist party, assumed a self-consciously moderate and responsible stance when he boasted in January 1947 that 'in the last years no political strike has taken place in Italy'. He indicated that it is 'the working class and the unions who are giving the best example and are taking all the necessary steps to preserve the discipline of production, order and social peace'.[27]

Despite the escalation of the Cold War – with its implication of a global conflict between two competing ways of life – on the domestic scene social and political disputes rarely threatened institutions of the state. Such disputes tended to be directed at influencing the state and consequently had the unintended consequence of legitimizing it. The Cold War served to foster a mood of unity and conformity within society. Geopolitical rivalries coexisted with acquiescence to order on the domestic plane.

De-politicization of ideologies

Although it was not noticed for some time, one of the consequences of the Second World War was to put an end to the Age of Ideologies. The most significant ideological casualty of the war were the ideas associated with the right and in particular with fascism. It is well known that fascism was militarily defeated. But it was also all but annihilated as an idea. Moreover Nazism succeeded in discrediting the political and moral credibility of all explicitly right-wing movements. Ideas about race, colonialism, Western superiority, the authority of tradition were significantly compromised by their direct or indirect association with fascism. As Paul Piccone, the maverick American social theorist indicated, the 'World War II defeat of fascism and Nazism led to the criminalization not only of both of these ideologies but of the "Right" in general'.[28]

The war had discredited nationalist attachments to the past and to tradition and dealt a blow to the ideal of national destiny. These values were closely identified with the Hitler regime as well as its allies in Italy and Japan. The association of reactionary values with fascism and with a catastrophic war forced explicit right-wing ideas to the margins of intellectual life.

The Second World War was far more ideological than the previous global conflict. The Nazi and fascist nations explicitly relied on the ideological appeal of nation, race and culture to mobilize the population. Their propaganda often assumed the character of a cultural crusade against the values of the Enlightenment, liberalism and modernism. In turn, anti-fascism emerged as a powerful counter-ideology that motivated the civilian population and armies of the Allied nations. As the barbaric consequences of the behaviour of the Axis powers became exposed, anti-fascist sentiment gained greater and greater force. The influence and appeal of anti-fascism directly benefited the Soviet Union and the communist movement. As democracy's ally against the fascist powers the image of the Soviet Union was rehabilitated in the West – at least for the duration of the war. The imperative of defeating fascism bound together otherwise hostile political forces.

The reputation of the Soviet Union was greatly enhanced by its military success against Nazi Germany. Its ability to more than match the military power of Germany as well as its considerable sacrifices for the war effort boosted its image. For a brief period of time the Soviet Union succeeded in enjoying acclaim in the West as a model progressive society. After the war 'the powerful myth of the Russian Revolution once again nourished the Utopian dream'. It appeared as if the left 'had been right about Russia after all'.[29] Furet goes so far as to say that the Second World War was 'even more of a political victory for the Communist idea than for the democratic idea'.[30] His argument is based on the claim that the 'end of the war marked the victory of anti-fascism rather than of democracy'.[31]

Furet is right to emphasize the significance of anti-fascism as a key motivational influence on the conduct of millions of people struggling for what they perceived as their freedom. And his argument that anti-fascism also boosted the appeal of communism is also persuasive. However, one significant – though often unnoticed – outcome of the war was the revitalization of democracy.[32] The Second World War exposed the horrible price exacted by the loss of freedom. Explicit anti-democratic and authoritarian philosophies were utterly discredited by the experience. As a consequence of the war, democracy was morally rehabilitated. Even those right-wing politicians who retained their suspicion of democracy felt uneasy about openly questioning the status of this creed.

In contrast to Furet, Bracher contends that one of the outcomes of World War Two was the reaffirmation for democracy. According to Bracher, in the years following the war there was both a 'positive assessment' of democracy and an 'unambiguous rejection of closed ideology'.[33] There is little doubt that 'anti-fascism' became one of the most effective themes promoted by the propaganda of the official communist movement. But part of its appeal was that it resonated with the experience of constituencies of the mainstream left and centre. Its main effect was that it limited the isolation of the communist movement, especially after the outbreak of the Cold War.

As an ideology, anti-fascism always bore the hallmark of an uneasy compromise among disparate parties with conflicting interests. To the extent that it endowed all anti-fascist forces with a focus of unity against a common enemy, it helped the communist movement overcome its isolation. But the reaction against fascism also contained a powerful reaction against all ideologies, specifically ones that appeared to be associated with totalitarianism. That is why in a relatively short period of time the reaction to totalitarian ideology would effortlessly shift its focus from fascism to communism.

In the 1940s it was the political right that faced isolation. Fascist regimes were identified with an authoritarian political style, which in the public mind they also shared with right-wing and conservative governments. In the post-Second World War climate it was difficult to gain public support for explicitly right-wing political projects. In Europe the ruling Christian Democratic or Social Democratic governments attempted to distance themselves from the right and projected themselves as parties of the centre. Indeed the newly founded Christian Democratic parties explicitly attempted to provide a centrist alternative, while hoping to retain the allegiance of the constituency of the old right.

One of the most important manifestation of the discrediting of the right was its marginalization in intellectual and cultural life. In a frequently cited statement, the American literary critic Lionel Trilling declared in his 1949 *Preface* to his collection of essays that right-wing ideas no longer possessed cultural significance:

> In the United States at this time liberalism is not only the dominant but even the sole intellectual tradition. For it is the plain fact that nowadays there are no conservative or reactionary ideas in general circulation. This does not mean, of course, that there is no impulse to conservatism or to reaction. Such impulses are certainly very strong, perhaps even stronger than most of us know. But the conservative impulse and the reactionary impulse do not, with some isolated and some ecclesiastical exceptions, express themselves in ideas but only in action or in irritable mental gestures which seek to resemble ideas.[34]

While Trilling's statement contains more than an element of exaggeration, there is little doubt that the experience of the interwar years and of the Second World War served to marginalize the influence of right-wing and conservative intellectual tradition in Western culture. Conservative and right-wing ideologies suffered a fate that was far worse and thoroughgoing than that experienced by liberalism after the Great War.

The widely shared conviction that the political right bore a singular responsibility for the outbreak of the Second World War led to its virtual disappearance as a force in intellectual and cultural life. As Daniel Bell recalled:

> Since World War II had the character of a 'just War' against fascism, right-wing ideologies, and the intellectual and cultural figures associated with those causes, were inevitably discredited. After the preponderant reactionary influence in prewar European culture, no single right-wing figure retained any political creditability or influence.[35]

The right never recovered its intellectual authority. Today, in the early twenty-first century, it is difficult to appreciate that not so long ago - in the first half of last century – right-wing thinkers and intellectuals still exercised a powerful influence over cultural life.

The dramatic marginalization of the right was inextricably linked to the thoroughgoing demise of fascism. There is simply no precedent in modern times for the annihilation of a political movement and ideology that had previously inspired and moved millions of people. Furet claimed that 'since the Crusades, history offers few examples of a political idea defended by armed combat that was subject to such radical interdiction as was the Fascist idea'.[36] The powerful reaction against fascism also fostered a climate of opinion that was intensely suspicious of the entire political right. This stigmatization of right-wing political views prevails to this day. Very few movements or people describe themselves as 'right wing' because of the negative connotations they convey.

Nor was the traditional right the only political movement faced with the necessity of distancing itself from the Nazi experience. Centrist and liberal intellectuals were forced to respond to the charge levelled by the Comintern that fascism was an outgrowth of capitalism. The German historian Hans Mommsen argues persuasively that the 'relative popularity' of the theory of totalitarianism 'can be explained 'by the need to provide a liberal alternative to the Comintern's theory of fascism'.[37]

In the long run, the demise of the right did not necessarily benefit the ideological movements of the left. But for a brief period the wartime record of the Soviet Union and the legacy of anti-fascism boosted the image and appeal of the left. However within a few years following the Second World War the benevolent image of the Soviet Union came under serious scrutiny. There was always a substantial body of Western opinion that was hostile and critical of communism and the Soviet Union. As the behaviour of the Kremlin assumed more and more the role of an imperial master in East Europe, it became easier and easier to cast the Soviet Union in the role of a dangerous totalitarian state.

Even among the non-communist European left, a sense of disillusionment towards the Soviet Union had become palpable. Victor Gollancz, a renowned British left-wing publisher, expressed this shift in attitude in his book, *Our Threatened Values*, published in 1946:

> While I by no means underestimate the dangers of resurgent fascism in many parts of the world, and particularly, owing to our own follies, in Germany, I am certain that it is in the spread of what is today called communism, and in the growing power

throughout Europe of Soviet Russia, that the strongest positive force opposed to stability and development of our western civilisation can be found.[38]

Gollancz's equation of Soviet communism with the danger of fascism expressed a sentiment that would gain a powerful influence in succeeding years in European public life. Such reactions expressed a sense of disillusionment not simply towards the Soviet Union but towards commitment to political ideologies in general. In some instances this reaction signalled a sense of betrayal and despair. The publication of *The God That Failed* in 1950 captured this sensibility of disillusionment. The book contained the testimonies of six well-known ex-communists about their loss of faith.[39] The discussion and reaction surrounding this publication indicated that the moral authority that the Soviet Union gained as a result of its achievement during the Second World War was gradually unravelling.

A collection of essays like *The God That Failed* ought to be situated in a political context where commitments to interwar ideologies came up against the sober reality of a world still confronted with a conflict between two powerful blocs. Memories of the bitter experience of a world war encouraged a sense of weariness and mistrust towards a new bout of ideological conflict. Daniel Bell argued in 1949 that a climate of de-politicization had enveloped intellectual life in Western societies:

> For out of the confusion and exhaustion of war, a new non-political attitude is spreading, typified by the French *je m'en fiche* (I don't give a damn), and the Italian *fanno schiffo tutti* (they all stink), in which the sole desire of the great mass of people is simply to be left alone. Conscripted, regimented, manipulated, disoriented in the swirl of ideological warfare, the basic and growing attitude is one of distrust. And [for] the intellectual, the seed-bearers of culture, the feeling is one of betrayal by power, and the mood is one of impotence.[40]

Bell may well have exaggerated the exhaustion of the impulse of radicalism. But, by all accounts, by the late 1940s the prospect of an indefinite era of ideological warfare provoked a sense of weariness against all forms of radical ideals.

Relegitimation of capitalism

War-weariness and exhaustion and the de-politicization of ideologies worked towards the consolidation of order and security. It also created the political conditions for the restoration of capitalist stability. Led by the United States, the capitalist world experienced an era of unprecedented expansion. The cumulative outcome of post-war reconstruction, massive expansion of state expenditure on the new arms race and welfare spending and consumer spending led to the restructuring of capitalist economies. These developments encouraged a massive rise in productivity and world trade. This post-war boom, which lasted until the early 1970s, led to a period of economic prosperity throughout most of the Western world. 'Within a few years following the two World wars, the standard of living of Western European countries, even those that were defeated and devastated, was higher than before', writes Kenneth Galbraith.[41]

The expansion of capitalist economies and of prosperity was paralleled by the extension of the provision of welfare benefits by the state. The coincidence of prosperity with an orientation to welfarism helped to rehabilitate capitalism and endow it with a more positive image. 'Capitalism now displayed an unexpected renewed vitality, and most significantly appeared to solve the problem of unemployment', states one review of this development.[42] The coexistence of full employment, welfare provisions and prosperity strengthened the impression that, despite previous misgivings, capitalism could be made to work for all. The sense of economic security was widespread, which significantly curbed the appeal of anti-capitalist movements.[43]

By the mid–1950s the traditional critiques of capitalism mounted by Marxists and socialists appeared even to their supporters as outdated and flawed. The tremendous expansion of production in the post-war boom served as proof of the vitality of capitalism. Reality seemed to reinforce the widely held claim that capitalism had been reformed to the point that mass unemployment could be abolished for ever. According to mainstream Western economic opinion, state intervention and regulation had succeeded in containing the destructive effects of the market. The British economist Andrew Shonfield expressed this conviction with confidence when he wrote:

> In the private sector the violence of the market has been tamed. Competition, although it continues to be active in a number of areas, tends to be increasingly regulated and controlled. The effort to secure an enlarged area of predictability for business

management, in a period in which technological change is very rapid and individual business investments are both larger in size and take longer to mature, has encouraged long-range collaboration between firms.[44]

From this perspective the economic chaos and insecurity of the 1930s had been left behind and superseded by a benevolent 'modern' capitalism exercising responsibility and control over the workings of the market. Galbraith's usage of the term 'affluent society' to describe the new stage of capitalism captured the consensus that prevailed among economists in the 1950s and 1960s.

Prosperity and a consciousness of unparalleled economic security helped to neutralize critics of capitalism. As one observer stated, 'there is little doubt that the growth of authority and control in free societies has been accompanied by great progress in production, in living standards, in security against many of the hazards of personal life, and in elevating the status of the individual in the community.[45] This was an era of remarkable growth and 'an era of unprecedented prosperity'. Judt wrote that 'in the space of a single generation, the economies of continental Western Europe made good the ground lost in forty years of war and Depression'.[46]

Economic success was its own justification and gradually capitalism, which bore the burden of responsibility for the depression and mass unemployment of the 1930s, succeeded in regaining its legitimacy. Its re-legitimation was not so much an outcome of its success in the battle of ideas but was founded on the fact that it seemed to work – not just for a small minority of elites, but for the benefit of all. The re-legitimation of capitalism was also assisted by the Cold War. As against the Soviet Union, the United States and the West appeared dynamic, productive and prosperous.

By the late 1950s and early 1960s the unprecedented expansion of economic life and of levels of living standards even forced the political opponents of capitalism to acknowledge that their previous predictions of crisis were seriously flawed. It was as if reality had demolished some of the most important assumptions of communist and socialist theories. By this point it was evident that the core constituencies of these movements – trade unions and working classes – had begun to identify with the new regime of welfare capitalism. It was the Italian Communist Party – the largest in Europe – that proved to be most responsive to these realities. Following Italy's economic 'miracle', Giorgio Amendola, one of the leaders of the PCI, warned that the economic boom had significant 'political and ideological consequences' – namely, a 'growing influence on working people'. He acknowledged that 'in spite of our criticism the influence exercised by the miracle succeeds in penetrating widely amidst the working class movement and even in the ranks of the Party itself'. For Amendola, 'evidence of the influence exercised by the "miracle" within the working class movement' necessitated a new, more positive orientation towards capitalism.[47] In effect the post-war boom had ideologically disarmed some of the most radical opponents of capitalism.

The re-legitimation of capitalism during the Cold War should not be perceived as the outcome of its intellectual or ideological triumph. Advocates of capitalism were continually forced to embrace the state as an instrument for market regulation and for curbing the forces of free competition. Arguably, as Favretto contends, 'under these conditions the Left exercised full "cultural hegemony" regardless of who was in power: the British Conservatives from the moment they returned to power in 1951, adhered strictly to Keynesian economic principles', as did De Gaulle and Christian Democrats in Italy.[48] Certainly the influence of free market capitalist ideas remained marginal and rarely succeeded in inspiring the imagination of the wider public. As Milton Friedman, one the most successful advocates of liberal economics, recalled, after 'World War II, opinion was socialist while practice was free market'.[49] In other words – the experience of the post-war boom notwithstanding – the argument for liberal economics had only a small audience in Western societies.

The idea of capitalism was only re-legitimized to a limited extent during the post-war boom. During this period many supporters of the 'Western way of life' lacked the confidence to mount a robust defence of the free market against alternative models. Symptomatic of this sensibility of intellectual insecurity was the equivocal approach adopted by the liberal French sociologist Raymond Aron. He argued that doctrinal disputes were a 'thing of the past' and that all 'regimes are imperfect' and neither the US nor the Soviet Union were all that bad.[50] By emphasizing the similarities of the two systems, Aron, like other theorists of convergence, evaded the attempt to construct a positive vision based on the distinct tradition of Western capitalism. Instead of insisting that 'we are morally superior', Aron's convergence theory simply claimed that 'you are no better than us'.

Theories of convergence argued that the technical imperatives of techno-logically developed societies tended to diminish the differences of ideologies between them. It was even claimed that economic progress would eventually overcome the antagonism between East and West. This outlook promoted by the American economist Walt Rostow and by the liberal thinker John Kenneth Galbraith showed a reluctance to make any serious claims about the virtues of capitalism.[51]

Despite this experience of the boom, capitalism enjoyed only a limited degree of an explicit intellectual and cultural affirmation. Its re-legitimation was directly linked to its evident success during the post-war boom. That is why, once this era came to an end, its legitimacy could be put to question yet again.

Cold War stability

Although periodically the Cold War appeared as if it was a direct prelude to World War Three and at times threatened to turn into a frightening confrontation between the major nuclear powers, its impact on global affairs was a conservative one. Paradoxically the Cold War worked to reinforce the stabilizing effect of the post-war boom. Cold War anxieties created a demand for security and in such circumstances the maintenance of the status quo was held to be a value in itself. Such sentiments resonated with a new economic climate that held out the promise of prosperity. The post-war economic boom encouraged a technical and de-politicized orientation towards the management of public life. In turn the Cold War provided both sides – but especially the West – with a focus for unity. During this time, the problems of legitimacy could be supressed by the intensity of a highly charged conflict between superpowers.

The Cold War provided both sides with a clearly identifiable external enemy. At the same time, given the ideological dimension of the rivalry between the two superpowers, the conflict also assumed a domestic dimension. Fear of the Soviet threat was paralleled by apprehension towards its domestic radical and communist allies. The threat of communism served as focus for unity among otherwise disparate parties of social democrats, of the centre and of the right. In some Western societies – particularly in the United States – anti-communism acquired a powerful momentum and served the role of a quasi-ideology. Hostility towards the menace of communism provided Western governments with an opportunity to avoid facing up to their own intellectual and moral crises. The absence of clarity about what constituted the foundational norms of liberal democracy and capitalism was effectively bypassed through the mobilization of an anti-communist consensus. The contrast with the Soviet Union worked to the benefit of Western societies and helped them gain the moral high ground without having to provide a compelling account of themselves.

Unlike the 1930s, when Soviet industrialization caught the imagination of millions of people trapped in the web of mass unemployment in the capitalist world, by the 1950s it was the West that was seen as dynamic and capable of improving living standards. Indeed, by the 1960s the internal flaws of the Soviet economy had become increasingly transparent and it was now perceived as a model to be avoided.

During the Cold War the advocates of Western capitalism sought to consolidate their position through counterposing their way of life against communism. By the time of the outbreak of the Korean War in June 1950 it was evident that anxiety about the intention of the Stalinist bloc was spreading rapidly among intellectuals and opinion-makers in Western societies. While such sentiments had been influential in the United States in the immediate post-Second World War years, they became noticeable in Europe in the aftermath of the blockade imposed on Berlin by the Kremlin between June 1948 and May 1949. At this moment in time, when the prospect of another global military conflict seemed imminent, many Europeans began to see the threat of a Soviet military occupation on their land as analogous to the danger posed by Hitler's armies in 1939. This outburst of fear towards the Soviet Union was well captured by the American historian of ideas, Stuart Hughes. An article, based on his journey to Europe during the summer of 1950 reported that, to many intellectuals and politicians, the danger of a Soviet occupation of Western Europe now seemed even more ominous than what occurred during the Second World War.

> A Westerner, even a left-wing intellectual, as he thinks back on the fascist experience, recalls a certain air of familiarity, of remaining within the European tradition. At the thought of Soviet occupation, whatever may be his conscious political affiliation, he instinctively shudders at something barbarous and alien.[52]

The Soviet Union, which had gained moral authority through its struggle against Nazi Germany, was now perceived by many as no better than its former enemy. Hughes observed that as a result of this reaction there was even a revision of the hostile attitude previously held towards Franco's Spain. He wrote that 'moderate leftists, who once could scarcely bear the mention of Franco's name' now 'grant that there is some merit in Franco's contention that his only sin was to recognize the communist menace somewhat earlier than the rest'.[53]

Although European communist movements continued to survive and at times gain significant electoral influence in Italy and France, their association with the Soviet Union meant that they could not make any serious claims to the moral high ground. Indeed communism could only survive through continually distancing itself from its ideological heritage and embracing a moderate political programme that at times was to the right of some of the socialist parties.

The negative example of the Soviet Union helped anti-communism gain influence. It also provided Western governments with their most powerful ideological weapon with which they could enhance their authority. At least while it lasted, the Cold War helped Western societies from having to deal with the issue of legitimate authority, which was so sharply raised during the Great War. However, in the long run, the negative worldview of communism lacked the moral and intellectual resources to legitimate a particular way of life. The failure to construct a positive worldview based on the affirmation of the virtues of liberal democracy would be exposed in the late 1960s and continues to haunt society to this day.

Half-hearted vindication of democracy

Liberal democracy, which as we noted was one of the principal casualties of the Great War, succeeded in regaining some of its legitimacy after the Second World War. Its re-legitimation was closely linked to the ideological decomposition of its most strident enemy – fascism. The necessity of countering the ideological appeals of the Axis powers provided an opportunity for waging a battle of ideas with the ideals of freedom and equality. The Allies represented their war effort as a crusade for freedom and democracy and succeeded in totally discrediting the ideology of their illiberal opponents. The defeat of fascism was portrayed as the downfall of the movement most associated with an explicit rejection of parliamentary democracy. After the Second World War it was unthinkable for any political movement – including the communist parties – to openly express any explicitly anti-democratic comments. Apologists for Stalin's regime frequently asserted that the constitution of the Soviet Union was the most democratic in the world. As for the West, its self-chosen description of itself as the Free World was incessantly coupled to its claim to uphold a democratic way of life.

Yet the official endorsement of democracy as the defining political philosophy of Western societies was rarely backed up by strong conviction and intellectual force. In the post-Second World Ware era policy-makers and their experts frequently equated the exercise of democracy with a problem. And the problem that such statements alluded to was with the capacity of the public to handle its freedoms and democratic rights in a responsible manner. In particular, popular sovereignty was castigated as an unreliable institution. It was frequently dismissed as an outdated concept that simply had no relevance in a mass society.

The questions raised during the Great War about the role of democracy in mass society remained unanswered. There has always been a degree of tension between liberalism and democracy. Classical liberalism was preoccupied with the protection of individual and minority rights and limiting the constitutional power of government and rule of law, while democracy stresses the role of popular sovereignty and participation. During the 1930s and 1940s the tension between liberalism and democracy gained force as a result of the rise of mass authoritarian movements. As one observer recalled, 'liberal political institutions collapsed like a house of cards tumbled over by a gust of wind'.[54] Often a fickle or irresponsible electorate was blamed for putting totalitarian regimes in power. Demoralized liberals represented the newly constituted totalitarian regimes as the outcome of the legacy of the excesses of democracy. In the aftermath of the Second World War this experience served to reinforce the disposition of classical liberalism to distrust majorities and mass society.

The experience of World War Two may have encouraged a revival in the authority of democracy, but in a form that was unapologetically elitist. Theories of mass society, which suggested that the public was an irrational and potentially dangerous force, were already widespread in the interwar decades. After 1945 there was no question that the masses were potentially even more destructive than previously suspected. In the minds of many commentators, the terrible catastrophe of the 1940s served as vindication of such theories. To this day the Second World War serves as a symbol of evil and of humanity's capacity for wicked behaviour. 'One intellectual legacy of the war was a profound anxiety about what it had revealed about humanity's capacity for evil', wrote Alan Brinkley.[55] Many American liberals argued that the 'experience of the war had brought a dark cloud of doubt and even despair to human society'. Some of them felt that 'humankind must move cautiously into its uncertain future, wary of unleashing the dark impulses that had produced these horrors'.[56]

This negative perception of humanity had important implications for how democracy itself was regarded. If indeed the dark side of humanity threatened to overwhelm existence, what hope could there be for a free and genuinely tolerant society? Writing in 1946, Waldemar Gurian declared that 'liberalism has become obsolete in a period of masses' because 'its concept of individualistic freedom appears as a concept meaningful only with the background of a comparatively secure world which accepts the common good as something self-evident'.[57]

Gurian's pessimism regarding the capacity of mass society to give meaning to the common good was shared by a significant number of intellectuals who drew the conclusion that the optimistic Enlightenment rendition of liberalism was inconsistent with the human condition. In his introduction to his classic *Life Against Death*, the American philosopher Norman O. Brown wrote that in 1953 he turned to Freud 'feeling the need to reappraise the nature and destiny of man'. He remarked that 'I, like so many of my generation, lived through the superannuation of the political categories which informed liberal thought and action in the 1930s'.[58] Brown observed that 'those of us who are temperamentally incapable of embracing the politics of sin, cynicism, and despair have been compelled to re-examine the classic assumptions about the nature of politics and about the political character of human nature'.

Brown drew the conclusion that the experience of the 1930s and 1940s called into question fundamental assumptions about Western rationality – hence his embrace of Freud. Not just of Freud but a distinctly pessimistic version of him. 'It is a shattering experience for anyone seriously committed to the Western traditions of morality and rationality to take a steadfast, unflinching look at what Freud has to say', he wrote. And the conclusion Brown drew was that 'it is humiliating to be compelled to admit the grossly seamy side of so many grand ideals'.[59]

Brown's vision of the 'superannuation of the political categories which informed liberal thought' was only a more radical version of the outlook that prevailed among liberal-minded thinkers on both sides of the Atlantic. Social historians of the post-1945 years point to a hardening of the mood of apprehension within liberal circles. Brinkley wrote that World War Two left a legacy of fear towards 'mass politics', 'mass man', a 'fear in short of the people' who could be so easily manipulated by demagogues'.[60] In Western Europe such apprehensions led the political classes to adopt institutional and constitutional arrangements that were designed to insulate them from the volatility of public opinion and the pressure of the masses. As Muller remarked,

> [...] insulation from popular pressures and, more broadly, a deep distrust of popular sovereignty, underlay not just the beginnings of European integration, but the political reconstruction of Western Europe after 1945 in general.[61]

During the 1940s and 1950s the cultural and rhetorical affirmation of liberal democracy coexisted with a determined attempt to control and restrict the scope for expressing public pressure. Motivated by the imperative of avoiding the upheavals of the interwar era and by an intense sense of suspicion of mass behaviour, the European elites 'fashioned a highly *constrained* form of democracy, deeply imprinted with a distrust of popular sovereignty – in fact, even a distrust of traditional parliamentary sovereignty'.[62] The post-war constitutional settlements sought to limit the role of parliament through assigning significant power to the judiciary and newly constructed constitutional courts. Bureaucratic institutions also gained significant influence, especially through the medium of the European Union. The project of taming democracy and preventing a return to the bad old days of the interwar years was most systematically pursued in West Germany. But the ethos of protecting democracy from the people pervaded the behaviour of the political elites throughout Europe. As Muller wrote, 'outside Britain the idea of unrestricted parliamentary supremacy ceased to be seen as legitimate'.[63]

In the United States the project of disciplining democracy was implicitly communicated through the belief that the institutions of the state had to be protected from the destructive impulses of the masses. Such sensibility among American liberals led to the conclusion that one of the objectives of politics was 'to defend the state against popular movements and their potentially dangerous effects'.[64] Political theorists expressed this agenda by arguing for a form of democracy that privileged the role of experts and elites. Arguing in this vein, the political scientist Robert Dahl proposed his theory of polyarchy, which assigned a special role for pressure groups in the political system.[65]

The tendency towards the bureaucratization of political life and the management of public opinion was expressed through a technocratic representation of democracy. Post-Second World War liberal democratic theory rarely reflected on the creative, truth-seeking dynamic of participatory democracy.

Instead democracy was reduced to the technical act of choosing representatives and leaders. The impulse to insulate the political elites from public pressure was often justified on the grounds that its emotional power could not be countered by rational arguments. This issue was increasingly depicted as one of psycho-pathology – one that demanded the intervention of psychology and behaviour management.

In his influential study *The Psychology of Hitlerism* (1933), Harold Lasswell attributed the success of this Nazi leader to his ability to 'alleviate the personal insecurity of many Germans'.[66] In the 1950s his version of political psychology became widely acclaimed and was used to explain the political behaviour of the public. Psychology was increasingly used as the instrument for diagnosing political behaviour. Indeed it was often claimed that politics served as the medium through which individual psychological problems were expressed. Political ideologies, such as communism, were now depicted as 'subterfuges for something else'.[67] Ideology was explained away as an expression of the emotional needs of people. This reduction of political ideologies to psychological issues absolved liberals from the challenge of fighting their opponents with their own political ideals. It also justified the attitude of suspicion towards mass behaviour. Rational debate was deemed as not a suitable means for engaging with a public that was simply not susceptible to persuasion through reasoned argument.

Historically, suspicion towards the lower orders was an integral feature of reactionary and conservative political theory. One of the legacies of the Second World War was to deepen mistrust towards the masses and to extend such senti-ments to sections of society who regarded themselves as democrats, liberals, even left-wing. So even the liberal-minded political theorist Peter Bachrach, who was critical of the elitism of democratic theory, concluded that the 'illiberal and anti-democratic propensity of the common man is an undeniable fact that must be faced'.[68] Bachrach himself alluded to the 'widespread support of totali-tarian movements in prewar Europe and the rise of powerful proletarian-based Communist parties in post-war France and Italy, of Peronism in Argentina and McCarthyism in the United States' to explain liberalism's loss of faith in the people.[69] Evidently the 'illiberal' propensity of the 'common man' means that it is pointless to treat them liberally.

By the 1950s many American liberal intellectuals regarded populist strands of public opinion with open hostility. According to one account, for fifties liberal intellectuals 'populism became the paradigmatic case of American-style xenophobia'.[70] In his important study *The Populist Persuasion*, Michael Kazin notes that in the United States during the Cold War, populism became the 'great fear of liberal intellectuals'[71]. They blamed mass democracy and an 'authoritarian' and 'irrational' working class for the rise of McCarthyism. Indeed their hostility to McCarthyism was underpinned by distrust and antipathy towards 'the very kinds of white American-Catholic workers, military veterans, discontented families in the middle of the social structure – who had once been the foot soldiers in causes such as industrial unionism, the CIO and the Popular Front in the 1930s and 1940s'. A decade later they were perceived as the enemy of liberalism. Whereas 'formerly liberals had worried about the decline of popular participation in politics', now 'they began to wonder whether "apathy" might not be a blessing in disguise', noted Christopher Lasch.[72]

The celebration of apathy by 1950s liberal theorists represented a remarkable departure from the significance that classical democratic theories attached to the value of public participation. This reversal in attitude to the involvement of citizens in public life was now justified on the grounds that stable democratic governance required widespread apathy and indifference to politics. Advocates of the virtue of political apathy argued that 'if the uninformed masses participate in large numbers, democratic self-restraint will break down and peaceful competition among the elites, the central element in the elitist theory, will become impossible'.[73] In 1954, the London School of Economics academic Wyndraeth Morris-Jones published a monograph, titled 'In Defence of Apathy'. Morris-Jones asserted that 'the ideas connected with the general theme of a Duty to Vote belong properly to the totalitarian camp and are out of place in the vocabulary of liberal democracy'.[74]

While Morris-Jones sought to provide an intellectual rationale for his defence of apathy, others were more cynical. Lester Milbrath's study of political behaviour noted that

> [...] it is important to continue moral admonishment for citizens to become active in politics, not because we want or expect great masses of them to be active, but rather because the admonishment helps keep the system open and sustains a belief in the right of all to participate, which is an important norm governing the behaviour of political elites.[75]

As Jack Walker commented in his critique of elitist theories of democracy, the arguments put forward by Milbrath transform the ideal of democratic participation into a 'noble lie'.[76]

From Milbrath's perspective, sustaining a belief in the right to participate has merely a propagandist function. The presumption that people are either incapable or uninterested in political participation deprived democracy of any inherent virtues or normative content. This half-hearted affirmation of democracy tended to reduce this system to a method for leadership selection. This model assigned primacy to the strength of character and wisdom of the political elites. Public opinion was regarded as an inconvenience that required skilful management and control. As Walker concluded

> democracy is thus conceived primarily in procedural terms; it is seen as a method of making decisions which insures efficiency in administration and policy making and yet requires some measure of responsiveness to popular opinion on the part of the ruling elites.[77]

The transformation of democracy into a technical procedure meant that it ceases to have any claim to a normative foundation or to any particular vision or future objective. During the decade following World War Two this value-free form of democracy was explicitly endorsed by political theorists and policy-makers uncomfortable with ideologies and values. As Bachrach commented, 'contemporary theorists generally agree that democracy has no overriding purpose to promote'.[78] Whether a democracy that makes no attempt to gain support for any normative ideals or purpose can motivate its citizens was a question left unanswered in the 1950s.

Certainly the defensive tone adopted by advocates of democracy suggested that its post-war re-emergence was not so much a result of its victory in the battle of ideas but an outcome of the collapse of the ideologies of the right and the slow decline of those of the left. Decades later, when Francis Fukuyama published his much-debated study, *The End of History*, he remained hesitant and ambiguous about the triumph of liberal democracy over its competitors. Fukuyama was sensitive to the mood of pessimism induced by the repeated failures of ideologies. He wrote that 'it is safe to say that enormous historical pessimism engendered by the twentieth century has discredited most Universal Histories'.[79] Yet, he also believed that pessimism was not warranted by the experience of the late twentieth century. He contends that 'while our pessimism is understandable' it is 'contradicted by the empirical flow of events in the second half of the century', the most important of which is the 'instability' of authoritarian forms of government and the 'complete absence of coherent *theoretical* alternatives to liberal democracy'.[80] The absence of a coherent alternative to liberal democracy was already evident in the 1950s. Yet the point that Fukuyama overlooked is that the absence of alternatives does not mean that liberal democracy had learnt to provide a convincing theoretical account of itself.

Despite the upheavals of the previous decades and the tragic experience of authoritarian dictatorships, democracy did not succeed in establishing a sturdy intellectual foundation to secure its future.

Notes

1   Zweig (1953) p.436.
2   Douglas (1945) p.7.
3   Wilkin (1945) p.116.
4   Gurian (1946) p.3.
5   Gurian (1946) p.6.
6   This analysis is based on inspection of Google Books Ngram Viewer on phrase 'world war three'.
7   See Lasch (1984) p.224.
8   Cited in Katznelson (2013) p.410.
9   Engerman (2010) p.34.
10   Whitfield (1996) p.5.
11   Kolko (1994) pp.225, 226.
12   Kolko (1994) p.303.
13   Milward (1984) p.xv.
14   Milward (1984) p.xvi.
15   Hobsbawm (2004) p.8.
16   Muller (2013) p.127.
17   Morgan and Evans (1993) p.29.
18   Cited in Morgan & Evans (1993) p.114.
19   Ropke (1958) p.21.
20   Cited in Furet (1999) p.368.
21   Ross (1945) p.649.
22   Hayek (1986) pp.6–7.
23   Koestler (1983) p.170.
24   Carr (1944) p.102.
25   Mannheim (1943) p.1.
26   Hopkins (1963) p.31.
27   Cited by Salvati (1972) p.197.
28   Piccone (1999) p.7.
29   Hopkins (1963) p.25.
30   Furet (1999) p.356.

31   Furet (1999) p.356.
32   As we shall explain, democracy was revitalized in a very restricted form.
33   Bracher (1984) pp.67–8.
34   Trilling (1964) p.ix.
35   Bell (1980) p.149
36   Furet (1999) p.368.
37   Mommsen (1981) pp.148–9.
38   Cited in Hewison (1981) p.24.
39   Hewison (1981) p.23.
40   Cited in Brick (1986) p.190.
41   Galbraith (1977) p.19.
42   Favretto (2003) p.17.
43   Marwick (1998) p.27.
44   Shonfield (1965) p.66.
45   Copland (1953) p.276.
46   Judt (2007) p.324.
47   Amendola (1961) pp. 46–7.
48   Favretto (2003) p.110.
49   Milton Friedman, 'The Battle's Half Won', *Wall Street Journal*: 9 December 2004.
50   Aron (1978) p.228.
51   For an illustration of this school of thought, see Tinbergen (1965).
52   Hughes (1951) p.153.
53   Hughes (1951) p.154.
54   Hallowell (1946) p.ix.
55   Brinkley (1998) p.105.
56   Brinkley (1998) p.108.
57   Gurian (1946) p.7.
58   Brown (1959) p.ix.
59   Brown (1959) p.ix.
60   Brinkley (1998) p.105.
61   Muller (2012) p.40.
62   Muller (2013) p.128.
63   Muller (2013) p.149.
64   Brinkley (1998) p.108.
65   See Dahl (1956).
66   See discussion in Robin (2001) p.65.
67   Robin (2001) p.95.
68   Bachrach (1967) p.105.
69   Bachrach (1967) p.8.
70   Singh (1998) p.13.
71   Kazin, M. (1995) *The Populist Persuasion: An American History*, Ithaca: Cornell University Press.
72   Lasch (1991) p.153.
73   Walker (1966) p.287.

74 Morris-Jones (1954) p.25.
75 Milbrath (1965) p.152.
76 Walker (1966) p.287.
77 Walker (1966) p.286.
78 Bachrach (1967) p.21.
79 Fukuyama (1992) p.69.
80 Fukuyama (1992) p.70.

5

From ideology to culture

Given the close association of ideological conflict with the two world wars and a series of revolutions and violent upheavals, it is understandable that the twentieth century is frequently remembered as the Age of Ideologies. Although in the twenty-first century the two powerful ideologies – communism and fascism – most associated with the dramatic events of the last century have lost their appeal, they still serve as the symbols of political catastrophe. Yet ideologies are by no means the only source of tension and conflict. The marginalization of communism and fascism has not led to the end of conflicts and wars. Conflicts that have assumed an ideological form in the past continue to influence events – albeit in a different form, such as culture. That by the end of the twentieth century global conflicts could be conceptualized as a *Clash of Civilizations* indicates that, for some, struggles between cultures appeared more significant than ideological disputes.[1]

Culture conflicts are not a recent phenomenon. It is important to note that the ideologies that emerged out of the turmoil of the Great War were preceded by conflicts that were often cultural in form and expressed unease and reaction to the experience of everyday life. A significant section of the German intelligentsia saw their nation's drive to war in 1914 as something of a crusade 'which would assure the victory of the German "ideas of 1914" over the Western "ideas of 1789"'. As the historian Hans Kohn pointed out, as far as they were concerned what was at issue was the 'liberation' of the 'German spirit from the "obsolete" Western principles of the nineteenth century'.[2] The war promised release from the confines of a stultifying routine that many young people regarded as a life without purpose or moral depth. The hope invested in the promise of liberation through World War One was often linked to a search for meaning and belonging. Later, in the interwar era, fascist ideology sough to recapture these sentiments and represented its mission as an affirmation of the destiny of culture.[3]

In his account of people enthusiastically acclaiming the coming war in August 1914, Stefan Zweig noted that 'as never before, thousands and hundreds of thousands felt what they should have in peace time, that they belonged together'.[4] However, the pre-war age of security and peace in Europe was not one where people felt that they belonged together. On the contrary, this was a time when a sense of alienation and estrangement from the workings of modern life pervaded society. Max Weber's writings on modernity, leading to his diagnosis of disenchantment with the impersonal and calculating practices and ethos of everyday life, reflected the spirit of these times. His analysis forced him to conclude that society lacked the cultural depth to give meaning to people's place in the world. But Weber believed that the 'calculating politics' which emptied political life of passion and emotion could be transcended in war.[5] Zweig's account of the crowd's excitement and solidarity accorded with Weber's argument. His description of the August days highlights the sense of excited anticipation among the urban crowd. He wrote how

> [...] a city of two million, a country of nearly fifty million, in that hour felt that they were participating in world history, in a moment which would never recur, and that each one was called upon to cast his infinitesimal self into the glowing mass, there to be purified of all selfishness.[6]

The intense passions and emotions that prompted millions to embrace the war as their own were difficult to forget, especially by those for whom this event provided the first experience of camaraderie and genuine belonging. Timothy Mason has argued that National Socialism 'can be understood as an effort to reproduce the experience of August 1914 as a permanent condition'.[7] Zweig knew that the unique sense of catharsis and belonging that people experienced in August 1914 would not endure for long. Nor would it reoccur during the days leading up to the outbreak of the Second World War. Why? 'The answer is simple: because the world of 1939 does not possess so much naïve credulity as did that of 1914', explained Zweig.[8] The sobering awareness that, far from noble, war's consequences were destructive and inhumane meant that its capacity to enthuse and motivate the Western publics had significantly diminished by 1939. This sensibility has become even more prevalent in the post-Hiroshima age. However, the search for meaning and belonging which influenced the behaviour of the enthusiastic crowds greeting news of the impending war in 1914 continues to play a decisive role in human existence.

As Fritz Stern pointed out in his 1974 *Preface* to his study of the cultural roots of the ideology of German fascism, the anti-modernist impulses that led to its crystallization persisted to his day. In words reminiscent of Zweig's observations of August 1914, Stern remarked that 'the present generation longs for a new communal existence, for a new faith, for wholeness'. As before during the interwar years, so too in the 1960s 'the deficiencies of liberal, bourgeois culture have been made shockingly clear in a decade of war, political divisiveness, industrial ugliness'. However, unlike in the past, the cultural reaction to modern society in the 1960s and 1970s was far less likely to assume a traditionalist nationalist or right-wing form. Fritz stated that 'although in many ways identical with the traditional laments of the right the outcry this time was linked to a vague leftist orientation'.[9]

At least in part, the interwar ideologies succeeded in gaining public support because, unlike liberal democracy, they promised to offer answers to people struggling to give meaning to their existence. Liberal democracy appeared to lack a normative foundation for motivating behaviour. Unlike its competitors, it failed to advocate values and goals which could capture the public's imagination. That liberal democracy survived the Second World War and regained credibility was not mainly due to its own accomplishment. During the Second World War the consequences of the loss of democracy in many parts of the world and the threat to freedom posed by the Axis powers offered an undisputable empirical argument for an open society. So it was not so much that liberal democracy won the battle of ideas as it was the case of its opponents losing it. However, liberal democracy remained a political institution that felt uncomfortable with the realm of values. Attempts to politicize values and culture were regarded by liberals with unease. It is worth noting that McCarthyism – one of the few genuine attempts to politicize Western culture – enjoyed fairly limited liberal support, even in the United States. It was also regarded by intellectuals with hostility.

One reason why liberal democrats were wary of the politicization of culture was due to their estrangement from the domain of morality and values. The version of democratic theory they favoured was typically elitist in form. It also purported to be value-neutral and eschewed any concern with 'human development' or with the potential for public participation to serve as the foundation for an enlightened community. In this Cold War version, democracy became a variant of the 'calculating politics' that bred the disenchanted cultural reactions that Weber wrote about. Liberal democracy not only failed to provide answers to the problems of existence but also contributed to the mood of moral disorientation that dominated the 1950s.

Writing in the late 1950s, Wilhelm Ropke described his world as one 'shaken by tremendous shocks and menaced by unimaginable disasters, the prey of anxiety, a world adrift and deeply unhappy'. He insisted that 'if anything, the crisis is getting worse rather than better'. Yet this was happening even though Communism was in decline as 'a spiritual and moral world power'.[10] Evidently the source of the problem facing the world was not so much an ideology external to capitalism and liberal democracy but a conflict that existed within itself.

Democracy in search of the normative

During the early years of the Second World it became all too evident to supporters of liberal democracy that something had to be done to rehabilitate its reputation if it was to flourish in the future. The democratic crusade against fascism reappropriated the language of equality and social justice and promised to improve the lives of people through a bold programme of radical reform.[11] In Europe, in particular, the cause of democracy was now closely allied with welfarism – a shift towards an egalitarian and interventionist form of social policy. However the questions that demanded an answer were what values did democracy stand for and did it have an aim or a purpose?

Haunted by the disturbing legacy of World War One, principally the demoralization of the democratic ethos, Karl Mannheim attempted to alert his colleagues to the necessity for providing democracy with moral depth. Writing in the early 1940s, Mannheim in his *Diagnosis Of Our Time* sought to fortify liberal democracy by appropriating a more militant and interventionist orientation to the world. 'Our democracy has to become militant if it is to survive', he declared.[12] He blamed democracy's previous reluctance to tackle the question of values for its political indecisiveness and defensiveness. In these wartime essays he assumed that *laissez-faire* stood discredited and that democracy was on the defensive. He noted that 'there is a growing disappointment with *laissez-faire* methods'. Not only because they 'have been destructive' in the economic field and produced 'devastating mass unemployment' but also because 'they are also partly responsible for the lack of preparedness in the liberal and democratic states'.[13]

Mannheim insisted at this critical conjuncture that 'the unbridled criticism of the form of freedom and democracy which has existed in the past decades must therefore cease'.[14] And rather defensively, he added that 'even if we agree that freedom and democracy are necessarily incomplete as long as social opportunities are hampered by economic inequality, it is irresponsible not to realize what a great achievement they represent and that through them we can enlarge the scope of social progress'.[15] To dispose of the argument that democracy was indifferent to the scourge of social inequality he proposed that society should become subject to the regime of economic planning. His compromise formula of 'planning for freedom' can be interpreted as an exercise in damage limitation.

Yet what concerned Mannheim was not simply democracy's failure to address questions relating to social and economic equality but its reluctance to engage with the cultural realm of values. The main point that Mannheim sought to convey was that society needed to believe in something and that democracy had to come up with some convincing answers regarding values that people should live by. His argument for a 'new militant democracy' was based on the conviction that the simple affirmation of *laissez-faire* liberalism lacked the cultural depth necessary to inspire the public. What he sought was an ethos that 'will differ from the relativist *laissez-faire* of the previous age' and 'will have the courage to agree on some basic values which are acceptable to everybody who shares the traditions of Western civilization'.[16] Mannheim was far from clear about the constitution of these values. His reference to values 'inherited from classical antiquity and even more from Christianity' showed a disposition towards the reappropriation of the legacy of Western civilization.

Mannheim's preoccupation with what he characterized as 'the crisis of valuation' anticipated some of the issues that were to be explicitly and stridently raised in the Culture Wars of the post-1960 era. The corrosive effects of the absence of consensus on basic values disturbed him. He wrote that 'there is nothing in our lives, not even on the level of basic habits such as food, manners, behaviour, about which our views are not at variance', and he observed that there is not even any agreement as to 'whether this great variety of opinions is good or bad, whether the greater conformity of the past or the modern emphasis on choice is to be preferred'. Nevertheless Mannheim was certain that it is 'definitely not good to live in a society whose norms are unsettled and develop in an unsteady way'.[17] The necessity for addressing this problem was particularly urgent for societies fighting for their survival in the middle of a war.

Mannheim went so far as to blame 'the slowness of democracies' to clarify values for helping fascism succeed and concluded that 'long before the outbreak of war a few far-sighted thinkers became aware of the dangers inherent in valuations, and tried to find the deeper causes of that crisis'.[18] The conclusion he drew from his assessment of the crisis of valuation was that 'the first step to be taken by democracies in contrast to their previous *laissez-faire* policy will consist in giving up their disinterest in valuations'.[19] He expressed the hope that the reaction to fascism will create a greater appreciation of the democratic way of life and for the emergence of a 'new consensus'.[20]

Mannheim had become acutely sensitive to the dangerous consequences of democracy's failure to adopt a grammar of moral values. He feared that democracy did not possess the cultural resources necessary to give meaning to people's lives. Mannheim stressed the necessity for tackling this problem through elaborating a narrative about the meaning of a democratic way of life. His awareness that liberal democracy lacked the resources necessary to motivate the public was paralleled by the concern that totalitarian ideologies were far more effective in this respect. This issue was frequently touched on by the literature on totalitarianism in the 1940s. Frequently totalitarian ideologies were interpreted as the functional equivalent of religion. Both were deemed to offer a focus for belief and faith.

The corollary of the thesis of ideology as faith was the claim that the lack of mass appeal of liberal democracy was due to its rationality and cold logic. Frequently, reason and rationality were deemed to be too cerebral and lacking passion – certainly not a brew for the emotionally driven masses. It was claimed that rationalism could make little headway among those inclined towards irrational behaviour. In other words, it was precisely the classical Enlightenment values of reason and rationality that accompanied the rise of liberal democracy which were held responsible for its inability to compete with the more emotionally appealing doctrines of totalitarian ideologies. In 1940, the historian Carlton Hayes explained this predicament in the following terms:

In the present crisis, when the historic Christian faith of the Western masses grows cold, a kind of religious void is created for them. But inasmuch as any such void is unnatural and eventually unendurable, the masses promptly seek to fill it with some faith. This they hardly find in 'humanity' or 'science' which are too abstract and intellectual and nowadays a bit stale. They find it rather in materialistic communism or its nationalistic deification of blood and soil.[21]

The implication of Hayes's argument was that liberal democracy was constantly at a significant disadvantage in competing with totalitarian ideologies for the loyalty of the masses.

Fascism and National Socialism had no inhibitions about conducting their propaganda war through the language of cultural values. These movements emphasized their hostility to Western civilization, materialism, liberalism and rationalism. Their reaction to the values of the Enlightenment was integral to what the American sociologist Talcott Parsons has described as a ' "fundamentalist" revolt against the whole tendency of rationalization in the Western world'.[22] Mannheim believed that this uncompromising cultural hostility towards modernism required a robust response. He understood that, unlike an authoritarian system, a democratic society could not impose an absolutist ethos on its citizens. Liberal democracy had to reconcile the right of individuals to act in accordance with their conscience and with the demands of community consensus. He stated:

> But militant democracy will accept from Liberalism the belief that in a highly differentiated society – apart from those basic values on which democratic agreement will be necessary – it is better to leave the more complicated values open to creed, individual choice or free experimentation.[23]

Mannheim's attempt to reconcile pluralism with adherence to basic values was rarely emulated by others. Throughout the post-Second World War decades liberal democracy was acutely aware of the absence of a normative foundation for its arguments.

Many liberal-minded thinkers were aware that their inability to offer a moral foundation for their doctrine significantly diminished its appeal. In the late 1940s, the recently established Mont Pelerin Society sought to develop a liberal creed that could influence public life in the post-Second World War world. However the debates among this society's members soon revealed that there was little consensus on fundamental questions of value. As one account of the proceedings of the Mont Pelerin Society stated, 'while there was agreement that liberalism was important, there was not agreement on the foundations of a liberal order, or on the fundamental reasons for its importance'. The 'lack of consensus on these foundational issues' meant that the focus of the society 'shifted from discussions of the ends which liberalism furthered to the means of furthering liberalism'.[24]

This instrumental orientation was criticised by some of the participants, who felt that liberalism had to have something to say about existential issues. Some looked outside the liberal ethos and sought to blend their liberalism with traditional religious and conservative values. Writing in this vein, Ropke acknowledged that 'I am not sure that I do not belong to the conservative rather than the liberal camp'.[25] Others, like Hayek, attempted to hold the line and affirmed the principles of classical liberalism.

Some American liberals adopted the pragmatic approach of Joseph Schumpeter, who avoided the question of values and insisted that democracy was mainly a method for choosing representatives.[26] From this standpoint democracy made no normative claims and its role was simply to offer a system of procedure for leadership selection. Indifference to the absence of a normative foundation to liberal democracy can be interpreted as an insecure and defensive responsive to the intuition that the promotion of values could serve as a focus for cultural conflict. This defensive posture was often expressed through a negative narrative that made no positive claims about the virtues of liberalism but merely pointed out the defects of its opponent's ideology. Louis Hartz, one of the leading theorists of American liberalism, explained that 'in the arguments with Communism we have more to hope from an inexorable disenchantment on its part' than from the 'attempt to recapture the Eighteenth Century on our part'.[27] In others words, Hartz invested hope in the failures of communism rather than on the intrinsic virtues of liberalism in the Cold War battle for ideas.

In the absence of clarity about foundational norms American liberalism opted for a self-consciously realistic orientation towards the advocacy of values. It attacked the politicization of values as illegitimate and decreed that ideologies and the extremism they bred represented a dead end for humanity. The strategy of targeting the politicization of values absolved liberalism of its own failure to elaborate a normative foundation for itself. One of the most coherent attempts to project a negative justification of liberalism was the essay *The Vital Center* by the American historian Arthur Schlesinger. *The Vital Center* attempted to counter the influence of Soviet communism and other ideologies by calling into question the legitimacy of all types of strongly held beliefs. These were dismissed as examples of extremism, utopianism or fanaticism. Schlesinger offered a hyper-realistic interpretation of the world which verged on the fatalistic. 'We must grow up now and forsake millennial dreams', he preached. His sobering words sought to deflate expectations which, he believed, were artificially inflated by ideologues. Schlesinger's alternative was the 'spirit of the new radicalism', which was 'the spirit of the center – the spirit of human decency opposing the extremes of tyranny'.[28]

Schlesinger attempted to resolve liberalism's problem of belief through the stratagem of de-legitimating all forms of strong beliefs. By renouncing all systems of strongly held beliefs he sought to make a virtue of the absence of the normative foundation of liberal democracy. Hostility to ideology was recast as a pragmatic alternative to the dead end of totalitarianism. As noted in the last chapter, liberal democracy relied on the promise of economic expansion and prosperity to legitimate itself. The assurance of economic security was offered as an alternative to the unrealistic and unreliable promises of radical ideologies. The French liberal social theorist Raymond Aron advanced this proposition in the following terms:

> Imperfect and unjust as Western society is in many respects, it has progressed suffi-ciently in the course of the last half-century so that reforms appear more promising than violence and unpredictable disorder. The condition of the masses is improving. The standard of living depends on productivity – therefore, the rational organisation of labor, of technical skills, and of investments.[29]

Through rendering the problems facing Western society as technical ones Aron sought to avoid normative problems. He, along with many Cold War liberal intellectuals, took the view that as long as the capitalist economy delivered the goods, engaging with the problem of values was unnecessary and should be avoided.

At a time of economic boom and prosperity, arguments that suggested that the problems facing society were susceptible to technical solutions retained a degree of plausibility. Certainly as far economic matters were concerned, by the mid-1950s the traditional conflict between socialist and capitalists ideologies had lost much of its relevance. As Martin Lipset recalled, the 'ideological issues dividing left and right had been reduced to a little more or less government ownership and economic planning'.[30]

Technical explanations regarding the nature and future of industrial societies avoided the sensitive issue of values. Since all economies seemed to be following a similar techno-rational imperative, observers often highlighted the irrelevance of competing political, ideological and cultural arguments on the subject. Even the radical sociologist C. Wright Mills believed that all the different modern industrial economies were converging on a similar path. Writing of the convergence of the societies of the US and USSR he stated:

> There are many other points of convergence and coincidence between these two countries, both in dream and reality. In surface ideology they apparently differ; in structural trend and in official action they become increasingly alike. Not ideology, but industrial and military technology, geared to total war, may well determine that the dreams of each will in due course be found in the realities of the other.[31]

Receptiveness to the influence of theories of industrial-technical convergence was partly a result of a sensibility that sought to avoid, or at least minimize, ideological differences. If ideological differences diminished in scope, then addressing the problem of values raised by Mannheim could be at least temporarily postponed.

The end of ideology

At the 1955 Milan Conference of the CIA-funded Congress for Cultural Freedom, a group of influential pro-Western liberals attempted to draw up a balance sheet of the state of play between liberal democracy and the ideology of communism.[32] The participants of this conference had little doubt that the economies of the Soviet Union and of Western capitalism were converging. According to their argument there was a similar logic at work in all industrial societies: as these economies developed and became more affluent they were destined to become less ideological and move closer together.

With the advantage of hindsight, it seems remarkable that Western liberal and anti-communist thinkers could have had such a high respect for the capacities of the Soviet social system that they would deem it to be equivalent to their own. One is struck by the hesitant and defensive tone of this argument. By stressing the similarities of the two systems, questions about the moral foundation of the Western way of life were avoided. The challenge posed by Mannheim in the early 1940s of constructing a positive vision of the future based on the foundation of Western liberal values was displaced with technocratic arguments about the logic of industrialism. Instead of claiming that 'we are morally superior', Western convergence theory merely hinted that 'you are no better than us'.

One reason why convergence theories were so readily embraced by Western liberal intellectuals was because they corresponded to the economic dynamics of the post-war boom. Similar ideas were circulating among social democratic and even among communist circles. Political commentators across the political divide interpreted the post-war boom as an experience that negated the traditional ideological difference between planning and the market. The successful blend of state intervention and organized competition practised in many Western societies called into question the historic ideological argument between capitalist and socialist economic regulation. At the Milan conference virtually everyone agreed that planning and competition were mutually compatible mechanisms. It was left to the lonely figure of the classical liberal Hayek to insist that the free market was incompatible with state regulation.[33]

But convergence theory was not simply an expression of post-war economic realities; it also provided a narrative through which the ideological debates that arose during and after the Great War could be disposed of as a historical relic. From this standpoint the absence of a robust affirmation of classical liberal values was not so much a problem as an opportunity to move forward with a technocratic and pragmatic fusion of a mixed economy. That is why the isolation of the classical liberal Hayek at Milan was not an accident. The participants at this conference did not want to be reminded of any ideology, even that of liberalism. The more ideological advocates of liberal democracy were actively discouraged from pursuing their agenda. In his classic *End of Ideology* thesis, Daniel Bell asserted that 'unadulterated liberalism and conservatism had lost their intellectual force'. With a dig at Hayek, Bell wrote that 'few "classic" liberals insist that the State should play no role in the economy, and few serious conservatives, at least in England and on the Continent, believe that the Welfare State is the "road to serfdom" '.[34]

One reason why the delegates at Milan could so casually dismiss the relevance of old doctrinal differences was because, by the mid-1950s, political ideologies seemed to have lost their capacity to inspire and enthuse. In Western societies, Marxism and communism were no longer seen as possessing the power to attract and mobilize a new constituency of discontented people. A few years after these proceedings Bell spelled out his thesis, which claimed that ideologies had become both exposed and exhausted by the experience of the previous decades:

Today, these ideologies are exhausted. The events behind this important sociological change are complex and varied. Such calamities as the Moscow Trials, the Nazi-Soviet pact, the concentration camps, the suppression of the Hungarian workers, form one chain, the rise of the Welfare State, another.[35]

In effect, Bell's argument about the exhaustion of ideology did not simply pertain to the decline of communism but to the loss of relevance of many of the political concepts that have inspired proponents of liberal democracy. He wrote that older 'counter-beliefs have lost their intellectual "force as well"'. The counter-beliefs that he alluded to were those of liberalism and conservatism.[36]

At one level the end-of-ideology thesis can be understood as a triumphalist acclamation of anti-communist sentiments. And certainly, as Scott-Smith observed, 'there seems to have been an air of complacency in Milan'. The sociologist Edward Shils reported the good news that 'there was a very widespread feeling that there was no longer any need to justify ourselves *vis a vis* the Communist critique of our society'.[37] In the face of the claim that 'communism had lost the battle of ideas' the gathering became 'something of a "post-victory celebration"'.[38] However the end-of-ideology thesis had as its main theme the **exhaustion** of ideology. It made no positive claims about the moral authority of Western liberal democracy. And it was difficult to ignore the possibility that exhaustion may have also afflicted the political doctrines associated with Enlightenment liberalism. Hearts and minds were not so much won by the West as lost by the Soviet Union during the Cold War.

Despite the occasional outburst of triumphalism, some of the delegates at the Milan Conference understood that what was still lacking was a positive account of the Western way of life. The exhaustion of communist ideology also served as a reminder of the inner deficiencies of the normative foundation of Western democracies. The British historian Max Beloff praised the proceedings at Milan as a tribute to the values of Western civilization, but he also warned that 'only occasionally were we reminded that the chief task of the Western intellectual today is to bear witness for cultural values in his own society'.[39] Beloff's statement served as an uncomfortable reminder of the fact that the problems raised by Mannheim remained not only unresolved but also studiously ignored.

By the 1950s, it was becoming evident that the real problem facing pro-Western thinkers was not the dynamism of its ideological opponents but its own deficiencies. The negative narrative of anti-communism was certainly not able 'to bear witness' to Western cultural values. Indeed, it often expressed itself in a language of realism that implicitly counselled the lowering of expectations. The tone of this narrative was typically defensive and often expressed disappointment with the values of the Enlightenment. As McAuliffe remarked, 'fundamental to pluralist thought in all its postwar manifestations – realism, consensus, and the Vital Center – was a loss of optimism, a dwindling assumption of progress, and a declining conviction of the fundamental goodness of mankind'.[40] Such views signaled a sensibility of misanthropy and cultural pessimism.

Whereas in in its classical form liberalism was an enthusiastic advocate of the idea of human progress, in the 1940s and 1950s Cold War liberalism became deeply troubled by it. To some extent the estrangement of liberalism from progress reflected the cultural temper of the post-Second World War decades. In his 1946 Presidential address to the American Historical Association, Sydney Fay explored the meaning of the idea of progress. He told his audience that:

> Optimism about the 'progress of civilization' received a rude shock from the war of 1914–18, the uneasy years of unemployment and depression, the failure of the League of Nations, and the frightful horrors and hatreds of World War II and its aftermath. Civilization seemed to be turned back several centuries.[41]

Fay hoped that the idea of progress could be revitalized. However many Western intellectuals had become distinctly uncomfortable with the ideal of progress. One reason for this stance was that the ideal of progress had become appropriated by hostile political ideologies – particularly by communism. The other reason for this estrangement from a concept central to Enlightenment philosophy was the difficulty of giving it meaning at a time when Western liberal culture was insecure about its own future.

In retrospect, liberal democracy missed an important opportunity to revitalize itself and tackle its crisis of valuation. It relied far too much on the Soviet Union discrediting itself and on exploiting this through negative anti-communist propaganda. Western Cold War ideology made an important contribution to the strengthening of stability and order, but it did not provide the normative foundation for a confident liberal democratic way of life. As we noted above, the reluctance of Western intellectuals to affirm the legacy of the Enlightenment betrayed an intense level of insecurity about the future. An intellectual defence of liberal democracy could not be conducted without upholding the ideal of progress and related Enlightenment values. Yet because in the context of the Cold War these ideas were also associated with the Soviet model, there was a reluctance to share them with the ideological enemy. The response of pro-Western intellectuals was to embrace a new narrative, one that communicated suspicion towards the idea of progressive change. Unable to dismiss the concept of progress altogether without inflicting damage on their own intellectual tradition, they sought to demote its status through a rhetorical strategy of devaluing its claims. Terms such as 'historical inevitability', 'historical determinism', 'the philosophy of history', 'historicism', 'teleological history' or 'ideological politics' were criticized for placing too much faith in progress.

Unable to reject progress entirely and yet reluctant to embrace it, liberal democrats in the Cold War opted for a compromise that projected the possibility of technical advance and development into the future. At the same time, such advance was posed as a sensible and steady process of development that stood in sharp contrast to the wild fantasies of ideologies. Such compromise was justified on the ground that unrestrained promises of ideologies had to be avoided. 'The degeneration of the Soviet Union taught us a useful lesson', 'it broke the bubble of the false optimism of the nineteenth century', stated Schlesinger.[42]

Having distanced itself from the ideal of progress, liberal capitalism now lacked a vision of the future. The post-war boom and prosperity encouraged a positive identification with capitalism. The Soviet Union did a good job of discrediting itself and thereby indirectly encouraged the Western public to react against it and identify with liberal democracy. But negative sentiments towards Soviet communism were no substitute for a positive identification with a system of values. This was a dilemma that exercised the minds of liberal intellectuals like Daniel Bell. Bell feared that Western societies lacked the cultural resources to motivate their public and particularly their intellectuals.

That the West had not actually won the arguments was evident even to the participants at Milan. While the Milan conference felt confident about defeating the ideological appeal of the Soviet Union, it was expressed concerns about the prevalence of anti-Western sentiment throughout the societies of Africa, Asia, Latin America and the Middle East. Many of the participants feared that just when the battle was won in Europe, the war could be lost in Asia and Africa. The defensive tone with which the predicament of the West in the Third World was discussed indicated that the questions raised through intellectual crisis of the interwar era remained unanswered. Something was clearly missing in this defensive narrative of the West. As the dissident Polish poet Czeslaw Milosz wrote in 1953:

> More than the West imagines, the intellectuals of the East look to the West for something. Nor do they seek it in Western propaganda. The something they look for is a great new writer, a new social philosophy, an artistic movement, a scientific discovery, new principles of painting or music. They rarely find this something.[43]

The quest for that 'something' would remain elusive so long as the question of the West's cultural values was avoided.

There was to be little solace in the end of ideology. In and of itself, the passing of political passions did little to provide society with a sense of purpose and direction. Bell himself sensed that the prerequisite for a genuine victory in the battle of ideas was the capacity for projecting a positive view of the future. If this challenge was not tackled then Bell feared that Western society would cease to inspire its intellectuals and youth. He warned that the younger generation of intellectuals was searching for a cause and that the 'welfare state and the mixed economy were not the sort of goals that could capture the passions of the intelligentsia'.[44]

The radical sociologist C.Wright Mills was defiant in his dismissal of the evasive strategy of the end-of-ideology movement. In his well-known 1960 statement 'Letter to the New Left' he argued:

> The end-of-ideology is on the way out because it stands for the refusal to work out an explicit political philosophy. And alert men everywhere today do feel the need for such a philosophy. What we should do is to continue directly to confront this need.[45]

By the time this letter was published, the celebration of the end-of-ideology was gradually coming to an end – not because of a revival of ideology, but because of the emergence of tensions and conflicts that would eventually mutate into the Culture Wars.

Problem of culture and reaction to it

The sensibility of exhaustion expressed through arguments about the end-of-ideology and other attempts to curb political passions were underpinned by an understandable aspiration for security and stability. The catastrophic legacy of decades of global conflict and the ever-present menace of nuclear conflict encouraged a disposition towards political restraint. During the 1950s ideologies that were identified with the destructive wars of the past had lost much of their capacity to inspire. That there was little attempt to formulate new ideological alternatives was significantly influenced by the unexpected success of post-war reconstruction followed by an unprecedented period of prosperity. In a very direct sense the post-war boom provided the conditions for the flourishing of end-of-politics arguments.

During the interwar era Keynes had alluded to the 'euthanasia of politics' in economic policy-making.[46] But it was only in the post-Second World War years that this ambition could be partially realized. The most powerful driver of the displacement of political ideology by economic policy was the global influence of the United States. In America, what Charles Maier has characterized as the 'politics of productivity' promised citizens steadily improving living standards and prosperity. This policy of economic engineering was 'based on the satisfaction of basic needs via a well-managed public-private "mixed economy"'. It also provided a focus for consensus and 'promoted a convergence of moderate leftist and rightist positions towards a broadly social democratic political centre'.[47] Through the Marshall Plan these ideas were internationalized and embraced by policy-makers throughout Western Europe.

In the US the culture of mass consumption acquired a veritable ideological dimension. As Lizabeth Cohen noted in her fine study, *A Consumers' Republic*, this orientation provided a 'powerful symbolism as the prosperous American alternative to the material deprivation of communism'. During the Cold War the politics of consumption emerged as the most effective antidote to the ideological appeal of radical ideologies. As Cohen wrote:

> No sooner had World War II ended than this new war raged, fought with ideological words as much as stockpiles of armaments and bombs. As the United States justified its superiority over the Soviet Union both at home and abroad, the mass consumption economy offered an arsenal of weapons to defend the reputation of capitalist democracy against the evils of communism.[48]

The claim that American capitalism worked and provided economic benefits to all succeeded in forcing its ideological opponents on the defensive. American policy-makers even tried to beat the Soviet Union at its own game by arguing that the distribution of material abundance to all ensured that theirs was a fair and just society.[49]

In Europe, the success of the mixed economy and economic planning served to vindicate the politics of productivity. Questions to do with the practical task of the technical management of the economy preoccupied policy-makers. In this conjuncture those who seemed to be still preoccupied with questions of class, exploitation, socialism or communism were easily marginalized and made to feel out of place. Hugh Gaitskell, the modernizing leader of the British Labour Party, accounted for the defeat of his party in the polls in 1959 by pointing to the weakening of working-class identity and the strengthening of consumerism. Gaitskell claimed that the factors responsible for Labour's defeat were the 'changing character of labour, full employment, new housing, the new way of living based on the telly, the fridge, the car and the glossy magazines'.[50]

The post-war boom and the expansion of mass consumption succeeded in neutralizing the political passions that gained such a powerful momentum in the interwar era. But prosperity on its own could not provide any durable answers to the question of value and norms. That is why even at the height of the post-war boom Anglo-American thinkers of virtually all shades of political opinion were deeply concerned about the absence of any positive vision of the future. 'No one could ignore the avalanche of works with such titles as "whither modern man?" or "good-bye to the West" or the "destiny of European culture"', wrote the political theorist, Judith Shklar in 1957.[51]

The project of turning consumerism into a political statement had succeeded in forcing socialists and communists on the defensive, but it could not provide a normative foundation for the Western way of life. In particular, it could not enthuse, inspire or give meaning to the life of its citizens, particularly the younger generations and intellectuals. At the time Bell recognized that there was a serious void within Western consumer culture. 'The young intellectual is unhappy because the "middle way" is for the middle-aged, not for him; it is without passion and is deadening', he wrote. Yet, he knew that 'the emotional energies – and needs – exist', and in a situation where 'politics offers little excitement' the question at stake is 'how one mobilizes these energies'.[52]

It is at this point in the late 1950s and early 1960s that commentators in many Western societies began to raise concerns about the apathy of young people, especially university students. Some commentators complained that

'politics is now boring'.[53] In the United States, a new genre of literature criti-
cizing the cynicism and disengagement of the young emerged. As Pells recalled:
'throughout the 1950s, magazines and newspapers berated the young as
members of a "silent generation" – politically apathetic, intellectually passive,
caring less for social causes than for economic security, preoccupied with their
lives.'[54] That apathy and political inertia was widespread was recognized by even
sections of the left and of the younger generations. The editorial of the first issue
of the Oxford-based *Universities & Left Review* in the spring of 1957 sought
to address this problem. It blamed the apathy of the young on the failure of
left-wing ideas to adapt and gain relevance to the times:

> The debate between those who clung to the slogans of the thirties and those who
> embraced the new orthodoxies of Welfare Britain, a debate which evaded the critical
> problems and the main frustrations of post-war society, appeared monstrously irrel-
> evant to the post-war generation. Its very irrelevance flattered their apathy. Given the
> feeble level of political controversy, and its internecine character, who could argue with
> the young intellectuals, when they said—they are still saying it.[55]

The first book published by New Left Books in 1960 in Britain was titled *Out
of Apathy*.[56] Tackling the problem of apathy was clearly seen as a priority by the
emerging New Left.

When the American sociologist Norman Birnbaum returned home after a
five-year absence in England he was surprised by the de-politicized climate
in his home. He wrote 'how tensions in the United States had shifted away
from politics'. He found Americans 'so preoccupied with problems of personal
identity that the population was politically passive, apparently existing without
an ideology or a politics'. Birnbaum observed that in America problems are seen
as 'exclusively, technical, matters of detail'.[57]

Whatever the merits of conformism and apathy for maintaining the status
quo it lacked the resources necessary for motivating people. Such a culture fails
to enthuse and provide people with meaning or a focus for belief. A culture that
lacked the resources to engage with people's quest for existential security and
meaning is likely to invite a reaction and a critique of itself. The conformism and
complacency of consumer culture always contained the potential for provoking
a reaction from those who regarded its materialistic ethos as crass and lacking
in purpose. Such reactions were widely articulated in the Western world. In
1960, Konrad Adenauer, the West German chancellor pointed to what he called

the 'most important problem of our epoch' – the 'inner political' weakness and superficiality of daily life in the Cold War. He derided empty 'materialism' and hoped for a revival of 'Christian belief in the simple devout life, free from military tensions, superficial consumerism, and impersonal bureaucratic institutions'.

Adenauer spoke a language that captured the essence of the Weberian concept of disenchantment with the process of rationalization. A regime of impersonal institutions which are underpinned by technical and pragmatic justification leaves open the question of how the institutions of society ought to be legitimated. That was the problem in Weber's era and in a different form provoked a sense of cultural estrangement in the 1950s and 1960s. The politics of productivity not only weakened hostile ideologies but also the normative foundation on which Western society was built. Its one-sided celebration of economic prosperity and materialism invited a reaction to consumer culture and conformism.

In his 1960 essay 'The End of Ideology?', Martin Lipset recognized that the decline of political ideological rivalries did not mean the end of conflict. Lipset took the view that conflict would continue but would not be expressed through a political ideological form. In this essay he anticipated that the revolt against 'many of the disagreeable aspects of American society which are now regarded as the results of an affluent and bureaucratic society' would assume a cultural form. He believed that with the erosion of ideology 'many intellectuals have turned from a basic concern with the political and economic systems to criticism of other sections of the basic culture of American society, particularly of elements which cannot be dealt with politically'.[58]

As examples of this turn towards a non-ideological critique of Western liberal democracy, Lipset cited the growing sense of disquiet towards consumerism and the conformist ethos of mass culture. Lipset pointed to the mounting concern with status – 'keeping up with the Joneses' – and to the 'related increase in the influence of advertisers and mass media as the arbiters of mass taste' to the evidence that Americans are overconformist – another side of keeping up with the Joneses.[59]

Reaction to consumer culture and conformism

The experience of the 1950s and early 1960s indicated that economic prosperity and security could provide a provisional, albeit limited solution to the problem of legitimation. However, it also demonstrated that a culture war could not be won with just dollars; it also requires a willingness to fight for a way of life and its values. At times, the one-dimensional emphasis of the United States on its economic accomplishments even threatened to undo its moral advantage relative to the Soviet Union. During the rivalry between the two super-powers it sometimes seemed that the US could not appeal to the idealism of neutral parties, since the only alternative to Soviet ideology was its culture of consumption.

The limits of the effectiveness of America's culture of consumption were exposed when Washington was forced to react to the unwelcome news that the Soviet Union had just successfully launched its first unmanned spacecraft. According to an interesting analysis of America's reaction – or over-reaction – to the launching of the Sputnik by the Soviet Union in October 1957, the West responded with a palpable sense of defensiveness regarding its intellectual and scientific achievements. This event was seen as not simply a great scientific achievement but as evidence of a failure of the American way of life. *Time* magazine reported that in 1957 'the world's balance of power lurched and swung toward the free world's enemies'.[60]

Not surprisingly, the Soviets went on the offensive and declared that they 'had found ways to mobilize the intellectual and economic capacities of its citizens while Americans frittered away their patrimony in mindless consumption and frivolous amusements'.[61] This Soviet attack on America's shallow culture of consumption succeeded in gaining some resonance within the United States and the Western public. Many American commentators claimed that the Soviets were far more effective at inspiring and motivating their people than Western capitalist societies. In particular it was frequently asserted that the Russian educational system was far superior to that of the United States 'in its ability to motivate youngsters and enlist them in the nation's enterprises'.[62]

Ever since the launching of Sputnik 1 the so-called crisis of education has become a constant subject of concern in Western society. This event detonated a veritable moral crisis that exposed consumer culture's limited capacity to endow life with purpose and meaning. The main manifestation of this crisis was the growing sense of doubt about the ability of the West to adapt successfully to rapidly changing circumstances. The defensive tone with which governments and intellectuals responded to Sputnik showed that the celebratory stance adopted by end-of-ideology theorists was the accomplishment of complacent thinking. Suddenly the old ideological enemy had resurrected itself. Some commentators went so far as to argue that the Soviet Union possessed the kind of formidable potential for innovation and dynamism that the West could simply not match. As one study of this crisis recalled:

> In a very real sense, in the late 1950s and early 1960s, Americans experienced a sort of 'moral crisis', triggered by Soviet scientific accomplishments, economic achievements, and diplomatic successes, and epitomized by the spectacular launch of Sputniks.[63]

The attribution of motivational and intellectual superiority to the Soviet Union by a significant section of the American cultural elite reveals far more about the moral climate that prevailed in the West in general and the United States in particular than about the dynamism of their opponent.

The tendency to experience the Sputnik-related moral crisis as that of education indicates that at some level it was understood as an issue that touched on the domain of norms and values. Education is frequently perceived as the mirror through which society becomes conscious of its blemishes. That is why often it is tempting to perceive schools as the source of a problem, the solution to the problem – or both. The 14 March 1958 cover of *Life* magazine stated: CRISIS IN EDUCATION. Inside the first of a five-part 'urgent' series of essays stated that 'the schools are in terrible shape, what has long been an ignored national problem, Sputnik has made a recognized crisis'.[64]

Since the late nineteenth century, the difficulties facing society have often been interpreted as the outcome of a failed system of education. At least in part, the perception that education is in crisis is symptomatic of the absence of consensus about the basic values of society. In the early 1960s, the political philosopher Hannah Arendt drew attention to the tendency to confuse the lack of moral consensus in society with the problem of schooling. She believed that there had to be a measure of consensus about the normative foundation of society before a system of education could affirm its virtues. In other words, a crisis of education is often a symptom of society's inability to provide a meaningful account of itself.[65] So the reaction to Sputnik 1 was far more about the confusion about how Western society understands its traditions and values than about the moral threat posed by the Soviet Union.

Western societies did not require an external foe to remind them that there was more to life than materialism and consumption. A veritable new genre of literature targeting the crass materialism and conformism of mass society emerged in the 1950s and 1960s. Influential texts such as Riesman's *The Lonely Crowd*, Galbraith's *The Affluent Society*, Vance Packard's *Hidden Persuaders*, Whyte's *The Organization Man* outlined a world of alienated and disconnected people. The authority of consumer culture was challenged and increasingly by a new generation of young people. By the late 1950s it was evident that those who voiced the concerns of this generation tended to reject the dominant form of cultural authority. An authority based on consumption and technical advance succeeded in preserving stability and political order, but it could do little to inspire or give meaning to people's experiences. As one study of this era in Britain concluded, young people's estrangement from authority was driven by a reaction against the 'age of affluence'. In this period the revolt against the conformism of Cold War society in Britain as expressed in the literary contribution of the so-called Angry Young Men took the form of a '*cultural* criticism of society'.[66] Soon such reactions would become more systematic, global and crystallize into a veritable counter-culture.

During the Cold War the cohesion of the rival blocs distracted attention from the conflicts within. Yet, particularly in the West, the Cold War inadvertently fostered a climate where dissatisfaction with everyday life acquired an increasingly cultural form. Suri argues that by the 1960s a new movement emerged that 'questioned the basic assumptions about the "good life" that underpinned social order'.[67] At least for some commentators, the reaction to the cultural authority that broke out in the West was reminiscent of the anti-modernist impulses detected in the years leading up to the outbreak of the Great War. Fritz remarked that, once again, 'implicit in the attack on modernity has been the repudiation, the hatred of the West'.[68] Whatever the rights and wrongs of his analysis, it indicated that prosperity alone could not provide a solution to the problem identified by Zweig and Mannheim in the early 1940s.

Notes

1 Huntington (1996) is the foremost representative of the culture conflict school.
2 Kohn (1964) pp.306, 307.
3 See Fritz (1974).
4 Zweig (1953) p.223.
5 Weber (1915) p.335.
6 Zweig (1953) p.223.
7 Mason is cited in Herf (1981) p.818.
8 Zweig (1953) p.225.

9   Fritz (1974) p.ix.
10 Ropke (1958) pp.11–14.
11 See Morgan & Evans (1993).
12 Mannheim (1943) p.7.
13 Mannheim (1943) p.8.
14 Mannheim (1943) p.10.
15 Mannheim (1943) p.10.
16 Mannheim (1943) p.7.
17 Mannheim (1943) pp.14–15.
18 Mannheim (1943) pp.14–15.
19 Mannheim (1943) p.26.
20 Mannheim (1943) p.26.
21 hayes (1940) pp.95–6.
22 Parsons (1964) p.123.
23 Mannheim (1943) p.7.
24 Hammond & Hammond (2008) p.2.
25 Ropke (1958) p.3.
26 Schumpeter (1976) p.250.
27 Hartz is cited in Bachrach (1967) p.25.
28 Schlesinger (1949) pp.254–6.
29 Aron is cited in Scott-Smith (2002) p.408.
30 Lipset (1964) p.404.
31 Mills (1959) p.27.
32 For a useful discussion of the CCF see Dittberner (1979).
33 See Scott-Smith (2002) p.452.
34 Bell (2000) p.402.
35 Bell (2000) p.402.
36 Bell (2000) p.402.
37 Shils (1955) p.54.
38 Scott-Smith (2002) p.445.
39 Beloff is cited in Scott-Smith (2002) p.445.
40 McAuliffe (1978) p.73.
41 Fay (1947) p.232.
42 Schlesinger (1949) p.viii.
43 Milosz is cited in Scott-Smith (2002) p.437.
44 Bell (1976) p.42.
45 See http://www.marxists.org/subject/humanism/mills-c-wright/letter-new-left.htm
46 Keynes is cited in Muller (2013) p.144.
47 Maier (1977) p.615.
48 Cohen (2004) pp. 8, 124.
49 Cohen (2004) p.125.
50 Cited in Freeman and Marshall (1978) p.19.
51 Shklar (1957) p.vii.
52 Bell (2000) p.404.

53 Lipset (1964) p.406.
54 Pells (1985) p.201.
55 Hall, Pearson, Samuel and Taylor (1957) no pagination.
56 See Hewison (1981) p.164
57 Birnbaum is cited in Dittberner (1979) p. 135.
58 Lipset (1964) p.409.
59 Lipset (1964) p.409.
60 See http://americanreviewmag.com/authors/view/25 .
61 Zieger (2004) p.88.
62 Zieger (2004) p.91.
63 Zieger (2004) p.93.
64 See http://www.pbs.org/wnet/need-to-know/the-daily-need/our-sputnik-moment-then-and-now/7286/ .
65 Arendt (2006) p.193.
66 Nelson (1989) p.35.
67 Suri (2009) p.69.
68 Fritz (1974) p.ix.

6

Why the 1960s hurt so much

The 1960s and the emergence of the counter-culture are the manifestations of trends that first gained a powerful momentum around the time of the outbreak of World War One. The period shared many of the assumptions of the turn-of-the-twentieth century romantic reaction to capitalist rationality. The post-war boom with its preoccupation with material possessions and consumption served to intensify the sensibility of alienation of the counter-culture. The 1960s intellectual revolt against capitalist culture coincided with the erosion of bourgeois self-belief in the legitimacy of its way of life. During the 1960s Western governments, influenced by technocratic modernizers, sought to distance themselves from the practices and traditions of the past. The convergence of the political elite's aspiration to leave the past behind with the 1960s revolt with the loss of bourgeois self-belief created the condition for the flourishing of the counter-culture.

Attitudes and sentiments that are associated with the counter-culture were already in evidence during the first two decades of the twentieth century. The rejection of materialism and the imperative of rationalization were central themes in the revolt against modernity in the early twentieth century. According to the historian Alan Kahan, 'World War I was a turning point in history, and it was a turning point in the struggle between mind and money'.[1] Kahan's reference is to the revolt of intellectuals against capitalist culture. Through this war intellectuals 'sought to re-enchant the world to find new sources of morality and meaning'.[2]

In the aftermath of the Great War the criticisms mounted against capitalism and liberal democracy tended to mainly assume the form of an ideological attack on socio-economic institutions. At this time the cultural expressions of this critique became less prominent. In the context of post-World War One economic dislocation, followed by a depression, ideologies – even those advocating a nationalist and racist programme – emphasized the economic dimension of their anti-capitalist doctrines.

As we noted in the previous chapter, during the Cold War and the post-war boom the socio-economic critique of capitalism was tempered by the reality of relative prosperity and security. In this conjuncture the reaction to capitalism lost some of its ideological impulse and increasingly acquired a cultural form. The cumulative outcome of this trend was the rise of the so-called counter-culture in the 1960s. The main target of this movement was the emotional attitudes, cultural values and lifestyles of post-Second World War consumer capitalism.

During the years leading up to the outbreak of World War One the principal target of the cultural critique of capitalism was the complacent and conformist middle class and its values. Cynicism directed at bourgeois lifestyle often conveyed an aristocratic disdain towards the compromises and shallow materialistic lifestyle of the money-obsessed middle classes.[3] The rejection of bourgeois lifestyle often meshed with a rejection of materialism and mass consumerism. Whereas initially this rejection had as its target the culture of materialism and consumption, by the 1950s it turned into an attack on mass consumerism and the tastes and dispositions of ordinary folk. The masses were accused of 'false consciousness' for their conspicuous consumption and their aspiration for material progress was denounced as shallow and selfish. Herbert Marcuse's *One Dimensional Man* (1964) offered a radical left-wing cultural critique of mass consumption. It claimed that mass culture had diminished the public's capacity to engage in a creative intellectual and spiritual life. His call for a cultural revolution resonated with the moment when, for many, the problem was not too few but too many material possessions.

The technocratic politics of the economic expansion of the 1950s which helped improve people's material circumstances created an unprecedented degree of economic security. It also provided an environment where many were freed to think about existential, moral and cultural issues. However the politics of economic productivity did little to offer people a moral universe which could provide them with a sense of purpose and meaning. Deprived of any inner moral sensibility, economic pragmatism failed to capture people's imagination. The incapacity of the end-of-ideology administrative regime of the modern welfare state to motivate the public encouraged a significant section of the younger generation to react against it. 'The 1960s were a time of acute disen-chantment with Western modernity', writes Richard Wolin. In a sense the revolt of 1968 can be seen as an expression of disenchantment with consumer society. Wolin notes that the 1968 'May movement targeted impersonal, bureaucratic, and highly formalized modes of socialization that operated "without regard for persons".[4] Unlike the reactions to the impersonal technocratic climate of pre-World War One, that of the 1960s was not restricted to relatively small groups of artists and intellectuals. It mobilized large constituencies of young people.

Accounts of the 1960s understandably highlight the revolt of students and of intellectuals. Consequently the behaviour and the reaction of the ruling elites is often overlooked. During the sixties the ruling elites frequently adopted a defensive tone, were hesitant in affirming their way of life and even expressed doubts about their right to exercise authority. Their behaviour suggested that they lacked a vision of the future and felt unable to engage either the intellect or the spirit of their citizens. Their intellectual energies were most enthusiastically and most effectively deployed against their Cold War enemy. But though Cold War and anti-Soviet ideology could secure order and loyalty, it could not offer a focus for the positive identification of values. As we noted previously, the Western elite felt exposed on the battlefield of culture. This point was acknowledged by Daniel Bell in the following terms:

> The traditional bourgeois organization of life – its rationalism and sobriety – has few defenders in the serious culture; nor does it have a coherent system of cultural meanings or stylistic forms with any intellectual or cultural respectability. What we have today is a radical disjunction of culture and social-structure, and it is such disjunctions which historically have paved the way for the erosion of authority, if not for social revolution.[5]

Unexpectedly, the booming economy only exposed the fragile foundation of the moral authority of the institutions of capitalist society. Ironically, at this point in time the crisis of nerve of the Western elites coincided with the disintegration of the old left. By the 1960s it was evident that the communist and socialist movements had lost their way. The 1950s was a decade of revisionism for left-wing parties attempting to redefine themselves. Brinkley points out that during the 1950s in the United States the old left had 'come closer to extinction than at any time in this century'.[6] The increasing irrelevance of what was now called the Old Left indicated that the traditional state-focused ideologies had also become exhausted. The left showed that it lacked a vocabulary with which to address the social conditions that were very different from the one it anticipated. Although social democratic and communist parties attempted to adapt to the new circumstances and revise their doctrines, they could not go too far down this road without obliterating their very identity.

The 1960s proved unkind to both sides of the old ideological divide. And both the old left and the right were soon overtaken by events.

The sixties – the revolt from within

The 1960s caught both the old left and the old right unaware. Political theorists and commentators whose outlook was shaped by the conflicts and disputes of the 1930s and the Cold War attempted to interpret events through a vocabulary of traditional political categories. As a result, relatively incoherent protest movements were perceived as if they were the reincarnation of interwar totalitarian organizations. Student protests and demonstrations were often denounced as the acts of fascist-minded radicals or of extreme revolutionaries. The conservative philosopher Alan Bloom depicted the New Left as the incarnation of Hitler Youth. He claimed that the 'American university of the 1960s was experiencing the same dismantling of the structure of rational inquiry as had the German university in the 1930s'.[7]

President de Gaulle's New Year's broadcast to the people of France condemned the May 1968 events and stressed the importance of fighting the 'materialist civilisation' that bred the individualistic chaos of the young radicals. He added:

> Otherwise, the fanatics of destruction, the doctrinaires of negation, the specialists in demagogy, will once more have a good opportunity to exploit bitterness in order to provoke agitation, while their sterility, which they have the derisory insolence to call revolution, can lead to nothing else than the dissolution of everything into nothingness, or else to the loss of everything under the grinding oppression of totalitarianism.[8]

De Gaulle's rhetorical association of May 1968 with the threat of totalitarianism indicated a disposition to interpret the revolt through the language of the past. However, his dismissal of those who called the May events a revolution as insolent indicates that he was sensitive to its defining feature as a negative counter-cultural phenomenon. What endowed De Gaulle's bitter denunciation of May 1968 with a passionate intensity was the recognition that this was a revolt from within French society and that he experienced it as the negation of everything that he stood for. That so many young people drawn from France's privileged elite were at the forefront of this movement served to emphasize that this was a revolt from within.

The counter-culture had its greatest impact on social layers who enjoyed a relatively privileged status in Western societies. Its leaders – on both sides of the Atlantic – were overwhelmingly drawn from individuals who came from an economically privileged middle-class background. One American official study observed the the influence of the counter-culture on 'housewives, corporate employees, and college students'. It indicated that those who 'questioned basic social assumptions were core political constituencies'. As the director of the CIA, Richard Helms reported, these were 'children of a generally affluent generation'.[9]

Apprehension coupled with an extravagant sense of foreboding was often evident in the political reaction to the 1960s movement. The intensity of the concern of the political elites towards the counter-culture is clearly articulated in a CIA study titled 'Restless Youth', published in 1968. The report predicted that the 'social and political malaise that underlies much of present-day dissidence will not be speedily cured; there are, in fact, striking parallels between the situation today and the conditions of cynicism, despair, and disposition toward violence which existed after World War I and which later helped produce Fascism and National Socialism on the Continent'.[10] No doubt this assessment was something of an over-reaction. While both the post-World War One decades and the 1960s were subject to a mood of cultural disorientation and cynicism, they expressed these sentiments in very different ways: in the post-1918 era through political ideology and in the 1960s through the politicization of culture.

That the CIA attempted to understand the 1960s counter-cultural movement through the historical experience of the post-World War One decades is significant. It indicated that the questions left unresolved during the interwar era had retained their salience in the 1960s. The CIA analysis also failed to note that the 1960s was principally cultural and rarely threatened the economic and social institutions of society. Its activities did not lead to the violence and political crisis of the interwar era. Its main effect was to intensify the sense of malaise and doubt about the conventions and rules of society.

Economic recovery proved to be a less challenging task than the moral rehabilitation of Western capitalism. So long as Cold War rivalry dominated domestic life, Western society was able to benefit from flattering comparison with the Soviet Bloc. The mere existence of the Soviet rival endowed the Western way of life with purpose and coherence. But unity against an external rival was not sufficient to provide Western elites with an *esprit de corps* and a sense of mission necessary for the authoritative management of political and cultural life.

The 1960s revolt was particularly successful in the domain of culture. Cultural institutions, especially schools and higher education but also music and the arts, swiftly internalized the new anti-establishment sensibility. The new counter-cultural movement explicitly opposed the values and norms associated with the old order. During the 1960s, establishment values were ridiculed and rejected by a vocal minority of young people – many of whom were the progeny of the old order. To the defenders of the old order it appeared as if their whole way of life was now under attack. National traditions were mocked and authority in all its forms was contested. The rapid advance of the 1960s counter-culture caught societies throughout the world by surprise. The CIA was overwhelmed by reports of political disruption on every continent. Its reports described it as a 'world-wide phenomenon' with potentially perilous consequences.[11]

One reason why the new counter-culture succeeded in making such a rapid headway was due to the weak resistance to its advance. By the 1960s the conventional norms and values had appeared to many as irrelevant and pointless. Instead of reinforcing conventional bourgeois norms, the consumer culture that arose in the 1950s appeared to diminish its relevance to people's lives. Some commentators blamed the new prosperity for helping to undermine conventional values; 'life has ceased to be as difficult as it used to be but it has become pointless', wrote the author of a study on *Permissive Britain*.[12] Though prosperity may have facilitated the growth of the 1960s counter-cultural lifestyle revolt, the real issue at stake was the loss of legitimacy of the norms that underpinned the institutions of Western societies. What many supporters of the Cold War political arrangement not could not openly acknowledge was the manifest irrelevance of the conventions and values that defined their way of life.

The strident denunciation of the 1960s counter-cultural movement by defenders of the status quo are best understood as expressions of deep insecurities regarding the moral status of their way of life. According to the chair of the Adenauer Foundation, 'the revolt of 1968 destroyed more values than did the Third Reich'.[13] However, by this time these values could only survive on life support. For the British historian J. H. Plumb the widespread derision towards 'hollow' values confirmed *The Death of the Past*. In a lecture given in 1968 he told his audience that 'wherever we look, in all areas of social and personal life, the hold of the past is weakening'.[14] Michael Stewart, the British Secretary of State for Foreign Affairs, responded to the upheavals of the late 60s by noting in his diary that the 'evening television news presents a depressing picture'. Stewart believed that it was 'the moral deficiencies of what should be the free world' that constituted the problem of his era. He wrote: 'Germany distracted, France selfish, ourselves aimless, USA in torment'.[15]

Reactions such as those of Stewart were widespread among the political elites. That is why it is possible to understand the transformation of cultural life in the 1960s as at least in part a result of a discrete or unconscious revolt of the elites. In his major study of this period, Arthur Marwick suggests that the outcome of the 1960s was in part influenced by a ruling elite ready to give way to new demands. Marwick indicates that the changes were not simply an outcome of protest but due to the reaction of enlightened elites. He characterized the sixties as due to a 'conjunction of developments, including economic, demographic, and technological ones and critically, to the existence in positions of authority of men and women of traditional enlightened and rational outlook who responded flexibly and tolerantly to counter-cultural demands'. He referred to this 'vital component of sixties transformations as "measured judgment" to signify [...] that it emanated from people in authority, people very much part of mainstream society'.[16]

There is little doubt that sections of the political elites responded to the cultural revolt with flexibility and, in some cases, embraced the demand for change with enthusiasm. But whether this response is best characterized as a case of 'measured judgment' or as a crisis of elite self-belief is a moot point. What mattered was that those in authority were reluctant to enter the battle-field of culture. Their equivocation indicated that there was little appetite for upholding the way of life into which they were socialized. Not all sections of society felt that there was little of value to defend. At least an influential minority of traditionally minded people drew the conclusion that there was something important to uphold. One of the outcomes of their backlash was to transform the cultural revolt of the 1960s into the Culture Wars of the decades to follow.

The changing battleground – pre-political

As noted previously, the post-war boom has served to significantly diminish the credibility of the critique of capitalism. Both communist and socialist arguments against the viability of capitalist prosperity were contradicted by the experience of the Golden Decades. As one review of this period noted, 'capitalism now displayed an unexpected renewed vitality' and forced left-wing movements to reorient their approach.[17] Instead of offering an economic critique of capitalism, the left offered one that was moralistic and cultural. Historically the cultural critique of capitalism and of middle-class lifestyles was associated with a conservative and aristocratic worldview. In the nineteenth century, philosophers like Kierkegaard and Nietzsche 'looked behind the façade of a seemingly stable society and found the inner castle empty'.[18] Now this traditional appeal to non-material and spiritual values was embraced by the New Left and reconstituted in a radical form. This 1960s cultural critique of modern society was expressed in a form that outwardly contrasted with that of the pre-1914 anti-modernist generation. What they both shared was what Bracher called a 'romantic declaration of war on the consequences of progress'.[19]

The pre-1914 movement 'found fault with the pomp, smugness and artificiality of bourgeois society'. It despised the masses for complacently enjoying the 'fruits of material growth' and disregarding 'the question of the soul'.[20] The 1960s movement developed this anti-materialist outlook into one that self-consciously sought to shift the focus from economics to culture. This critique accepted that capitalism was productive and efficient but questioned how resources were distributed. Criticisms directed at inequality were co-joined to ones that queried the culture of consumption. Such arguments did not so much query the capacity of capitalism to deliver the goods as the culture of acquisitiveness it fostered. Increasingly radical opponents of the status quo began to question 'artificial' wants and desires promoted through consumerism and advertising. It also focused its wrath against the materialism of consumer society. In effect the socio-economic-based anti-capitalist critique of the first half of the twentieth century gradually mutated into a cultural one.

That the 1960s cultural revolt was a product of prosperity and economic security highlighted its character as a movement that rejected a way of life or a lifestyle wedded to prosperity, efficiency and material progress. It represented 'an explosion of doubt about the quality and direction of life' and 'a rejection of affluence as an adequate justification for the existing social arrangements or as a sufficient goal for political action'.[21] Just when advocates of capitalism expected that the economic achievements of their system would endow it with credibility and moral authority, the terrain on which the battle of ideas was fought fundamentally altered. The main issue at stake was not the economic but moral and cultural consequences of free-market capitalism. Since the nineteenth century, the 'valueless' empty materialist lifestyle of the middle class had been the object of bohemian scorn.[22] Its condemnation had led a minority of artists and intellectuals to embrace the heroic lifestyle that glorified and welcomed World War One. Half a century later – in the 1960s – the cultural critique of conventional middle-class lifestyle acquired a far wider audience than in previous times. By the 1960s it was evident that whereas the economic case against capitalism had been marginalized, the cultural critique against this society possessed an unanticipated vitality and momentum.

Irving Kristol, who would later become one of the leading figures of American neo-conservatism, told the Mont Pelerin Society in 1972 that winning the ideological war against the Soviet model of the planned economy was the easy part of their struggle. Having triumphed in the economic war, liberals and conservatives still felt that real victory had eluded them. Kristol noted that 'it is therefore a source of considerable puzzlement to the free marketers that, though the other side seems to have lost the argument, their side seems somehow not to have won it'.[23] The question posed by Kristol was: 'if the traditional economics of socialism has been discredited, why has not the traditional economics of capitalism been vindicated?'

Kristol answered his rhetorical question by indicating that the reason why triumph eluded the victors in the economic war was because the left had changed the battleground on which the struggle was fought. He wrote:

> The Old Left has been intellectually defeated on its chosen battleground, i.e., economics. But the New Left is now launching an assault on liberal society from quite other directions. One of the most astonishing features of the New Left – astonishing, at least, to a middle-aged observer – is how little interest it really has in economics. I would put it even more strongly: The identifying marks of the New Left are its refusal *to think economically* and its contempt for bourgeois society precisely because this is a society that does think economically.[24]

At a relatively early point in time Kristol had identified a disquieting development in the long war of ideas – which was its transformation into a struggle about competing visions about the meaning and conduct of everyday life. What was now at issue was not so much the economic realities of capitalism but its moral and normative foundation.

Despite the persistence of significant pockets of poverty and hardship in the 1960s, the counter-culture demonstrated relatively little interest in material deprivation. Indeed, the most strident criticism of capitalist consumer society was mounted by individuals who were relatively indifferent to material needs. Those involved in the counter-culture rejected society on the grounds that it was emotionally and spiritually alienating and repressive and did not provide an outlet for self-fulfilment and happiness. Their disenchantment with a life they considered to be empty and soulless was often expressed through arguments that were either explicitly anti-modernist or deeply sceptical of the claim that a modern industrial society could provide a space for the realization of the individual. As Wolin remarked, the 'denizens of advanced industrial society discovered that not only did affluence fail to coincide with happiness, but that the two often seemed to operate at cross-purposes'.[25]

Hostility to industrial society was often fuelled by an outrage against its potentially destructive impulses. Theodor Roszak described this society as 'fatally and contagiously diseased' and pointed to the threat posed by thermo-nuclear annihilation. Roszak claimed that nuclear weapons symbolized the wider ethos of destruction that dominated a technological society. In his influential text *The Making Of A Counter Culture*, he denounced 'technocracy's essential criminality', which, he claimed, 'insists, in the name of progress, in the name of reason, that the unthinkable become thinkable and the intolerable become tolerable'. He added that the youthful counter-cultural activists refuse 'to practice such a cold-blooded rape of our human sensibilities' which is why generational conflict 'reaches so peculiarly and painfully deep'.[26] The approach proposed by Roszak explicitly called into question the ideals of Enlightenment modernity. He dismissed technocratic assumptions about science and intellect and argued that 'nothing less is required than the subversion of the scientific world view, with its entrenched commitment to an egocentric and cerebral mode of consciousness'. In its place, he demanded that 'there must be a culture in which the non-intellective capacity of the personality – those capacities that take fire from visionary splendour and the experience of human communion – become arbiters of the good, the true, and the beautiful'.[27]

One important observation made by Roszak pointed out that for the first time since modern times the anti-modernist rejection of technocratic society had gained the support of a substantial body of opinion, including those who were at the 'center of our society' – particularly middle-class university students.[28] What Roszak referred to was actually a deep-seated expression of generational discontent which rejected the ethos of technological progress and economic growth. This rejection of the spirit of capitalist modernity had important political implications, since it directly called into question the principles on which the legitimation of the system was based. The legitimacy of the capitalist order was based on its ability to deliver economic growth and prosperity. Once economic growth came to be contested as a value in its own right, the legitimacy of the prevailing order stood exposed.

It was significant that this new moral rejection of capitalist modernity acquired its greatest support among the principal beneficiaries of the system. Although the cultural revolt against capitalism was often portrayed as 'left-wing' or 'progressive', it did not express the classical political ideology associated with radical ideologies of the past. This was a movement that expressed the disenchantment and disorientation of sectors for whom everyday life had little meaning. Indeed, at the time, the politicization of everyday life permitted radical 1960s youth to distance themselves from the doctrines of the Marxist and socialist movements. This embrace of everyday personal issues allowed 'activists to address a variety of prepolitical, "existential" concerns: issues pertaining to psychology, sexuality, family life, urbanism, and basic human intimacy', claims Wolin.[29] The rhetoric of the 'personal is political' and the attachment of the term political to activities carried out in the private sphere – politics of the family, politics of sex, politics of identity – indicated the energies devoted to activism were now focused on battles that contrasted strikingly with those of the past.

At the time, the politicization of everyday life was interpreted by some as simply an expression of the libertine impulse of 'anything goes' and a rejection of all forms of authority. The term loss of respect for authority was frequently repeated in an attempt to account for the escalation of conflict over issues that had a direct bearing on the conduct of everyday life. Western capitalist society appeared to lack the moral resources with which to legitimize itself and, as a result, authority in all of its different dimensions was exposed to contestation.[30] The most striking manifestation of the moral crisis of the West was that it was not simply one form of authority but the authority of authority that was put to question.

Already, back in the 1950s, Hannah Arendt claimed that authority had become 'almost a lost cause'. In an essay that referred to authority in the past tense self-consciously titled 'What Was Authority?', Arendt insisted that 'authority has vanished from the modern world, and that if we raise the question what authority is, we can no longer fall back upon authentic and undisputable experiences common to all'.[31] Arendt's narrative of loss left little room for retaining illusions that authority in its classical form could survive. Arendt drew attention to a dramatic development in the 'gradual breakdown' of 'the authority of parents over children, of teachers over pupils, and generally of the elders over the young'.[32] She observed that this is 'the one form of authority' that existed in 'all historically known societies', as it is 'required as much by natural needs, the helplessness of the child, as by political necessity'. But 'ours is the first century in which this argument no longer carries an overwhelming weight of plausibility and it announced its anti-authoritarian spirit more radically when it promised the emancipation of youth as an oppressed class and called itself the "century of the child"'. Arendt was less interested in the implosion of generational authority itself as in the extent to which it signified 'to what extremes the general decline of authority could go, even to the neglect of obvious natural necessities'.[33]

In Arendt's account, the crisis of authority is not confined to the domain of the political. Indeed what gives this crisis its 'depth and seriousness, is that it has spread to such prepolitical areas as child-rearing and education', she concluded. That the contestation of authority dominated the pre-political spheres of everyday life was shown by the eruption of acrimonious debates in the 1960s over issues such as child-rearing, health, lifestyles, education and the conduct of personal relationships. Arendt intuited that the devaluation of authority had spread beyond the political sphere to capture all domains of social and cultural experience. This trend was expressed through the powerful counter-cultural movement of the 1960s. At the time, the so-called crisis of legitimation tended to be perceived as a political problem afflicting the state. However, as Eric Hobsbawm noted almost four decades after Arendt's 1956 contribution, the loss of authority was principally a cultural phenomenon. In his account of what he called the 'cultural revolution', he wrote of 'the breaking of the threads which in the past had woven human beings into social textures'. Echoing Arendt's point about the far-reaching effect of the loss of pre-political authority, Hobsbawm stated that 'what children could learn from parents became less obvious than what parents did not know and children did'.[34]

The main impact of the 1960s revolt was on the sphere of culture rather than on political institutions. Although the legitimacy of these institutions came under attack, they were able to weather the challenge. Matters were very different in the pre-political sphere where the cultural revolt struck deepest. The writer Umberto Eco remarked that 'even though all visible traces of 1968 are gone, it profoundly changed the way of all of us, at least in Europe, behave and relate to one another'. He added that 'relations between bosses and workers, students and teachers, even children and parents, have opened up' and therefore 'they'll never be the same again'.[35]

Although the advance of this cultural revolution was at times fiercely resisted – particularly by the more conservative and traditionalist sectors of the Establishment – at times it appeared that the 1960s radicals were kicking against an open door. There were, of course, numerous examples of firm and repressive reactions to the activities of the 1960s radicals. For sections of the political and cultural elites, the attack on their authority was often experienced as not just a threat to their roles but their way of life. For many who were used to the exercise of unquestioned authority, the world appeared to have turned upside-down. However, although their response was sometimes violent and often forceful, it lacked moral and cultural depth. This was a response that also expressed an evasive sense of bad faith, for it was difficult to accept the bitter truth that it was the moral depletion of bourgeois values and convention that invited the radical challenge to its cultural authority. Demonizing the sixties helped the old establishment to avoid take responsibility for its retreat from the battlefield of culture.

In one sense the 1960s radicals carried on where the pre-World War One intellectuals left off in their attempt to re-enchant their lives. Their reaction to rationalization and loss of community was, if anything, far more comprehensive and radical than that of early twentieth-century romantic reaction to industrial capitalism. Certainly, the 1960s movement achieved far more than its romantic predecessors in terms of transforming everyday life. However, the experience indicated that the revolt against disenchantment did not lead to the re-enchantment of human experience.

The moral depletion of Western capitalism

Daniel Bell's verdict on the outcome of the 1960s cultural revolution was that it undermined 'the social structure itself by striking at the motivational and psychic reward system' of capitalism.[36] Bell believed that the erosion of values associated with the Protestant work ethic, rationalism, sobriety and ambition for material and psychic rewards had struck a serious blow to the mechanisms of legitimation in a capitalist society. It was as if the world had changed, as

'it is the very idea of economic growth that is now coming under attack –
and by liberals'. With a hint of amazement he explained that 'affluence is no
longer seen as an answer' and 'growth is held responsible for the spoliation of
the environment'.[37] Bell interpreted that loss of the 'traditional legitimacy' of
capitalism as evidence that the cultural authority of capitalism has been significantly undermined. 'Who in the world today, especially in the world of culture,
defends the bourgeoisie?' he asked.[38]

The reason why the 'motivational and psychic reward system' of capitalism
lost much of its force was because it was so closely linked to the valuation
of economic efficiency and success. Until it was challenged, economic and
technical efficiency could help legitimate the institutions of society. 'Instead
of having to use "spiritual" values as a way of bypassing the social instability
induced by a zero-sum game, modern industrial societies used increased
productivity', wrote the American sociologist Alvin Gouldner.[39] But such a
solution could not serve as a durable alternative to a normative foundation for
society's institutions. Gouldner argued

> [...] the moral crisis has not so much been solved as deferred by the strengthening
> of the non-moral bases of social order, particularly the growth of the increasingly
> abundant gratifications that an industrial civilization is able to distribute.[40]

The problem of motivation alluded to by Bell and Gouldner was characterized
as a motivational crisis by the German social theorist Jurgen Habermas in his
path-breaking essay, *The Legitimation Crisis* (1973). Habermas explained that
the problem of legitimacy confronting post-1960s societies 'must be based on a
motivation crisis – that is, a discrepancy between the need for motives declared
by the state, the educational system and the occupational system on the one
hand, and the motivation supplied by the socio-cultural system on the other'.
According to Habermas, the imperatives of the welfare state-guided economic
system lacked the spiritual or cultural resources necessary for maintaining its
authority. His analysis suggested that capitalist institutions which have historically relied on cultural and traditional resources to legitimate themselves were
now forced to find new sources of validation.[41]

Habermas claimed capitalism had historically found it difficult to create
or produce values and norms that could provide a moral foundation for
its authority. He wrote that 'bourgeois culture as a whole was never able
to reproduce itself from itself' and as a result 'it was always dependent on

motivationally effective supplementation by tradition world-views'. Habermas went so far as to argue that it was precisely because capitalism could not provide a normative foundation for its institutions that it was forced to rely on economic incentives to forge popular support. He claimed that 'the less the cultural system is capable of producing adequate motivations for politics, the educational system, and the occupational system, the more must scarce meaning be replaced by consumable values'.[42]

The devaluation of norms through the dominant imperative of rationalization has decoupled authority from a system of moral meaning, leading to what Habermas characterized as a legitimation crisis. Writing more of less at the same time as Bell penned his thesis on the cultural contradictions of capitalism, Habermas stated that 'while organizational rationality spreads, cultural traditions important for legitimation are undermined and weakened'.[43]

The problem of cultivating a normative foundation for capitalism was a constant subject of discussion among social theorists during the decades leading up to World War One. In his review of the rise of sociology in the nineteenth century, Gouldner noted how sociologists understood that 'utilitarianism has a built-in tendency to restrict the sphere of morality' so that it bred a culture that is estranged from moral norms. Consequently, a rationalized utilitarian culture possessed a ' "natural" or built-in disposition towards moral normlessness', a tendency that the French sociologist Emile Durkheim characterized through his concept of *anomie*.[44] For Durkheim, this concept refers to a historical moment 'when society is disturbed by some painful crisis or by beneficent but abrupt transitions'. In such moments 'the scale is upset; but a new scale cannot be immediately improvised' and therefore 'time is required for the public conscience to reclassify men and things'.[45] Rational authority can do little to counteract this weakening of public conscience because it does not speak the language of moral norms.

In his analysis of the modern rationalized state, the German sociologist Ferdinand Tonnies noted the 'veiled hatred and contempt' of this institution towards the customs and traditions of community life. He described this as a 'revolution in social order', which led to the contract becoming the foundation of the new system and where the 'rational will of *Gesellschaft*' dominates institutional and cultural life. Tonnies noted that depth of moral life diminishes as religion and traditional values are displaced by science.[46] Paradoxically the very process of rationalization deprives the state of the fundamental moral values that it requires to validate it. He predicted that it was 'highly improbable' that the state could invent or construct a morality that would provide its authority with a normative foundation.[47] His analysis of this process concludes on a pessimistic note. The rationalized modern state 'means the doom of culture itself'.[48]

Throughout the twentieth century, liberal capitalism constantly faced difficulty in developing a moral and cultural foundation for its authority. Joseph Schumpeter explained that through its commitment to rationalization, calculation and efficiency, capitalism undermines 'its own defenses' because it 'creates a critical frame of mind which, after having destroyed the moral authority of so many other institutions, in the end turns against its own'. Schumpeter claimed that 'the bourgeois finds to his amazement that the rationalist attitude does not stop at the credentials of kings and popes but goes on to attack private property and the whole scheme of bourgeois values'.[49] Schumpeter feared that rationalization 'spreads rational habits of mind', which has the effect of destroying 'those loyalties and those habits of mind and those habits of super- and subordination that are nevertheless essential'.[50]

What Schumpeter and other observers pointed to was the perennial tension that appeared to exist between capitalist economic rationality and the cultural reaction to it. Furet's analysis is in accord with Schumpeter. He points out that the bourgeoisie was always the target of cultural scorn. He wrote that 'virtually everywhere in European culture, the bourgeois were on the receiving end of that mixture of contempt and hatred which was the price paid for the very nature of their being'.[51]

Alan Kahan has described this conflict as 'the war between mind and money', which he identified as 'the great unresolved conflict of modern society'.[52] What's interesting about this conflict is that it exposes capitalist society's unease with the way the imperative of economic instrumentalism comes to dominate human existence. Indeed, capitalism is the first social system that through its very emergence posits the very possibility of its own alternative or counter-systems. Unlike previous societies that regard themselves as natural or based on tradition, capitalism possesses a strong sense of contrast between itself and previous ways of organizing society. Consequently capitalism possesses a unique sense of historical consciousness, which at times fosters an orientation towards change and an anticipation of alternatives. Its sensibility of change and variation means that capitalism not only throws up ideas that validate its existence but also critiques of itself.

From its inception, capitalism could not take itself for granted and has always faced the challenge of explicitly justifying itself against criticisms that it is unfair or outdated or that it exacts an unacceptable price on humanity or the planet. Since the interwar era of the twentieth century, capitalism as a social system has found it increasingly difficult to positively justify itself against its critics.

The absence of an intellectually compelling normative foundation for capitalism meant that, even at the height of the post-war boom, capitalism was exposed to a cultural critique of its values. Consequently, even in these very favourable circumstances, capitalism acquired only a limited influence over intellectual and cultural life. This estrangement of capitalism from its own culture emerged with full force in the late 1960s when many of its values were explicitly challenged in what would turn out to be an interminable Culture War.

Samuel Brittan, the British economist and journalist, offered a sobering analysis about the difficulty that capitalism faced in offering a compelling and authoritative account of its values. Like Schumpeter, Brittan lamented the loss of the pre-modern traditions that provided the foundation for capitalist morality. He argued that:

> For a long time capitalist civilization was able to live on this feudal legacy, and the aura of legitimacy was transferred from the feudal lord to the employer, from the mediaeval hierarchy of position to that derived from the luck of the market place. But this feudal legacy was bound to be extinguished by the torchlight of secular and rationalistic inquiry, which was itself so closely associated with the rise of capitalism.[53]

Brittan believed that modern politicians and middle-class leaders lacked the 'glamour' and the 'heroic qualities' of the leaders of the past and therefore their authority over the masses is limited. 'At most they are tolerated on the strict condition that they bring results', he stated. Brittan asserted that the 'personal qualities of middle-class leaders did not help to kindle that affection for the social order which is probably necessary if it is not to be blamed for the inevitable tribulations and disappointments of most people's lives'.[54]

Brittan's concern about the quality of leadership in the UK and Europe was shared by American pro-market liberals and conservatives. At the time *Fortune Magazine* journalist John Davenport sought to explain to members of the Mont Pelerin Society why their liberal ideas failed to resonate with the times. He told the society's 1970 meeting to look beyond 'utilitarian economics' and 'to re-examine our own political and philosophical premises'. He claimed that the society's single-minded focus on economic efficiency distracted from its advocacy of values. 'Economics, we say is neutral', he noted. But he went to claim that

> [...] in seeking to maximize human choice and options, we have, I submit, been far from neutral. We have to some degree, smuggled in ends or values, and we have to this extent tried to define the political and human good. My suggestion is that the smuggling process should stop and that our choice of values be made explicit.[55]

Davenport urged his audience to replenish the ideological armoury of the free-market army with the weapons of conservatism. He argued that 'at least in the matter of morality' the 'libertarian should move over a bit to make room for what some of our conservative friends have been long urging – namely that the end of man is not just the pursuit of pleasure, but of something quite different – the pursuit of excellence, the pursuit, let us say it, of *virtue*'.[56] A study of this discussion contends that in effect Davenport called for a return to the society's original hope of developing a 'comprehensive moral worldview' which was the prerequisite for making 'free markets' 'compelling to the public'.

The question that neither Davenport nor the leaders of the Mont Pelerin Society explicitly addressed was why it failed to develop a 'comprehensive moral worldview'. This was not an oversight and numerous members of the society – including its most prominent representative, Hayek – drew attention to the import of this project in the 1950s and 1960s. The society's focus on economics was in part a consequence of the fact that this was the territory where the greatest gains in the battle of ideas could be made by liberals. In contrast, any attempt to recast traditional moral virtues as the foundation for modern capitalist life was likely to prove a far more challenging and ultimately unsuccessful project.

Nevertheless, the 1960s helped focus the Establishment mind on the problem of the moral depletion of capitalism. This issue was of particular concern to those disposed towards a conservative sensibility. The 1960s cultural revolt also served as a catalyst for a conservative reaction that would subsequently be known as the birth of 'neo-conservatism'. According to Robert Nisbet, one of the leading American neo-conservative thinkers:

> Neo-conservatism was born in the mid-1960s. It is almost inseparable from the 'Student Revolution' which played something of the role in the conservative renaissance

that the French revolution played in the rise of philosophy at the end of the eighteenth century.[57]

In 1972 the neo-conservative ideologue Irving Kristol warned that capitalism was living off the 'accumulated moral capital' of the philosophies that preceded it.[58] He was critical of the market advocates for their one-dimensional focus on the promotion of materialism and their failure to recognize the perils of cultural decline. Sensitive to the absence of a moral foundation for capitalism, he exhorted members of the Mont Pelerin Society to enter the battle for cultural values. Kristol believed that his liberal colleagues' emphasis on winning the argument for free-market capitalism had become redundant and that they 'were still fighting a battle that they had already effectively won'. He told the 1972 meeting that 'this ideological battle is over', and the dispute over the relative economic merits of central planning vis-a-vis the market had been settled. Kristol asserted that the war now had to be fought on the battleground of culture. He argued that the New Left had abandoned the battle over efficiency in favour of values. Kristol represented the New Left's moralistic critique of capitalism as not progressive but 'utterly regressive' and accused them of adopting the approach of the Old Right that 'never did accept the liberal-bourgeois revolutions of the eighteenth and nineteenth centuries'.[59] Kristol had concluded that secular libertarian philosophy 'simply had too limited an imagination when it came to vice' and therefore its economic insights needed to be situated within 'a comprehensive moral framework that preserved a place for virtue'.[60]

The exhortation by Kristol to reclaim traditional virtues and morality echoed a theme that was to become a central feature of the neo-conservative project. However the attempt to revitalize the tradition of the past could not provide the moral and intellectual resources necessary to provide a cultural validation for capitalism. This was a point that Daniel Bell understood better than most. Bell's *Cultural Contradiction of Capitalism* provided an astute analysis of the conflict between capitalist economic growth and the cultural hostility to it. The power of this hostile 'adversary culture' literally 'shattered' bourgeois culture to the point that almost no one is prepared to defend it.[61] Without any significant cultural support, capitalism lacked a 'moral justification of authority'. As a result 'in periods of crisis it has either fallen back on the traditional value assertions, which have been increasingly incongruent with social reality, or it has been ideologically impotent'.[62]

A painful reminder

During the 1960s, currents that regarded them as repressive and authoritarian explicitly challenged the hitherto taken-for-granted values associated with everyday life. In both Europe and America the conventional family became an object of scorn and traditional values were dismissed as either irrelevant or as a constraint on self-expression and the realization of the individual. For those whose values were the targets of this culture war, the 1960s represented an era where the traditions of the past were so marginalized that they could be ridiculed with impunity. That is why the language they use to describe the sixties evokes the sense of pain brought by a sense of humiliation. One retrospective account of the 1960s written in 2005 refers to this era as the 'undead decade', which apparently is still 'decanting its poisonous old wine into new bottles, fomenting our culture wars, and picking the scabs off the angry social wounds that have been with us for a generation'. This study claimed that at this point in time the 'collection of values that provides guidelines for societies as well as individuals – was assaulted and maimed'. The authors remark that 'we likened this inchoate attack to an assault on our culture's immune system'.[63]

In reality the 1960s brought to the surface trends that were at work for many decades. The contestation of conventional values began a long time before the 1960s. From its outset capitalism always had an uneasy relationship with the values embodied in its historical legacy. This issue preyed on the mind of thoughtful advocates of capitalism such as Hayek and Schumpeter.

As many students of capitalism observed, this social system itself found it difficult to coexist with the traditional values on which it was built. Capitalism contains an inherent tendency towards expansion and change, one that by its very nature regards tradition as a restraint on its ambition. Yet the traditions of the past provide a market-oriented society with many of the values that govern everyday life. In this respect, as Schumpeter pointed out, capitalism undermines the foundation on which it emerged. For Schumpeter the tendency of capitalism to destroy the normative foundation on which it was built represented a constant challenge to maintenance of order.[64]

Capitalist rationality inadvertently negates the norms and values that it itself requires for the maintenance of its credibility. The erosion of traditional values exposes the instrumental behaviour of profit-focused institutions and individuals to critical scrutiny. Attempts to endow business with a measure of moral authority have, even at the best of times, enjoyed only a modicum of success. Even in the United States, where the spirit of enterprise has enjoyed great influence over public life, the culture of capitalism did not escape unscathed. During the 1960s the ethos associated with capitalism was forced on the defensive. Looking back on this decade, the neo-conservative commentator Norman Podhoretz stated that 'by the end of the 1960s the values of the business class were no longer dominant in America'. Podhoretz believed that, judged by the 'readiness with which it assented to attacks on its own position', even the business class had been influenced by this trend.[65]

That even the business class was less than inspired by its own values was most strikingly confirmed by the difficulty it had in transmitting them to its own progeny. The evident estrangement of significant sections of the most well-to-do youth in the sixties exposed this problem. At the time, terms like 'self-hatred' and 'self-loathing' were used to describe this negative reaction of the privileged against the ethos that underpinned its way of life. Furet wrote of this group's 'infinite capacity to produce offspring who detest the social and political regime into which they were born'. He suggested that this disposition towards self-hatred was informed by an awareness of the fragile moral foundation for its elite status. Furet argued that this trait 'turns them against what they are: all-powerful in economic terms, in control of things but without legitimate power over others and devoid of moral unity deep down inside'.[66]

The uncomfortable truth alluded to by Furet, which was that the capitalist ethos had lost its capacity to enthuse even its own beneficiaries, was noted by observers during the late 1960s and early 1970s. Lipset and Dobson wrote how in the US 'many in the governing elites exhibit a failure of nerve'. They concluded that 'the basic tension of the contradictions within the system, come from within the elite itself – from its own intellectual leaders supported by large segments of its student children'.[67] What was frequently diagnosed as a failure of nerves can be interpreted as an awareness of a failure to transform power and wealth into legitimate authority. The very moment when the post-war boom was at its high point forced a section of the Western establishment to react to the moral depletion of its economic system. As Kristol wrote in retrospect:

> It is the ethos of capitalism that is in gross disrepair, not the economics of capitalism—which is, indeed, its saving grace. But salvation through this grace alone will not suffice.[68]

That economic success and growth was not enough and that something more was needed to legitimate society could not be ignored after the experience of the 1960s. Without a convincing ethos, capitalist society could not forge a moral consensus necessary for the conduct of everyday life.

The metamorphosis of the age-old reaction to the business ethos into what became known as the Culture Wars was brought about by the expansion of the questioning of its legitimacy. Although this ethos has always been a target of criticism in the early past of the twentieth century, all but a small section of society accepted or acquiesced to the prevailing moral consensus. It took over half a century for what was a sentiment held by a small minority to gain significant influence within Western culture. The unravelling of this consensus opened up the realm of values, lifestyles and personal life to conflicts that were hitherto conducted through the language of politics. Gabriel Kolko was one of the first scholars to pick up on this 'cultural realignment', which he claimed led to conflicts which were 'prepolitical' rather than class. He asserted that what 'ultimately explains the realignment in America's public culture are *allegiances to different formulations and sources of moral authority*'.[69]

Although matters came to a head in the 1960s, it is important to note that already in the 1940s and 1950s the weak cultural infrastructure of Western societies had gained the attention of numerous commentators concerned with the future of capitalism. Hayek wrote in 1949 that liberal capitalism needed 'intellectual leaders who are willing to work for an ideal, however small may be the prospects of its early realization'. He recognized that the usual language of economics was not 'likely to inspire any enthusiasm' and that therefore he hoped that younger liberal intellectuals would prove equal to the task of elaborating 'liberal Utopia'.[70] However, liberals who possessed a relatively libertarian orientation towards everyday life were no more likely to invent a Utopia than tackle the question of values. This project was more in tune with the disposition of conservative thinkers who embraced tradition as the key issue facing society.

During the high tide of the Cold War, the formidable influence of anti-communist ideology was harnessed by some American conservatives towards realizing the project of consolidating support for traditional values. The rise of McCarthyism in the United States is often associated with the attempt to deploy anti-communist hysteria to silence political dissent. However, it can also be seen as an attempt to roll back the cultural influences that were damaging to the survival of traditional norms and values. 'McCarthyism in the 1950s represented an effort by some traditionalist forces to impose a uniform political morality on the society through conformity to one ideology of Americanism and a virulent form of anti-Communism', observed Bell.[71]

Although at the time McCarthyism represented an influential current in public life and succeeded in intimidating many liberal and left-wing individuals with a legacy of dissent, it failed to establish cultural hegemony. In particular, McCarthy never succeeded in making any serious headway among intellectuals or gaining any cultural credibility. McCarthyism's failure to gain and retain moral authority is demonstrated by its inability to leave behind a positive legacy. As one critic of Cold War liberals recalled in 1997, McCarthy had become a symbol of the moral exhaustion of the right to the point that he is generally held in cultural contempt.[72]

McCarthy's anti-communist crusade and the reaction to it can be seen as one of the earliest post-Second World War attempts to revitalize traditional values in the face of their rapid demise. Although conducted through the medium of a shrill anti-communist crusade, what was at the centre of this project was a struggle over the meaning of the American way of life. One of the most astute analyses of this episode was provided by Jeane Kirkpatrick. Although a passionate anti-communist, Kirkpatrick understood that in the interaction between McCarthy and his opponents the 'actual prize was jurisdiction over the symbolic environment'.[73] What was at issue was who would serve as the arbiter of culture and whose narrative of meaning would prevail.

Kirkpatrick contends that McCarthy confused communism with non-conformism. In turn, his opponents challenged 'social conformity' and called into question the right of a government to possess 'any jurisdiction over the attitudes of its citizens'. She added that 'McCarthy served then and now as a symbol of the demands that intellectuals support the values and beliefs of society, revere what the society defines as sacred, and respect whomever the society defines as authorities and whatever it defines as authoritative'.[74]

The failure of McCarthy to hold the line and the rapid decline of his reputation had important implications for subsequent developments. It indicated that although a potent political resource, anti-communist ideology on its own could not contain the corrosive outcomes of the moral depletion of capitalism. Kirkpatrick asserted that McCarthy's demise and victory of his critics was a 'precondition of the rise of the counterculture in the 1960s'.[75] Whereas during the McCarthy era the term loyalty, with all of its implications, was rarely openly contested, by the 1960s it had lost some of its cultural valuation. Anti-war demonstrators, draft-dodgers and ordinary members of the public rejected loyalty as an unwelcome imposition on their ability to be themselves. As Kirkpatrick recalled, the 'peace marchers were far more aggressive in their defiance of traditional taboos than the timid victims of Joe McCarthy' which 'reflected the distance that the cultural revolution had proceeded'.[76]

The casual manner with which traditional taboos were derided in the 1960s indicated that those who upheld traditional values could no longer assume that they occupied the moral high ground. The cultural assault on the values of capitalist consumer society played a significant role in the realization of this outcome. However this assault should be seen as catalyst for, rather than a cause of, the unravelling of the Cold War Western values consensus. The inner corrosion of the ethos of capitalism had been at work for many decades and the lack of self-belief of the ruling elites contributed to its diminishing influence. However, the contribution of the elite's crisis of confidence for the ascendancy of counter-cultural influences was difficult to openly acknowledge.

At the time and during subsequent decades, most members of the Establishment found it difficult to openly accept their role in the defeat of their way of life in the Culture War. Unable to come to terms with the decline of traditional ideas, conservative intellectuals blamed 'insidious' influences for seducing youth. It seemed incomprehensible to them as well as their more liberal colleagues that at a time of relative prosperity the legitimacy of society could face such concentrated criticism and hostility. From their vantage point something insidious appeared to be at work.

That something was identified as the betrayal of social values by the 1960s intellectual. The failure to counter the cultural critique of capitalism was sublimated into a denunciation of a new cohort of perfidious intellectuals who subverted the institutions of Western societies. **In effect the intellectual crisis experienced by Western capitalism was recast as the crisis of the intellectual.** Intellectuals were represented as adversaries who had consciously participated in the construction of an 'adversary culture'. The term adversary culture was coined by the American literary critic Lionel Trilling, who detected its influence in the writings of modernist authors. Trilling claimed that the work of these authors was oriented towards estranging their readers from their traditional culture and inculcating them with values that contradict it. He stated that:

> Any historian of the modern age will take virtually for granted the adversary intention, the actual subversive intention, that characterizes modern writing – he will perceive its clear purpose of detaching the reader from the habits of thought and feeling that the

larger culture imposes, of giving him a ground and a vantage point from which to judge and condemn, and perhaps revise, the culture that has produced him.[77]

The adversary intention of modernist writers was represented as but one variant of a wider project of the intellectual subversion of traditional Western culture.

Like the stab-in-the-back myth that appealed to Germans who could not accept the military defeat of their nation in the First World War, the theory of subversive sixties intellectual allowed its proponents to avoid facing up to the unexpected and humiliating loss of their cultural influence in the 1960s and 1970s.

Notes

1   Kahan (2010) p.173.
2   Kahan (2010) p.173.
3   See Kahan (2010) for an analysis of this critique.
4   Wolin (2010) pp.11, 107.
5   Bell (1972) p.30.
6   Brinkley (1998) p.224.
7   Bloom (1987) p.313.
8   Speech in *Le Monde*; 2 January 1969.
9   Suire (2009) p.49.
10   Cited in Suri (2009) p.57.
11   Suri (2009) p.47.
12   Davies (1975) p.202.
13   Cited in *The Nation*; 22 May 1989.
14   Plumb (1986) p.66.
15   Cited in Suri (2009) p.57.
16   Marwick (1998) p.13.
17   Favretto (2003) p.17.
18   Neuman (1946) p.34.
19   Bracher (1984) p.228.
20   Neuman (1946) p.34.
21   Berger (1979) pp.32, 33.
22   See Kahan (2010) p.116.
23   Kristol (1973) p.3.
24   Kristol (1973) p.5.
25   Wolin (2010) p.11.
26   Roszak (1970) p.47.
27   Roszak (1970) pp.50–1.
28   Roszak (1970) p.51.

29   Wolin (2010) p.10.
30   This point is developed in Chapter 16 of Furedi (2013).
31   Arendt (1958) p.81.
32   Arendt(1956) p.403.
33   Arendt,(1956) p.404.
34   Hobsbawm (2004) pp.327, 334.
35   Eco is cited in Muller (2013) p.200.
36   Bell (1976) p.54.
37   Bell (1976) p.80.
38   Bell (1976) p.40.
39   Gouldner (1973) p.276.
40   Gouldner (1973) p.276.
41   Habermas (1976) pp.73, 75.
42   Habermas (1976) p.93.
43   Habermas (1976) p.47.
44   See Gouldner (1973) p.67.
45   Durkheim (2002) p.213.
46   Tonnies (1955) pp.263–5.
47   Tonnies (1955) pp.268–9.
48   Tonnies (1955) p.270.
49   Schumpeter (1976) p.143.
50   Schumpeter (1976) p.423.
51   Furet (1999) p.12.
52   Kahan (2010) p.4.
53   Brittan (1975) p.149.
54   Brittan (1975) p.149.
55   Cited in Burgin (2012) p.209.
56   Cited in Burgin (2012) pp.209–10.
57   Nisbet (1985) p.77.
58   Cited in Burgin (2012) p.211.
59   Cited in Burgin (2012) pp.211–12.
60   Cited in Burgin (2012) p.212.
61   Bell (1976) p.40.
62   Bell (1976) p.77.
63   Collier & Horowitz (2006) pp.1, 4, 6.
64   Schumpeter (1976) pp.139, 143.
65   Podhoretz (1979) pp.29–30.
66   Furet (1999) pp.14, 16.
67   Lipset and Dobson (1972) p.184.
68   Kristol (1979) p.12.
69   Kolko (1968) p.118.
70   Hayek (1949) pp.383–4.
71   Bell (1976) p.77.
72   'The Blacklist Revisited' in Kramer (2000).

73   Kirkpatrick (1979) p.42.
74   Kirkpatrick (1979) p.42.
75   Kirkpatrick (1979) p.43.
76   Kirkpatrick (1979) p.44.
77   Trilling (1965) pp.xii–xiii.

7

The 1970s war without victors – modernity under attack

The oil shock of 1973 dramatically brought the so-called Golden Years of the post-war boom to an end. Today it is difficult to imagine what a disproportionate impact this event had on the psyche of the time. For a brief moment in time in the 1970s it appeared that the decade would turn into a rerun of the interwar era. At the time the significance of this event was interpreted through the idiom of economic and political crisis, since it was widely understood that the boom played an indispensable role in the securing of stability. Governments feared order and stability would be seriously threatened by the kind of anti-democratic movements that caused chaos in the aftermath of the ending of World War One.[1] Apprehensions about a return to the bad old days of economic stagnation captured the public mood and to many the future looked unusually bleak. The oil shock was not simply interpreted as the outcome of economic dislocation and of dysfunctional global markets but also as something far more ominous – a warning from nature. It was at this conjuncture that environmentalist consciousness, with its insistence on natural limits and warnings of resource depletion, inserted itself into mainstream culture in the West.

Predictions that the unravelling of the global economy would lead to the revival of post-World War One chaos and instability proved to be incorrect. The sudden disruption of arrangements established during the aftermath of the Second World War did not lead to the radicalization of political life. Indeed, it forced political movements of both the left and the right to question their ideological and intellectual legacy and identity. The concurrence of the oil shock and economic crisis in the West with the immobility of Soviet society and the Welfare State meant that none of the competing systems and institutions escaped unscathed.

Numerous observers have claimed that one consequence of this experience was the emergence of a mood of pessimism towards the future. This sensibility of low expectations towards the future served to diminish the attraction of political utopia. But at a more fundamental level, the future of politics itself, or at least the capacity of politics to influence the future, was implicated in what turned out to be a deeply pessimistic reaction to the end of the post-war boom.

During this decade, simplistic accounts of global affairs still continued to speak the language of the Cold War and attempted to mobilize public opinion against the Soviet threat. Despite the easing of tension between the two super-powers from 1971 onwards, which led to the policy of détente, Cold War ideology continued to retain an important status in the political vocabulary in the 1970s. Indeed the economic upheavals following the oil shock intensified the insecurity of the Western elites to the point that they actually attributed a degree of power and influence to the Soviet Union which it clearly did not possess. One otherwise useful account of the 1970s actually claims that during this decade 'Communism had enjoyed its greatest series of advances since the late Forties'. This observer also asserted that at this time the Soviet Union was 'stronger than ever'.[2] Yet this was the conjuncture when the failure of the reform programme in the Soviet Union forced its leadership to realize that its system lacked an economic mechanism capable of stimulating technological progress and innovation and of matching the dynamism of Western capitalist societies.[3] It was also in the 1970s that the so-called Crisis of Marxism erupted, leading to the demise of the movements associated with it.

In retrospect, it appears that the continued promotion of Cold War propaganda, which reached its high point in President Ronald Reagan's 'Evil Empire' speech on 8 March 1983, was an expression of a confused reaction to political insecurities that were endogenous to Western society. As events would soon show, the Cold War was a blessing in disguise as far as the maintenance of political order was concerned. By the end of the twentieth century the Cold War could appear as a time of stability, legitimacy and relatively high trust. The coexistence of the Golden Years of economic boom with the Cold War reinforced stability to the point that the ideologies that emerged during and after World War One had lost much of their force. That is why the end of the post-war boom inevitably led to speculation that the economic crisis of the 1970s might lead to the revival of these ideologies.

Outwardly, Cold War rivalry in the 1970s remained an important feature of global affairs. As before, its main accomplishment was to freeze geopolitical realities. It also displaced serious conflicts and wars to the societies of the former colonial world. In this region superpower rivalries did cause problems for the

West. The relationship of the West to the Third World was deeply problematic. As we argued previously, the moral status of Western colonial empires was one of the casualties of World War One. A succession of colonial wars fought by Western powers in the post-Second World War decades culminating in the American fiasco in Vietnam served to further compromise the image of the West. By the 1960s this erosion of moral authority had reached the point where it was continually forced on the defensive by movements opposing it. This was not simply a geopolitical issue. Within Western societies anti-imperialism occupied the moral high ground. Many commentators erroneously attributed the success of anti-imperialist ideology to the powerful influence of Soviet propaganda. However, the near annihilation of the imperial ideal was directly linked to the dramatic erosion of belief in it within Western societies.

The inability of Western propaganda to justify its activities in the Third World allowed various liberation movements to gain a significant degree of credibility. For the New Left of the 1960s and 1970s, support for the Third World liberation movement served as a unique source of radical identity. In many Western societies the very absence of any radical impulses in the domestic sphere disposed the New Left to search for causes abroad. In France, for example, the left's identification with the Chinese Cultural Revolution assumed a character of an exercise in such a displacement activity.[4] Such attitudes blended in with the counter-cultural hostility to the dominant worldview of Western societies.

Counter-cultural hostility against the old order never acquired a systematic political existence to the point where it could generate its own ideology or pose a serious alternative. The cultural divisions over lifestyles and values that erupted in the 1960s and gained momentum in the 1970s did not turn into the interwar anti-parliamentary movements that were feared by some. Instead they tended to consolidate around competing lifestyle and identity claims and became drawn towards single-issue protest.

Instead of a revival of the appeal of interwar ideologies, the 1970s saw their gradual disintegration. During the 1970s the manifest inefficiencies of the planned economy of the Soviet Union showed to many of its Western supporters that this system had reached an impasse, if not a dead end. In the Soviet Union the constant calls for reform indicated that the ruling elite had lost faith in the social system. Although still using the rhetoric of socialism, the calls for reform usually represented a demand for the expansion of the market and the privatization of the state's resources.[5] In the West, the hope invested in the Welfare State was dashed by the realization that an ever-expanding public sector deficit was a burden that could not be indefinitely ignored. It is at this conjuncture that the Welfare State became divested of its optimistic reformist ideology. By the late 1970s the moral authority of the Welfare State was often effectively challenged by liberal economists, who portrayed it as a problem rather than as a solution.

Identity crisis of left and right

At the time, the 1970s appeared as a decade where the *status quo* was subjected to radical challenges on different fronts. Western societies faced a variety of radical social movements that demanded a significant reordering of public and private life. The sexual revolution and the women's and gay liberation movements came into their own and gained a significant constituency of support. Movements for racial equality and advocates of minority causes proved successful in gaining major concessions in society. The Cultural Revolution in China, the defeat of the US in Vietnam, the Iranian Revolution, the Nicaraguan Revolution and the Portuguese Revolution created the impression of an old order crumbling in the face of mass radicalization.

The rise of new social movements and the political upheavals of the 1970s occurred at a time when circumstances conspired to de-politicize public life. Many participants of 1970s movements were aware that, compared to those of the 1960s, their activities lacked the vision and ambition of their predecessors. Even during the early years of the 1970s there was an awareness of the fact that the radical moment had passed. At the time, the 1960s tended to be perceived as far more radical, optimistic and innovative than the decade that followed. 'The contrast between the widespread activism of the 1960s and the relative calm of the 1970s in the American universities is dramatic', concluded a study published in 1979. It asserted that 'in general, American students are not now politically active, although there have been a small number of demonstrations'.[6] At least in part, such contrasts tended to be overdrawn because of a sense of disappointment with the experience of the 1960s.

Nevertheless many activists of the 1960s' revolt experienced the 1970s as a decade of de-radicalization. Outwardly, the counter-culture was in the ascendancy and had gone from strength to strength. Its gradual institution-alization and new respectability meant that its broader transformative social liberationist impulse became more muted as it opted for the advance of its particular identity and lifestyle. The logic of the counter-culture led it towards the embrace of identity politics, which meant a move 'away from mass constituencies to single issue campaigns'.[7]

Although expressed through a radical rhetoric of liberation and empowerment, the shift towards identity politics tended to reflect a conservative sensibility that celebrated the particular and regarded the aspiration for universal values with suspicion. The politics of identity focused on the consciousness of the self and on how the self was perceived. It was and continues to be the politics of 'it's all about me'. Even when self-identity was expressed through a group form, the imperative of recognition by others remains its axial principle.[8] As the historian Tony Judt stated, the doctrines that were developed to express the politics of identity were directed towards psychology and were often indifferent to the 'traditional projects of social revolution'. Indeed 'they sought to undermine the very concept of the human subject that had once underlain them', argues Judt.[9] People whose identity is defined by their biology, emotional disposition, history and culture have as their focus what they are rather than what they could be. As we shall see, such low expectation towards the exercise of human subjectivity interlocked with a tendency to devalue the ideas of progress and development.

If anything, the de-radicalization of the traditional left was even more profound than that of the counter-cultural movements. At the time many observers assumed that the end of the post-war boom would provide the old left with an opportunity to expand its constituency. However, the left was far too overwhelmed by the experience of economic expansion of the boom to develop a credible anti-capitalist alternative. During the boom, years of economic prosperity and growth helped create the impression that in a modern industrial society problems could be solved by administrative and technical means and that political intervention was unnecessary. The efficacy of state intervention and its apparent autonomy from any distinct political direction had encouraged belief in the 'diminishing importance of choice and conflict within industrial societies'.[10] This belief was so deeply entrenched that when the boom came to an end it still influenced the thinking of left-wing political parties. Although from time to time trade unions and radical left-wing forces attempted to offer an alternative economic strategy, their doctrine lacked conviction and force.

Instead of encouraging the radicalization of the Old Left, the cumulative impact of the 1970s was to tame it and become reconciled to prevailing economic realities. One symptom of this new realism was the emergence of Eurocommunism. Although some of the more doctrinaire communist parties refused to embrace the banner of Eurocommunism, they all tended to move in its direction. With the rise of Eurocommunism one of the most important sources of anti-capitalist ideology became extinguished. Santiago Carrillo, the former leader of the Spanish Communist Party and the father of Eurocommunism, explained his thinking in the following terms:

> Formerly we Marxists thought that, when a certain ceiling was reached, the capitalist system would become an almost insurmountable obstacle to its own development. But practice has shown that, one way or another, the law of human progress breaks the strait-jacket of the social system.[11]

Carillo's statement of faith in the ability of capitalism to solve its own structural problems in the midst of a decade of economic insecurity indicated that belief in the transient nature of this social system – one of the distinct and fundamental elements of communist doctrine – had become lost. After their exhaustion during the post-war boom, not even the global economic disturbances of the 1970s could stimulate the revival of the anti-capitalist ideologies.

One of the most startling developments of the 1970s was the survival of the post-war boom technocratic approach that claimed that the management of the economy was more an administrative issue than a political one. The premise of this approach was that economic life had an inner logic that policy-makers had to respect and abide by. This left little space for political debate on this subject. When on 25 June 1980, the British Prime Minister Margaret Thatcher made her famous 'There is No Alternative' speech, she drew on an uneasy consensus established during the previous years. At the time her electoral victory in 1979 was interpreted as a victory for the political doctrines of the right. Yet, as events indicated, the 1970s proved to be no kinder to the right than it was to the left.

To be sure, the Keynesian economic consensus forged during the post-war boom fragmented during the seventies. By the second half of the decade there was a general awareness that public expenditure had to be reined in and that a more market-oriented investment strategy was needed to provide the foundation for the expansion of capitalism. However the ascendancy of free-market economics was not so much an outcome of the triumph of the political ideas of the right as a response to new circumstances.

Milton Friedman, who was one of the most prominent exponents of the revival of free-market economics, was not in doubt about the provisional and limited scope of the ideological victory of the right. Looking back on the previous decades, he wrote in 2002 that the 'dramatic shift in the climate of opinion' towards his version of economics 'developed while and partly because the role of government was exploding under the influence of initial welfare state'.[12] Friedman understood that he was the beneficiary of the post-war economic boom and of global economic conditions that readily resonated with his ideas. During the period between the late 1960s and the mid-1970s, 'his ideas seemed irresistibly prescient, and those of his numerous opponents repeatedly wrong'.[13] By this time the problems associated with the massive expansion of public expenditure and the inefficiencies of welfarism had diminished the appeal of planning. The disintegration of the Soviet system of planned modernization was all too apparent. Unlike post-World War One and World War Two liberals, Friedman did not face an environment where economic planning enjoyed ideological hegemony. In such circumstances his free-market liberalism was of the moment and his receipt of a Nobel Prize in 1976 constituted a recognition of this fact. However he also understood that the 'change in the climate of opinion was produced by experience, not by theory or philosophy'. The setbacks suffered by advocates of big government provided an environment where free-market ideas gained a new respectability. Nevertheless this triumph of free-market capitalist ideas had a restricted scope and rarely succeeded in inspiring the imagination of the wider public. Moreover, while Friedman and his allies made significant headway on the economic front, they did not manage to elaborate a broader narrative about its vision for society.

The failure of liberalism to push home its advantage on the economic front and offer a coherent political alternative was all too apparent to centrist and right-wing intellectuals. Irving Kristol went to the heart of the matter when towards the end of the 1970s he wrote:

> Meanwhile, Liberal Capitalism survives and staggers on. It survives because the market economics of capitalism does work—does promote economic growth and permits the individual to better his condition while enjoying an unprecedented degree of individual freedom. But there is something joyless, even somnambulistic, about this survival.[14]

The reservations expressed by Kristol – liberal capitalism 'survives and staggers' – were widely echoed by commentators and intellectuals who identified with this system. The language they used and the literature they produced communicated the absence of conviction and identification with liberal democratic ideas and a concern for a society that was characterized by aimless survival. Isaiah Berlin, one of the leading liberal political theorists of his era, was haunted by the idea that his generation had failed to provide young people with a cause. 'The Gods of yesterday have failed the young', he wrote. He went on to state that we feared 'war, economic collapse, totalitarianism' but 'ennui is worse'.[15]

Berlin's reference to his generation's fears towards some of the dangerous events that followed in the wake of World War One indicated that this legacy continued to shape the outlook of the Cold War political thinkers. Yet this focus on the threats of yesterday meant that far too little attention was paid to the emergence of a problem that would continue to dominate public life to this day. For Berlin it was as 'ennui', while Kristol used the word 'joyless' to describe the state of affairs where society found it difficult to motivate and inspire its public. What they were both describing was the powerful mood of disenchantment which reigned not only among the young but also among sections of the older generations. One compelling account of the 1970s in Britain described the decade as 'a time when, in politics, in the arts or in almost any other field one considers, the prevailing mood was one of a somewhat weary increasingly conservative, increasingly apprehensive disenchantment'.[16] What characterized this disenchantment was its highly privatized and fearful quality. Unlike the romantic disenchantment of the pre-World War One generations who regarded the impending conflict as an opportunity to forge new communities and loyalties, their 1970s equivalent adopted a more fearful orientation towards constructing such attachments. The disenchantment of the 1970s had little of the idealism of its earlier pre-1914 counterpart.

During the 1970s almost all the values that were upheld by the pre-1914 cohort of young intellectuals – loyalty, heroism, commitment, sacrifice – had lost much of their cultural affirmation. In his superb study of this important cultural shift, Christopher Lasch attributes this development to the prominence that Western societies in general and America in particular gave to the question of survival from the early 1970s onwards. One symptom of this obsession with survivalism was the normalization of crisis and a tendency to perceive every issue, no matter how 'fleeting or unimportant', as a 'matter of life or death'.[17] The tendency to inflate risk and danger was paralleled by the idealization of safety and survival as values in their own right. From this perspective the exaltation of struggle and sacrifice by young romantics attempting to re-enchant their existence on the battlefield of 1914 was entirely incomprehensible. 'Survivalism leads to a devaluation of heroism', remarked Lasch, as did the 'entire stock of allegedly outworn ideals of honor, heroic defiance of circumstances, and self-transcendence.[18]

In his analysis of the 1970s peace movement, Lasch explained that it was motivated not simply by hostility to an unjust war but to any demand for personal sacrifice. 'This attitude reflects a widespread reluctance not merely to die in an unjust war but to die for any cause whatsoever', he argued.[19] The conviction that nothing was worth dying for is a roundabout of arguing that nothing is worth fighting for. The devaluation of idealism was one of the most powerful legacies of the 1970s.

The difficulty that 1970s society had in finding a language with which to express idealism was to a significant extent the outcome of the political impasse reached by both the left and the right. Neither the left nor the right were able to develop a political strategy that was capable of offering a future-oriented vision for society. One of the consequences of the failure of either the left or the right to develop a powerful narrative about its vision of the world was that it encouraged the questioning of all values associated with modernity and Enlightenment thinking. The political right has always been ambivalent towards its relationship to the Enlightenment; in the 1970s the left also adopted a more hesitant orientation towards it.

In the 1970s the counter-cultural left's anti-capitalist critique hardened into a more expansive reaction against Enlightenment liberal ideals such as development and progress. Karl Dietrich Bracher believed that this reaction expressed the conservative impulse of resisting change. He claimed that in the 1970s – and especially after the oil crisis of 1973 – there was a 'virtual reversal of battle-lines'. The left 'became "value conservatives", using the value concept of the "quality of life" to defend the *status quo* against the dangers of material progress', argued Bracher.[20] The mutation of anti-capitalist sentiment into a critique of consumer culture acquired a systematic form in this period. Traditional conservative condemnation of mass culture was internalized by 1970s lifestyle radicals and anti-consumerists and gained a new lease of life in an apparently left-wing form.

Scepticism towards Enlightenment ideals such as that of universalism and progress expressed a dramatic alteration of the configuration between left and right. As the political scientist Brian Barry argued, 'during most of the nineteenth and twentieth centuries, attitudes to the Enlightenment marked the main division between left and right'.[21] With the erosion of this historically significant dividing line, the distinction between left and right lost its classical meaning. This development challenged the old political categories and made it difficult to give them relevance in the 1970s setting. Lasch argued that 'long-established distinctions between left and right, liberalism and conservatism, revolutionary politics and reformists politics, progressives and reactionaries are breaking down in the face of new questions about technology, consumption, women's rights, environmental decay, and nuclear armaments, questions to which no one has any ready-made answers'.[22]

However the breakdown of the old political classification is interpreted, it definitely expressed the problem of identity for both the left and the right. This identity crisis was not simply an expression of doctrinal confusions but struck at the foundation on which left and right were based. Historically the left was wedded to the idea of progressive change. By the end of the decade it found it difficult to provide an intellectual defence of its traditional belief in the ideals of reason, progress and universalism. Its equivocation towards its traditional ideals was brought to a head in France, where by the end of the 1970s the so-called New Philosophers had succeeded in forcing the left on the defensive. The New Philosophers – most of whom were ex-leftists – promoted a stridently anti-universalist and anti-Enlightenment outlook which effectively marginalized the French Communist Party.[23] The very foundation on which French leftist culture was constructed since the 1920s was severely weakened by this assault. Even the French Revolution, which served as the historical symbol of left-wing radicalism, came under sustained attack by a new breed of intellectuals. They denounced it as an early manifestation of the totalitarian impulse. According to one account, the New Philosophers 'rapidly marginalized Marxist thought and undermined the legitimacy of the French revolutionary tradition paving the way for the postmodern, liberal and moderate republican alternatives of the 1980s and 1990s'.[24]

As for the right, they too experienced the 1970s as the annihilation of their identity. It is to this development that we now turn.

The enemy is at home – crisis of authority[25]

At the time and also in retrospect, the 1970s appears an unusually dreary and undistinguished decade. And yet it is difficult to disagree with Christopher Booker's verdict that it was 'the most important decade of the twentieth century'.[26] This was not a decade of global wars. Nor did these years see the emergence of new radical transformative movements that captured the imagination of millions. As Judt recalled, these were 'mediocre times', for it was 'an age depressingly aware of having come *after* the big hopes and ambitious ideas of the recent past, and having nothing to offer but breathless and implausible re-runs and extensions of old thoughts'.[27] Many of those old thoughts were ones that gained influence in the years that preceded and followed the Great War. As we noted, the liberal ideal was one the main casualties of the Great War. The unexpected scale of slaughter and destruction called into question liberal ideas of freedom, democracy, reason and progress. This reaction fostered a political climate that threatened to engulf Western civilization into a new Dark Age. However, the barbaric outcome of the Second World War forced society to draw back and offered democratic culture a second chance to revitalize itself. Despite the constant state of tension induced by the Cold War, the post-war boom provided a breathing space where the promise of prosperity offered the kind of security unknown since 1914. However, with the end of the boom, many old problems returned to haunt society. At this historical conjuncture it became difficult, if not impossible, to externalize the tensions and conflicts that were endogenous to Western capitalist society.

In his review of the long twentieth century, Eric Hobsbawm wrote that the twenty years that followed the end of the Golden Years were 'that of a world which lost its bearings and slid into instability and crisis'.[28] There are many ways of interpreting the post-1973 crisis. Lasch surely has a point in his diagnosis of the tendency to normalize the idea of a crisis. The constant impulse to perceive new events and different dimensions of experience through the prism of crisis was a manifestation of the difficulty that society had in interpreting them. Daniel Bell used the phrase 'the loss of nerve of the Establishment' to account for the consciousness of crisis articulated by this group.[29] The phrase loss of nerve goes some way towards explaining the mood of pessimism and low expectations communicated by this group during the 1970s. But what underpinned this mood of demoralization was the discovery that the real threat faced by Western society was the loss of cultural and moral authority of its way of life and of those who represented it.

Alexander Solzhenitsyn, in his famous address to students at Harvard University in 1978, put matters bluntly. This former Russian dissident, now an exile living in the US, was appalled by the atmosphere of nihilism and weariness that dominated Western societies. 'The Western world has lost its civil courage, both as a whole and separately, in each country', he warned his Harvard audience. He observed that 'such a decline in courage is particularly noticeable among the ruling groups and the intellectual elite.'[30]

Solzhenitsyn's lament about an elite that has lost its way highlighted a problem that could no longer be ignored – which was the difficulty that society had in positively affirming its institutions of authority. By the mid-1970s this problem of legitimacy could not be avoided and doubts were raised about its capacity of reconciling political order with the ethos of democracy.

One of the symptoms of the loss of nerve of the 1970s establishment was their constant over-reaction to what were in historical terms relatively limited political challenges to their rule. Their inflated sense of peril was linked to their inability to find a language with which to express their authority and hence to an awareness that they lacked the resources to act authoritatively. Their insecurity was often focused on the unpredictability of public opinion and democracy which was frequently depicted as a source of unreasonable expectations that could not be met by government. Whereas in the interwar era the threat to democracy itself was principally attributed to the ambition of totalitarian movements, in the seventies the unrealistic expectations of the public cast it into the role of the villain.

'The conjecture to be discussed in this paper is that liberal representative democracy suffers from internal contradictions, which are likely to increase in time, and that, on present indications, the system is likely to pass away within the lifetime of people now adult', wrote Samuel Brittan in 1975.[31] The pessimistic prognosis offered by this British commentator indicated he believed that this conjecture had considerable merit. In line with the thinking of the time, Brittan pointed the finger of blame on 'the rising expectations' of the electorate. The thesis of rising expectations sought to attribute political instability and the weakening of authority to the unreasonable aspirations of the public. It shifted the focus of the problem from the institutions of the state to the pathology of mass democratic politics. One significant consequence of this interpretation of the malaise facing Western societies was to displace the problem of authority with that of trust. Historically, authority as a problem was associated with the weakening of the foundational norms on which it stood. It represented a statement about the relative lack of legitimacy of the ruling elites. In contrast, the problematization of trust was principally focused on the attitude of the public and its reluctance to respect or believe in the institutions of society. The main challenge posed by the problem of trust was to regain the loyalty and respect of the public by changing their attitudes through accommodating their aspirations or changing the way that institutions work. In effect, the fundamental issues constituted by the erosion of authority were redefined as ones of behaviour management or institutional reform.

The narrative of rising expectations obscured a more fundamental problem, which was the failure of the Establishment to win the argument about what was reasonable for citizens to expect. The implications of the narrative of rising expectation for governmentality were spelled out in great detail by a report that captured the Spirit of the Age. Titled *The Crisis of Democracy; Report on the Governability of Democracies to the Trilateral Commission*, it offered a depressing account of the challenges facing democratic societies. The Trilateral Commission, a global network of leading Western political leaders, policy-makers, prominent opinion-formers and business executives, was preoccupied with the apparent loss of legitimacy of the institutional arrangements that successfully managed capitalist economies during the post-war boom. One of the most striking features of the report is that although it recognized that there was no serious political alternative confronting Western capitalism, it nevertheless concluded that the system was in trouble. Its downbeat verdict was only marginally offset by its assessment that 'with all the dissatisfaction, no significant support has yet developed for any alternative image of how to organize the politics of a highly industrialized society'.[32]

Despite the absence of serious political alternatives, the authors of the report claimed that what is 'in doubt today are not just the economic and military policies but also the political institutions inherited from the past'. It argued that throughout the world, observers predict a 'bleak future for democratic government'. Such predictions projected a world 'of the disintegration of civil order, the breakdown of social discipline, the debility of leaders, and the alienation of citizens'. Even the most stable and successful democracies are said to be prey to the forces of disintegration and 'so observers speak of the Vietnamization of America and the Italianization of Britain'.[33]

The study made a genuine attempt to grapple with a problem of legitimacy, which would in subsequent decades be characterized as the crisis of trust in Western societies. It offered a variety of explanations to account for the demise of trust and authority. The most significant insight it offered was what one the report's authors, Michael Crozier termed a 'cultural failure'. The outcome of this failure was that the West's 'values are not rejuvenated in a convincing way'. Crozier asserted that behind all the 'governability problems of modern Western societies lie some more basic problems of values', which is why he believed that a 'cultural crisis may be the greatest challenge' confronting society.[34]

Crozier blamed the 1960s for forcing a 'moral showdown' that destabalized traditional authority. He seemed unaware of the long-term historical roots of the estrangement of capitalism from its own cultural foundation. The other chapters of the report confined themselves to discussing the symptoms of the cultural crisis rather than in analysing its causes. Repeatedly, the authors drew attention to one symptom of the loss of their cultural authority, which was the ascendancy of values that are antithetical to the traditional norms. They drew attention to a 'shift in values' away 'from the materialistic work-oriented, public-spirited values'. However, instead of explaining why old values have lost their influence, they claimed that new self-oriented values were the outcome of economic affluence. They also opted for the tactic of deflecting the problem through blaming 'cultural failure' on adversaries whose behaviour was motivated by their hostility towards the culture of Western capitalism.

Although it was still officially the Cold War, the Trilateral Report was far less worried about the Soviet Union than it was about the enemy at home. This enemy was the adversary intellectual. The authors explained that though in the past the challenge to democracy came from the 'aristocracy, the military, the middle classes, and the working class', in the 1970s the threat emanated from 'the intellectuals and related groups who assert their disgust with the corruption, materialism, and inefficiency of democracy and with the subservience of democratic government to "monopoly capitalism"'. It argued that the 'development of an "adversary culture" among intellectuals has affected students, scholars and the media'.[35]

In the mid-1970s the concept of an adversary culture served to communicate a narrative of wilful subversion by a group of highly committed oppositional intellectuals. The prominent status achieved by this group was attributed to the expansion of higher education, mass media and the knowledge economy, which created new opportunities for this so-called 'new class' of adversarial intellectuals. The report claimed that these intellectuals 'often devote themselves to the derogation of leadership, the challenging of authority, and the unmasking and deligitimation of established institutions'. As far as the authors were concerned, 'this development constitutes a challenge to democratic government which is, potentially at least, as serious as those posed in the past by the aristocratic cliques, fascist movements, and communist parties'.[36]

The representation of the adversarial intellectual as a threat that was the equivalent of radical mass movements of the interwar era was at the very least a misguided over-reaction to the social weight and power of this group. However the threat assessment issued by *The Crisis of Democracy* was not simply a case of wilful scaremongering. The intellectual serves as the focus for the sublimation of elite insecurities. It was easier to visualize the implosion of the Establishment's cultural authority as the outcome of conscious sabotage by resentful intellectuals than to acknowledge the elite's responsibility and failure of nerves.

The weakening of intellectual and cultural authority meant that the authors of the Trilateral Report were intensely insecure about the capacity of Western governments to guide and manage the expectations of a democratic electorate. One of the most fascinating feature of *The Crisis of Democracy* was its open acknowledgement of a lack of confidence about the ability of the political elites to make democracy work. This apprehension was based on an intuitive grasp of a historically significant development, which was the depletion of the cultural and moral capital of the political elites. However, instead of probing the implications of this development, the authors evasively pointed the finger of blame on democracy itself. 'There is deeper reason for pessimism if the threats to democracy arise ineluctably from the inherent workings of the democratic process itself', it warned, before asserting that indeed this political system was responsible for encouraging the unrealistic expectations of the public. The report argued that 'in recent years, the operations of the democratic process do indeed appear to have generated a breakdown of traditional means of social control, a delegitimation of political and other forms of authority, and an overload of demands on government, exceeding its capacity to respond'.[37] In particular the so-called 'democratic surge' of the 1960s was held responsible for the declining authority of institutions and conventions of social control.

The anti-democratic ethos of this report was most systematically expounded by the American political scientist and policy advisor, Samuel Huntington. In his chapter on the situation in the United States, Huntington claimed that it was the increased and widening of popular participation of the public in the 1960s that led to the 1970s crisis of governability. The effect of what he characterized as the 'democratic surge' was to substantially increase 'governmental activity', which in turn led to a 'substantial decrease in governmental authority'. Huntington contends that the democratic imperative is to continually expand the state's activity at the expense of authority.[38] Consequently the 'democratic surge of the 1960s' challenged and weakened all forms of authority in public and private life. 'Authority based on hierarchy, expertise, and wealth all obviously ran counter to the democratic and egalitarian temper of the times and during the 1960s, all three came under heavy attack', he observed.[39]

According to Huntington, authority was now confronted by an 'adversary media' and a 'critical intelligentsia'. The cumulative impact of their activity was to weaken the 'coherence, purpose, and self-confidence of political leadership'. The question posed implicitly by Huntington was how to deal with what he characterized as 'democratic distemper'. To this question Huntington had no clear answer other than to attempt to downgrade the status of democracy. Thus he suggested that 'democracy is only one way of constituting authority' and it was 'not necessarily a universally applicable one'. Hinting at one approach to confining the status of democracy, he asserted that 'in many situations the claims of expertise, seniority, experience, and special talents may override the claims of democracy as a way of constituting authority'. However, his main focus was the project of limiting the pressure exercised by the public. For Huntington, apathy was political virtue since it diminished pressure on the political elites, and he therefore concluded that democracy worked best when it was detached from popular pressure and participation. He stated that 'the effective operation of a democratic political system usually requires some measure of apathy and non-involvement on the part of some individuals and groups'.[40]

For Huntington and his fellow authors, the solution to the crisis of authority was the institutionalization of a form of insulated democracy that substantially reduced popular pressure on the institutions of the state. The problem they identified was labelled as the 'overload' of demands on the state. The concept of overload suggested that rising expectations had led to a situation where the demands on the state exceeded its capacity to respond.[41]

The concept of overload, which was introduced by the Trilateral Report, sought to give expression to elite anxieties about delegitimation and ungovernability.[42] As one review of this concept stated, it was in 'practical terms' not 'very different from the idea of a decline in political authority leading to ungovernability'.[43] Typically, the high expectations that result from democracy were identified as the source of ungovernability. This thesis made its first appearance in Britain with the publication of 'The Economic Contradictions of Democracy' in 1975 by Samuel Brittan and Anthony King's 'Overload: Problems of Governing in the 1970s'. Giovanni Sartori, the Italian political scientist echoed this argument in his essay 'Will Democracy Kill Democracy'.[44]

The concept sought to represent the erosion of cultural authority as the problem of unrealistic or rising expectations. Implicitly the solution it suggested was the lowering of expectations. One way of lowering expectations was to adopt authoritarian solutions and measures that would limit opportunities for the public to pursue new demands on governments. As much as this course of action appealed to some of the advocates of the concept of overload, it was also recognized that this was not a suitable strategy to pursue. One interesting approach was offered by Brittan, who raised the possibility of restraining expectations through channelling anti-consumerist sentiment towards the acceptance of lower living standards. He stated that:

> Many of our present tensions would become much less important in the unlikely event of a genuine revulsion against materialism or the 'consumer society'. Modern technology does make it possible to reduce the obsession with procuring ever more material products without having to submit to a life of ascetic poverty. It is unfortunate that the leadership among those who talk of an 'Alternative Society' should have been taken over by intolerant and envious political revolutionaries and that those most concerned with freedom, personal relations and the devising of new life styles for themselves should have lost ground.[45]

This very early argument for what would come to be characterized as sustainable capitalism attempted to offer a novel approach towards restraining pressure on economic resources. What Brittan's proposal amounted to was the mainstreaming of counter-cultural anti-materialist culture in order to lower expectations regarding the desirability of economic goods. In the event, it turned out that expectations did not have to be manipulated or consciously lowered. There were at work powerful cultural forces in motion which worked towards the lowering of expectations of Western societies.

Lowering of expectations

In his speech on the crisis facing strike-torn Britain during the three-day week in December 1973, Prime Minister Edward Heath attempted to strike a Churchillian tone. Referring to the hardships of the last World War, Heath warned that we shall have 'a harder Christmas than we have known since the War'. Heath's evocation of the trials and tribulations of war served as a prelude to his statement that we shall have to 'postpone some of the hopes and aims for expansion and for our standard of living'.[46]

Both at the time and in retrospect, the contrast between the optimism of the 1960s and the pessimism of the 1970s is striking. Booker's verdict on the decade was that 'the truth is that, in the past ten years, the old sources of optimism which have sustained the human race throughout the twentieth century (and which began to emerge a very long time before that) have begun to collapse on an unprecedented scale'.[47] This diagnosis was echoed throughout the Western world. 'It was an age depressingly aware of having come *after* the big hopes and ambitious ideas of the recent past, and having nothing to offer', wrote one historian.[48]

In most accounts of the 1970s the sudden outburst of cultural pessimism is usually represented as a by-product of the oil crisis. Marwick, in his magisterial study of the 1960s, claims that 1974 should be seen as the cut-off point for the 60s since this was the year when the public began to 'feel the effects of the oil crisis'. Horowitz argued that the 1970s energy crisis 'sparked a discussion about an era of diminished expectations'.[49] The oil crisis played an important role in fostering a climate where social and economic insecurities towards the future could be represented through the language of natural limits. It was at this point in time that the ecological sensibility of limited resources began to grip the imagination of a significant section of the Western public. Booker recalled that 'on all sides we began to hear talk of "zero growth" and "diminishing expectations"'.[50] Another study of the 1970s claims that environmentalism was sustained by 'a sense of impending doom'.[51]

The rhetoric of environmental anxiety seamlessly merged with the narratives of cultural pessimism and economic insecurity. All of these themes were drawn together in what was one of the most remarkable statements made by an American President. On 15 July 1979, President Jimmy Carter gave what is known as his 'Crisis of Confidence' speech. Although the statement was ostensibly about the destabilizing consequences of the oil crisis and about how to 'win the war on the energy problem', it attempted to address a much wider issue, which was that of the moral malaise afflicting the United States. The speech openly acknowledged the malaise of pessimism and apathy afflicting the nation and all but called for a moral crusade.

'The erosion of our confidence in the future is threatening to destroy the social and the political fabric of America', warned Carter in a tone that was unusually downbeat and alarmist for an American President. Carter stated that the threat facing society was 'invisible'. He added:

It is a crisis of confidence. It is a crisis that strikes at the heart and soul and spirit of our national will. We can see this crisis in the growing doubt about the meaning of our own lives and in the loss of unity of purpose from our Nation.[52]

As evidence of this crisis, Carter remarked that 'as you know, there is growing disrespect for government and for churches and for schools, the news media and other institutions'. His home truths about the absence of respect and trust, conveyed in a therapeutic language, failed to rally public opinion. Tackling the problem of moral malaise required more than an open acknowledgement of the problem.

In this statement to the nation the President used the rhetoric of war to mobilize public opinion. He cited with approval an anonymous labour leader who allegedly told him: 'when we enter the moral equivalent of war, Mr President, don't issue us BB guns.' Time and again Carter drew an analogy with the Second World War to indicate that the nation possessed the will to triumph over adversity. The terrain on which Carter claimed that America could regain its confidence had little to with morality. It was, after all, the energy crisis that preyed on his and the public's mind. The oil crisis, which forced America to confront the reality of its limited power, served as a catalyst through which a wider culture of low expectations came to dominate public life. That is why in Carter's statement, energy and morality were meshed to the point where the two were all but the same. 'On the battlefield of energy we can win for our Nation a new confidence', declared Carter.

To promote this crusade Carter promised to create an 'energy mobilization board which, like the War Production Board in World War II, will have the responsibility and authority to cut through the red tape'. And he asserted that 'I firmly believe that we have the national will to win this war'. The ease with which Carter made a conceptual leap from the energy crisis to that of confidence and malaise anticipated a sensibility which would become crystallized in the late 1980s and 1990s, when ethical and moral issues became increasingly articulated through the medium of environmental consciousness. In this sense Carter was ahead of his time. In another sense he was very much a prisoner of the Golden Years of the post-war era. His belief that the means for solving the crisis of confidence was through the winning of the energy war saw the solution as the recovery of economic prosperity. As events would prove, whatever the benefits of economic recovery it would do little to restore the loss of respect and trust that Carter warned about.

American policy-makers have a formidable track record of using the metaphor of war to address domestic and social issues; war on poverty, war on drugs, war on crime are only a few examples of this trend. Most of the time the use of this metaphor has only a limited rhetorical significance. In the case of Carter's appeal to nation, something more was at stake. The aim of his crusade was not simply the resolution of the energy crisis but also to regain a sense of national unity and purpose. However the statement, which was derisively described by the press as the 'malaise' speech, failed to galvanize public opinion. Carter's call to cut fuel consumption, curtail travel and lower the thermostat was rightly interpreted as a conservative call for lowering living standards. On the thirtieth anniversary of this speech one conservative commentator recalled that this statement was about demanding restraints and setting limits.[53]

Carter's malaise speech sounded positively upbeat in comparison with Alexander Solzhenitsyn's lament about the decline of the West. Solzhenitsyn's audience at Harvard were taken aback by his brutally direct denunciation of the Western way of life. Pointing to what he characterized as a cowardly, mindless and self-indulgent culture, his verdict was that the 'western way of life is less and less likely to become the leading model'. He expounded on what he perceived as the moral crisis of the West, stating:

> There are meaningful warnings that history gives a threated or perishing society. Such are, for instance, decadence in art, or lack of great statesmen. There are open and evident warnings too. The centre of your democracy and of your culture is left without electric power for a few hours only, and all of a sudden crowds of American citizens start looting and creating havoc. The smooth surface film must be very thin, then, the social system quite unstable and unhealthy.[54]

Like Carter, Solzhenitsyn was drawn towards the metaphor of war. His belief that 'the fight for our planet, physical, spiritual' was a 'fight of cosmic proportions' led him to warn against appeasing the forces of evil. But unlike Carter, who regarded the energy war as a means to regain national confidence, Solzhenitsyn argued the moral and psychological challenges had to be tackled before entering the field of battle. He insisted that 'no weapons, no matter how powerful, can help the West until it overcomes its loss of willpower'. Taking a long view of the wars of the twentieth century, he predicted that the next one would not be a simple variation of the two previous global conflicts. He concluded with the warning that the 'next war (which does not have to be an atomic one and I do not believe it will) may well bury Western civilization for ever'. Solzhenitsyn did not expand on this warning and the meaning of the 'next war' was not clarified. What concerned him was that the West appeared far too defeatist and far too cowardly to mobilize for it. Instead it appeared paralysed in the face of what he saw as a 'calamity of a despiritualized and irreligious humanistic consciousness'.

Solzhenitsyn's criticism of the West had as its target the secular values of the Renaissance and the Enlightenment and the modernizing and liberal impulses it set in motion. His statement condemned modernity and indicted all the usual targets of anti-Enlightenment thinkers. Materialism, consumption, individualism, individual rights, freedom of the press, humanism and progress were some of the values held responsible for the 'harsh spiritual crisis' and 'political impasse' of the West. His condemnation of technology and rationalization echoed the sentiments of the romantic intelligentsia searching to re-enchant the world during the years leading up to the Great War. 'All the glorified technological achievements of Progress, including the conquest of outer space, do not redeem the Twentieth Century's moral poverty which no one could imagine even as late as in the Nineteenth Century', he warned.

Estrangement from modernity

Solzhenitsyn's rejection of the political and philosophical premise of modernity was expressed in unusually irrational and intensely illiberal form. For that reason his Harvard audience found it difficult to sympathize with the sentiments expressed by the Russian dissident. However his critique of the Western way of life resonated with the spirit of the times. During the 1970s, anti-modernist sentiments gained cultural affirmation and migrated from the margins to the mainstream of society. A number of distinct currents – counter-cultural sentiments, powerful sensibility of ecological limits, anti-consumerism – converged with one another to reinforce attitudes that were uncomfortable if not always self-consciously hostile to modernity and the ideal of progress.

One conservative commentator who was drawn to the new conservative sense of limits wrote of a 'growing sense of horror at what our wonderful runaway technology was doing to our cities, to our countryside and rivers and seas, to other species, to the whole balance of nature on the planet'.[55] And reviewing the 1970s reaction to the accomplishments of modernization, he wrote that 'for the first time in centuries, if not in millennia, it became apparent in the Seventies that the whole advance of human technology was beginning to operate on the law of diminishing returns.[56] Disappointment with the impact of technology was paralleled by the tendency to regard it with suspicion. Consequently technology and even science were often framed through a narrative that stressed their potentially harmful consequences. In the early twentieth century, romantic and anti-modernist movements stressed their alienation from technology and the inconsistency of spiritual values with rationalization. In subsequent decades, this concern with the dehumanizing consequences of technology turned into a condemnation of the peril represented by its destructive effects. During the 1970s such sentiments acquired substantial influence over mainstream culture.

The ascendancy of the theme of technology getting out of control served as testimony to the extraordinary shift from the optimistic/modernist zeitgeist of the post-war boom years to the cultural pessimism of the 1970s. The strikingly different response to the destruction of the first Apollo spacecraft in January 1967 and the space shuttle Challenger nineteen years later is illustrative of this shift. When Apollo caught fire and three astronauts were killed, the American public was shocked and horrified. However, despite widespread anguish about the accident, the future of this space project was not seriously questioned. In contrast, the response to the destruction of Challenger indicated that a significant section of the public regarded this tragedy as proof that technology was out of control and that space travel was not a good idea. Most accounts confirm that there occurred a dramatic change in attitude towards technology at the end of the 1960s.[57]

Western society's estrangement from modernity itself was a clear expression of the regime of low expectation that dominated the climate of opinion of the 1970s. As one commentator pointed out, 'until recently' anti-technological concerns 'were the exclusive property of small segments of the academic community'. However 'during the last several years the idea of autonomous technology has gained considerable public attention'.[58] Technophobia was a key component of a survivalist ideology that accorded little scope for human agency. 'The rise of notions of autonomous technology in Western literature has in fact, come side by side with frequent and enthusiastic attacks on the idea of human autonomy', observed one contribution on this subject.[59]

The growth of technological and ecological determinism was inversely proportional to the diminishing influence of Enlightenment values. One of the most coherent statements of the turn against Enlightenment modernity was

The Making Of A Counter Culture: Reflections on the Technocratic Society by
Theodor Roszak. The target of Roszak was the process of rationalization and
its impact on life, which he condemned as 'absolutely evil'. Adopting a tone of
alarmist urgency – society was faced with a 'historical emergency' – he called
for a wholesale rejection of modernist thinking:

> [...] nothing less is required than the subversion of the scientific world view, with its
> entrenched commitment to an egocentric and cerebral mode of consciousness. In its
> place, there must be a culture in which the non-intellective capacity of the personality
> – those capacities that take fire from visionary splendour and the experience of human
> communion – become arbiters of the good, the true, and the beautiful.[60]

Roszak 's condemnation of rationality and the power of human reasoning was
uncompromising. In this respect his critique was directed at humanism and
implicitly at its liberal and left-wing variant. He criticized old radicals who
believed that science was an 'undisputed social good' and sought to offer as an
alternative a form of anti-modernist radicalism.[61]

The emerging anti-rationalist and anti-modernist currents can be interpreted as a variant of the cultural criticism of capitalism discussed previously.
However, what was now at issue was not only the values of materialism and
consumption but of the Enlightenment itself. Although not always noted at
the time, this new critique was as much anti-capitalist as it was anti-liberal and
anti-left. The new anti-modernist outlook of the 1970s represented a synthesis
of traditional right-wing conservative themes with radical counter-cultural
ideals. Bracher concluded that 'left-wing and right-wing anti-capitalism – that
intellectual concept of civilizational critique more than a century old – has been
revived as a romantic declaration of war on the consequences of progress'.[62]

No alternatives – or double crisis

'The talk now is of an exhaustion of modernism and its idea of progress
altogether', observed Karl Dietrich Bracher. In line with numerous other
observers, he pointed to Western society's failure of nerve: 'At the moment
of greatest extension and highest material achievements, western thought
finally seems to be losing confidence in itself, undermined and exploded by its
own ideas and their realization.'[63] This was not the first time that there was a

major outcry about a 'crisis of nerve' and the 'decline of the west'. However, in contrast to the late nineteenth century or the interwar era, what was lacking was the emergence of a self-consciously political alternative. His 'pessimistic perspective notwithstanding', Bracher hoped that, as before, the 'search for an ultimate value' will lead back to 'finite and not chiliastic solutions'. The really important question for this writer is whether the idea of political democracy can still inspire and offer an alternative.[64]

By the time Bracher penned these thoughts, the left had more or less given up on the idea of elaborating credible anti-capitalist alternatives. In both Italy and France – where official communist parties possessed a mass constituency – left-wing ideals lost much of their authority. In November 1977, the leading French communist ideologue, Louis Althusser gave his famous 'Crisis of Marxism' speech, where he more less acknowledged the intellectual poverty of his movement. He stated:

> The crisis which we are living through has been aggravated by a special circumstance. Not only has something 'snapped' in the history of the Communist movement, not only has the USSR 'moved on' from Lenin to Stalin and Brezhnev, but the Communist Parties themselves, organisations of class struggle claiming to base themselves on Marx, have not really provided any explanation of this dramatic history—twenty years after the 20th Congress of the Soviet Party! They have either been unwilling or unable to do so.[65]

Others were less ready to acknowledge the irrelevance of their movement. But soon the exhaustion of classical anti-capitalist politics became all too evident to ignore.

The 1970s called all forms of classical political alternatives into question. By the end of the decade neither the left nor the right could feel that this was their decade. Outwardly, the growth of the influence of anti-modernist and anti-progress thinking appeared as confirmation of traditional conservative thought. Conservative and right-wing parties made some headway in the early 1980s and the election of Thatcher and Reagan was greeted by many as the dawn of a new era of conservatism. These electoral triumphs combined with the all-too-apparent demise of the Soviet Union and the left led many observers to draw the conclusion that conservatism had made a comeback.

However, the decline of the left and of values associated with progress and modernity did not help to strengthen the political identity of the right. In particular, the retreat of the left did not mean that the right could now possess moral authority. The reason for the failure of the right to capture the moral high ground was due to the fact that in the 1970s the norms and values that underpinned authority had lost their capacity to motivate large sections of the public. Bell has convincingly argued that the distrust of authority was the principal feature of the 1970s:

> If there was a dominant theme in American *culture* in the 1970s, one sufficiently distinct to be identified in some encapsulated way [...] it was the widespread skepticism toward, if not the revolt against, authority – of professionalism, of expertise, of elites and the restraints of law and traditional morals.[66]

At the time and since, such anti-authority sentiments are difficult to ignore. But what observers often overlook is that this scepticism was preceded by the emptying out of the normative content of authority. In this way the gradual unravelling of the authoritative is confused with the reluctance of people to defer to it. Since the 1970s the crisis of authority is frequently one-sidedly perceived as a change in public attitude and represented as the problem of trust. During the 1970s the rejection of authority to the point where the authority of authority was called into question gained a potent cultural dynamic. Historically the contestation of authority has a specific focus. It was often linked with the attempt to reconstitute authority on a different foundation. In the 1970s authority itself was queried. But the questioning of authority was not so much driven by the aspiration to gain freedom from it as by a loss of belief in the legitimacy of institutions.

Numerous studies and surveys noted that in the 1970s trust and respect in the institutions of Western societies took a dramatic fall. Since this era, the problem of trust has become entrenched and constitutes one of the most important and distinct features of public life of the past four decades. The decline of trust was often represented as the outcome of the activities of assertive and radical movements which refuse to defer to traditional authorities. While the contestation of cultural authority by new social movements has been a constant feature of the 1970s and the decades that followed, their activities have been facilitated by the internal corrosion of authorities. Bell pointed to the 'loss of nerve' of the American Establishment and the inability of the elites to reproduce themselves.[67] What is most interesting about the deepening mood of distrust is its coincidence with a climate of de-politicization and a general sense of disenchantment with public life.

An essay titled 'A Quarter-Century of Declining Trust', published in 2000 to commemorate the twenty-fifth anniversary of the publication of the Trilateral Report was relatively optimistic about the durability of democratic institutions compared to the 1975 report. This assessment was based on the conclusion that Western democracies did not face any coherent alternatives. Nevertheless, this conclusion was tempered by the realization that public life had become emptied of content and that the citizens of Western societies were alienated from their institutions. It noted that:

> Nevertheless, to say that democracy per se is not at risk is far from saying that all is well with the Trilateral democracies. In fact, public confidence in the performance of representative institutions in Western Europe, North America, and Japan has declined since the original Trilateral Commission report was issued, and in that sense most of these democracies are troubled.[68]

Insofar as this mistrust was linked to suspicion towards the state, it appeared to benefit advocates of 'small governments' and social conservatives. However, mistrust was not confined to the institutions of the state. It was also directed at non-political institutions such as the professions and the media and, as it soon became evident, towards pre-political ones as well, such as the church and the family.

The point that many observers failed to pick up on at this time was that one of the most important drivers of the crisis of trust was crystallization of a culture war that had been brewing for decades. The counter-cultural movement continually challenged conventions, lifestyles and traditions associated with the past. Their challenge helped mobilize a social conservative backlash. Conservatives also shared some of the anti-modernist concerns of the counter-cultural movement and were therefore prepared to contest the authority of science, education, professions and the university. Bell sought to make sense of the dynamic whereby left and right appeared to reinforce one another's revolt against authority. He concluded that the 'revolt against authority' came from the left while the 'revolt from modernity' came from the right.[69] In reality, matters were not so clear-cut.

Notes

1   See Pharr & Putnam (2000) p.6.
2   Booker(1980) pp. 15, 63.
3   See Chapter 7 in Furedi (1986).
4   See Wolin (2012).
5   See Furedi (1986) p.206.
6   Altbach (1979) p.609.
7   Judt (2007) p.486.
8   On the politics of recognition, see Furedi (2004).
9   Judt (2007) p.479.
10 Berger (1979) p.30.
11 Carrillo (1977) p.155.
12 Friedman (2002) pp.vi, vii.
13 Burgin (2012) p.204.
14 Kristol (1979) p.12.
15 Cited in Dalya Alberge, 'Philosophers despaired of UK youth, letters reveal', *The Observer*, 16 June 2013.
16 Booker (1980) p.5.
17 Lasch (1984) p.60.
18 Lasch (1984) pp.72–3.
19 Lasch (1984) p.75.
20 Bracher (1984) p.218.
21 Barry (2001) p.9.
22 Lasch (1984) p.197.
23 See Christofferson (2004).
24 Christofferson (2004) p.1.
25 On the crisis of authority see Chapter 16 in Furedi (2013)
26 Booker(1980) p.5.
27 Judt (2007) p.478.
28 Hobsbawm (1984) p.403.
29 Bell (1985) pp.47–8.
30 A transcript of this speech given on 8 June 1978 is available on http://www.columbia.edu/cu/augustine/arch/solzhenitsyn/harvard1978.html .
31 Brittan (1975) p.129.
32 Crozier, Huntington and Watanuki (1975) p.159.
33 Crozier, Huntington and Watanuki (1975) p.2.
34 Crozier (1975) pp. 30, 34.
35 Crozier, Huntington and Watanuki (1975) p.6
36 Crozier, Huntington and Watanuki (1975) pp.6–7.
37 Crozier, Huntington and Watanuki (1975) p.8.
38 Huntington (1975) pp.64, 103.
39 Huntington (1975) p.75.
40 Huntington (1975) pp.113, 114.

41   Crozier, Huntington and Watanuki (1975) p.8.
42   For a discussion of this concept, see Birch (1984).
43   King (1975) p.288.
44   See Parsons (1982) for a discussion of these texts.
45   Brittan (1975) p.157.
46   The speech given on 13 December 1973 can be heard on http://www.youtube.com/
     watch?v=bj9OlIiHFo4 .
47   Booker (1980) p.5.
48   Judt (2007) p.478.
49   Marwick (1998) p.18 and Horowitz (1985) p.1.
50   Booker (1980) p.11.
51   Beckett (2010) p.234.
52   A transcript of this speech is available on http://millercenter.org/president/speeches/
     detail/3402
53   Sean Scanlon 'Carter Conservatism', *The American Conservative*, 6 April 2009.
54   http://www.columbia.edu/cu/augustine/arch/solzhenitsyn/harvard1978.html .
55   Booker (1980) p.11.
56   Booker (1980) p.11.
57   See for example Feenberg (2003) p.4.
58   Winner (1977) p.13.
59   Winner (1977) p.16.
60   Roszak (1970) pp. 51–2.
61   Roszak (1970) p.56.
62   Bracher (1984) p.228.
63   Bracher (1984) p.220.
64   Bracher (1984) p.220.
65   Speech published in Louis Althusser, 'The Crisis of Marxism', *Marxism Today*, July 1978.
66   Bell (1985) p.42.
67   Bell (1985) pp.46–7.
68   Pharr, Putnam, Dalton and Russell (2000) p.9.
69   Bell (1985) p.53.

8

Culture wars

The dissolution of the Soviet Union on 26 December 1991 appeared to bring to an end the era of ideological conflict that erupted in the midst of the Great War. The end of the Cold War marked the culmination of the type of ideological clashes that dominated the interwar years and continued to shape global political life in the post-Second World War years. But as we shall see, the wars conducted through ideology did not entirely disappear, they merely assumed a different form.

The triumph of the West in the Cold War did not mean that it had won the battle for ideas. The Soviet Union and the official communist movement had for a long time sought to rid themselves of their traditional beliefs and by the 1980s they more or less acknowledged the irrelevance of their ideology. The subsequent implosion of the Soviet Union and of the political movements inspired by the Revolution of October 1917 were far more the result of loss of belief and an act of self-destruction than of a defeat on the battlefield of ideas. Indeed at times it appeared that the leaders of the official communist movement were far more committed to burying their ideological heritage than to preserving it. As Furet indicated, 'former Communists seem obsessed with the negation of the regime in which they lived'.[1]

The most significant outcome of the disintegration of the Soviet Bloc and of the communist movement was that it strengthened the view that there was no alternative to the capitalist market. Former opponents of capitalism drew the conclusion that this system was the most efficient regulator of economic life and by the 1980s the critics of the market were far weaker than at any time in the twentieth century.

Francis Fukuyama, who responded to the end of the Cold War with his statement that History has Ended, found it easier to explain the success of the capitalist economic system than the 'victory of liberal democracy in the political sphere'.[2] Indeed, he found it difficult to provide a compelling account of democracy's alleged triumph. On the contrary, he suggested that on their own, democratic values lack the power to inspire and therefore require that citizens establish some form of emotional identification with their system. He concluded that 'they must come to love democracy not because it is necessarily better than the alternatives, but because it is *theirs*'.[3]

One of the most important insight that Fukuyama offered in his *End of History* was that liberalism in its classical form contained insufficient moral content to provide guidance to people and to provide a normative foundation for authority. He explained that 'beyond establishing rules for mutual self-preservation, liberal societies do not attempt to define any positive goals for their citizens or promote a particular way of life as superior or desirable to another'.[4] In reality no society – liberal or otherwise – can evade the challenge of providing norms and ideals for guiding people's lives and for validating itself. Security, efficiency, material well-being are indispensable for community life but on their own are insufficient for its flourishing.

Of course, security and material prosperity make an important contribution to the promotion of stability and order. Indeed, during the decades that followed the Second World War prosperity and economic security created the conditions for the consolidation of stability and order within Western democracies. Marwick has argued that in the US 'affluence and consumerism were taken as validating the perfections of existing society'.[5] A similar pattern was evident throughout Western Europe and Japan, where the decades of prosperity and security served to legitimate the institutions of society. However, by itself economic success does not provide the values and norms that society requires to validate it. Indeed it invites criticism from those who ask, 'is this it?' Already in the 1950s, claims that capitalism invented 'artificial wants' through manipulating the public with mass advertising raised questions that would give impetus to the counter-culture in the 1960s. By the 1970s the very values of materialism, productivity and economic success were directly questioned by a shift in values towards what was characterized as post-material norms. The Trilateral Commission feared that such values ran counter to the imperatives of democratic stability and order. It claimed that this was a shift in values 'away from the materialistic work-oriented, public-spirited values towards those which stress private satisfaction, leisure and the need for belonging and intellectual and aesthetic self-fulfilment'.[6]

Ronald Inglehart, who developed the concept of post-material values, represented their emergence as the counterpoint to the decline of the traditional ones such as nationalism, patriotism and deference to authority.[7] In his account, the conflict between traditional and post-material values appears in a relatively benign form. But what happens when competing values become politicized? This was the question facing Western societies in the late 1970s. The polarization of values contains a powerful tendency towards conflict. Because such conflicts touch on the fundamental principles that guide people's conduct in their everyday life, they have the potential to mobilize our emotion towards bitter conflicts. As Fukuyama noted, 'conflicts over "values" are potentially much more deadly than conflicts over material possessions or wealth'.[8] It is always possible to come to a sensible compromise over the way that material resources are divided up or the way that political offices are distributed. Values express a person's identity and beliefs to the point that if they are not affirmed, an individual may experience it as a slight on their persona or as an existential crisis. That is why conflicts involving religion or moral claims are rarely resolved through compromise.

The ideologies that emerged out of the experience of the Great War attempted to provide an answer to the quest for positive norms and values that could motivate and inspire. That so many young intellectuals could actually regard this war as an opportunity to realize their aspiration showed that the search for community could follow the most unlikely directions. The demise of interwar ideologies does not mean that the problems they sought to solve have been resolved. Fukuyama himself noted that something more than instrumental rationality and security are needed for a liberal society to flourish. He claimed that 'for democracy to work' citizens 'must forget the instrumental roots of their values, and develop a certain irrational thymotic pride in their political system and a way of life'.[9]

Constructing a way of life demands that communities mobilize cultural resources and values that provide an idiom through which people can identify with another and interpret their experience. A way of life is a cultural accomplishment and provides the medium through which citizens are socialized and express their community's norms and values. Fukuyama claimed that such a civic culture is 'critical to the long-term health and stability of democracies, since no real-world society can long survive based on rational calculation and desire alone'.[10]

Historically, democratic societies have attempted to construct their way of life by cultivating the sensibility of a distinct national culture. National pride, cultural uniqueness, economic and scientific achievements were some of the resources through which claims about a way of life were expressed. During the post-war era France stressed its civilizational accomplishments and its republican traditions. Britain boasted about its National Health Service – 'best in the world' – and its Welfare State. The United States went to great lengths to elaborate an American Way of Life, which was a synthesis of economic might, Hollywood glamour and pioneering ethos.

During the Cold War, the construction of a way of life – at least in the West – was facilitated by the ominous presence of a negative despotic model. For decades the Soviet threat, which served as the symbol of evil, provided Western societies with an opportunity to legitimate – at least negatively – their way of life. President Ronald Reagan's Evil Empire speech on 8 March 1983 was not simply a denunciation of the Soviet Union but the affirmation of the American way of life:

> Yes, let us pray for the salvation of all of those who live in that totalitarian darkness— pray they will discover the joy of knowing God. But until they do, let us be aware that while they preach the supremacy of the state, declare its omnipotence over individual man, and predict its eventual domination of all peoples on the Earth, they are the focus of evil in the modern world.[11]

This speech, which was made to a group evangelical Christians, had a quasi-religious tone to it. It provided a powerful illustration of the way that Cold War ideology could be used as an instrument for moralizing the American way of life.

Reagan's Evil Empire speech is often presented from the perspective of its geopolitical impact on US-Soviet relations. But this was not simply a speech about international affairs. This was also a sermon that Reagan targeted at a domestic audience and which sought to undermine the moral authority of his 'liberal' and 'leftist' opponents. That is why supporters of Reagan interpret this speech as a challenge to the so-called liberal elites in what would soon be called the Culture Wars.[12]

Western societies have not proven equal to the challenge of cultivating a way of life that resonates with the experience and emotions of citizens. Almost a quarter of a century has gone by since the end of the Cold War and since that time clarity about what constitutes a nation's way of life has diminished significantly.

The loss of the Cold War

Cold War ideology was always more than empty rhetoric in service of a public relations exercise. The narrative of the Cold War provided Western societies with a language through which they could define themselves and validate their institutions. Anti-communism proved to be an extraordinarily powerful vehicle for providing disparate groups on the centre and the right with a counter-ideology that validated their way of life. A fascinating study by Lisa McGirr showed how anti-communism cemented an alliance between different wings of conservatism in Orange County, California during the 1950s and 1960s.[13] In effect, during the Cold War, anti-communism served to validate the claims that conservatives and centrists made about the moral superiority of their society's way of life. Once anti-communism lost its immediacy and relevance, its capacity to validate a way of life was also severely weakened.

At a time when conflicts over values within Western society threatened to weaken domestic consensus, Cold War ideology provided a unique resource for minimizing its effects. Consequently the influence of Cold War ideology was not simply confined to the governing of East-West relations; it also guided policy-makers in the domain of domestic policy. One of the unexpected outcomes of the end of the Cold War was that it made the ideology linked to it irrelevant and deprived Western governments of one of the most effective instruments of validation. That is why since that time politicians and policy-makers have continually betrayed their yearning for the certainties of the Cold War years. As Dick Cheney, the former Vice-President of the US, recalled in February 2002, 'when America's great enemy suddenly disappeared, many wondered what new direction our foreign policy would take'.[14] Confusion about the future direction of foreign policy was by no means the only outcome of the demise of the Cold War. A similar pattern of disorientation is evident in relation to domestic affairs.

For a very brief moment the end of the Cold War was greeted with a tone of triumphalism by Western commentators, particularly those of a right-wing and conservative disposition. They could look back upon the demise of their traditional opponents on the left and conclude that their marginalization represented the vindication of the Western way of life. They rightly noted the political disintegration of the alternatives of the left and, along with numerous academic observers, they represented the 1980s as decade of the victory of neo-liberalism or neo-conservatism. Such reactions were integral to a consensus that tended to regard the Thatcher-Reagan years as an expression of the triumph of neo-liberal ideology.

During this short interlude between the late 1980s and early 1990s, it seemed that the end of the Cold War would lead to an era where neo-liberal economics and conservative politics would come to define the political cultures of Western societies. Such perceptions were based on an outlook that drew a direct causal link between the demise of the Soviet Union and left-wing ideals and the moral rehabilitation of Western capitalism. The electoral triumphs of Reagan and Thatcher appeared to confirm the presumption that right-wing political movements were in the ascendancy. Such assumptions faithfully noted the demise of left-wing ideologies but overlooked the weakness and limited appeal of the worldview of the right.

Right-wing sentiments were most influential in the domain of economics. From the late 1970s onwards pro-market consensus led to the hegemony of liberalism in the economic sphere. However, success in establishing a consensus upholding the free market was not paralleled by a similar process in politics and culture. Governments found it difficult to gain public support for the reduction of public expenditure, despite the discrediting of state socialism and the Welfare State. Even though public opinion was won over by the argument for a reduced government, politicians found it difficult to gain support for policies designed to cut back on the Welfare State. This was the case even in the United States, 'where though certain parts of the conservative project resonated with the broad public, the rollback of government programs that benefited the middle class did not.'[15]

The end of the Cold War served to expose the relatively fragile normative foundation on which authority in Western society was based. Almost immediately after the disintegration of the Soviet Union, the reliance of Western governments on Cold War ideology became evident. The negative validation of authority provided by an anti-Soviet and anti-Communist narrative had lost its capacity to legitimate. As Zaki Laidi argued, 'to define oneself by contrast with communism no longer has any meaning'.[16]

The end of the Cold War made it difficult for Western societies to retain unity and consensus through externalizing the challenge they faced. No sooner did the Cold War terminate before they were confronted with problems that were integral to their society. Almost instantly the triumphalist tone gave way to the realization that compared to the certainties of the Cold War the new world was a confusing, unpredictable and dangerous place. Already in the early 1990s there was a perceptible mood of nostalgia towards the certainties of the Cold War years. The suspension of Cold War rivalries brought to the surface the divisive issues surrounding the question of legitimacy, which were suppressed during the ideologically driven global conflict.

In retrospect it was soon evident that for the West, the Cold War represented an era of stability, legitimacy and relatively high levels of trust. In January 1991, the *Financial Times* reported that the 'West's relief at the ending of the Cold War is history'. Instead of relief, the predominant reaction was now one of fear of 'political instability and the awareness that integrating Eastern Europe, not to mention the Soviet Union, into the world economy poses difficulties of a hitherto unimagined complexity'.[17] An even more pressing matter confronting societies in the post-Cold War era was the necessity to develop a positive account of their way of life. During the Cold War the effectiveness of the anti-communist crusade meant that this challenge could be evaded and postponed. However, with the disintegration of the Soviet Union the quest for norms and values that could help define a way of life became more pressing.

One reason why the defeat of the Soviet Union did not lead to the strengthening of the normative foundation of liberal democracies was because the West did very little to develop a positive account of it during the Cold War. Aside from the rhetoric of freedom versus enslavement and good versus evil, the West was almost entirely dependent on the appeal of its economic success during its ideological confrontation with the communist world. As Bracher explained during the Cold War, the idea of freedom was attractive, but 'previously unknown prosperity' helped and its appeal was 'made more conspicuous by contrast with the repulsive picture of communist coercive rule and coercive economy'. He added that at this time attempts to develop 'a philosophical and moral foundation of libertarian-democratic policies were lagging behind a pragmatic orientation'.[18] In other words, people were drawn towards the West in the Cold War mainly because of its economic superiority and its promise of prosperity. So it was not enthusiastic approval and support for liberal democracy but pragmatism that underpinned the calculation of citizens on both sides of the East-West divide.

After the end of the Cold War, Western governments could no longer rely on the legacy of economic efficiency and prosperity to spare them the responsibility of validating their way of life in the language of politics and culture. As we noted throughout this book, in the long run capitalist efficiency and calculation does not provide a sufficient basis for order. As the experience of the years leading up to World War One or the 1960s indicate, the culture of rationalization and calculation constantly invited its counter-critique. In any case, by the 1990s the era of post-war boom had given way to that of global economic insecurity and instability.

For all its limitations, Cold War ideology at least provided policy-makers and society with an explanatory framework for interpreting global events. Its loss, which led to the rapid disintegration of assumptions, conventions and practices associated with the Cold War order, has led to what Laidi has characterized as a 'world crisis of meaning'.[19] This crisis of meaning is the outcome of the incapacity of public institutions and conventions to provide clarity of purpose for the conduct of policy. As one contributor to a post-Cold War discussion on the 'Winds of Change' asserted, a 'plausible vision of common good remains stubbornly elusive'.[20] The absence of a vision of a common good was most strikingly demonstrated by the continuing decline of 'public confidence in the performance of representative institutions in Western Europe, North America and Japan'.[21] The post-Cold War 'feel-good' factor soon gave way to a new era of mistrust and alienation from public life.

One symptom of the post-Cold War malaise was the inability of Western societies to forge the consensus and unity of that era. The problem of galvanizing public support around a common objective became evident to policy-makers in the years following the so-called war on terrorism. One study of British public diplomacy concluded that it is far more difficult to convince citizens to back the official line on the war on terror than it was during the Cold War.[22] This loss of Cold War certainty was coupled with the awareness that society's capacity to integrate its citizens had become seriously compromised. So a study published in 2008 about the security threat facing Britain reported that 'we are in a confused and vulnerable condition'. It indicated that one reason for this sense of insecurity was because 'we lack the certainty of the old rigid geometry' of the Cold War.[23] Confronted by what it perceived as the 'loss of confidence' and the absence of an overarching moral purpose in British society, the authors could not but mourn the loss of the Cold War.

This acknowledgement of the loss of Cold War certainty and the consequent emergence of a sense of vulnerability was directly equated to the conditions that led up to the outbreak of World War One. The authors argued that the 'stiff geometry of the Cold War world has given way to a less predictable (although actually older and familiar) flow of forces in world affairs'. The 'older and familiar' global dynamic it referred to was that of the early years of the twentieth century. Pointing to the absence of social cohesion and agreement about fundamental values, it stated that 'in all three ways – our social fragmentation, the sense of premonition and the divisions about what our stance should be – there are uneasy similarities with the years just before the First World War'.[24]

The analogy that the authors of the report, *Risk, Threat and Security; The case of the United Kingdom* drew with the conditions that led up to the outbreak of the Great War was not a little overdrawn. The Great Power Rivalries that provided the geopolitical context for the catastrophic Great War are of a qualitatively different scale than the conflicts that have erupted since September 2001. Despite domestic tension and conflict, national unity behind the 1914 War was far more robust than domestic consensus in the twenty-first century. The report recognized this development when it argued that the UK 'presents itself as a target, as a fragmenting, post-Christian society, increasingly divided about interpretations of its history, about its national aims, its values and its political identity'.[25] Nevertheless, this historical analogy contained one important insight, which is that despite the massive upheavals and changes that occurred during the twentieth century, it is still possible to identify the 'flow of forces in world affairs' as bearing some resemblance with the conditions that led to World War One.

De-politicization experienced as the triumph of the Right

At the end of the 1980s many observers looked back on the bad old crisis-ridden decade of the 1970s and drew optimistic conclusions about the future of the West. It was widely claimed that neo-liberalism had won the battle of ideas and that a mood of conservatism had captured the imagination of the wider public. At least superficially it seemed to many that the post-Cold War era would constitute a new Golden Age of global capitalism. As Muller recalled, 'in retrospect it can easily seem that the 1980s were a decade of renewed confidence and optimism – in both Europe and the West as a whole – leading right up to Francis Fukuyama's 1989 thesis about the "end of history"'.[26] Yet, once the Berlin Wall came down and the Soviet Union followed it onto the scrap heap of history, ending the Cold War, the Western elite was faced with the fundamental questions that it had evaded for so long. The question of what society stands for could no longer be answered by the statement 'its hostility to communism'. It was at this point in time that policy-makers and their intellectual consultants unleashed a quest for a 'big idea' to replace the now irrelevant anti-communist crusades of the Cold War. What President George Bush described as 'that vision thing' in 1987 continues to elude policy-makers to this day.

Observers were quick to point out that all the alternatives to Western liberalism had been exhausted. Fukuyama used the metaphor of war to suggest that liberalism had 'conquered rival ideologies'.[27] Whatever liberalism accomplished during the Cold War, it certainly did not conquer its ideological opponents. Liberalism itself, particularly in the form of so-called neo-liberalism, remained an intellectually underdeveloped outlook and possessed relatively limited cultural support. In a very short period of time the term neo-liberal was far more likely to be used as a term of abuse than as a positive form of identification. Studies of the career of this term indicate that since the 1990s neo-liberalism became a 'negative term' used to denounce political opponents.[28] The absence of any significant cultural affirmation for neo-liberalism is demonstrated by the near total absence of voices who describe themselves as one. As Hartwich wrote, 'the most curious characteristic of neoliberalism is the fact that these days hardly anyone self-identifies as a neoliberal'.[29]

The Nobel Prize-winning liberal economist, Milton Friedman was not in doubt about the fact that liberalism did not conquer its ideological opponents. He acknowledged that by the late 1970s support for the free market and capitalism had overwhelmed its opponents. But he also knew that the shift in public opinion in this direction was due to the apparent failures of state socialism rather than to the compelling force of the ideals of liberalism. He insisted that the 'change in the climate of opinion was produced by experience, not by theory or philosophy'. After summarizing the numerous setbacks suffered by advocates of big government and the Welfare State, he asserted that it was 'these phenomena, not the persuasiveness of the ideas expressed in books dealing with principles' that explain the 'transition from the overwhelming defeat of Barry Goldwater in 1964 to the overwhelming victory of Ronald Reagan – two men with essentially the same program and the same message'.[30] In other words, the success of liberal economics was contingent on the experience of failure of its opponents.

In any case, liberalism had by the 1980s lost much of its original meaning. Milton Friedman claimed that this term confused as much as it clarified. 'Because of the corruption of the term liberalism, the views that formerly went under that name are now often labelled conservatism', he observed. Nevertheless, he opted to embrace it: 'partly because of my reluctance to surrender the term to proponents of measures that would destroy liberty and partly because I cannot find a better alternative, I shall resolve these difficulties by using the word liberalism in its original sense – as the doctrines pertaining to a free man.'[31] Friedman and Fukuyama were part of a small minority of individuals who still used liberalism in the classical sense of the term. In America, those who identified themselves as liberal were anything but. As George Packer stated, 'a creed that once spoke on behalf of the desire of millions of Americans for a decent life and a place in the sun shrank to a set of rigid pieties preached on college campuses and in eccentric big-city enclaves'. Packer concluded that 'the phenomenon of political correctness [...] for a period during the 1980s and early 90s became the most visible expression of liberalism'.[32] However liberals and their opponents conceived their creed, at the very least it faced a profound crisis of identity.

The termination of the Cold War proved to be a mixed blessing for the parties of the centre and the right. Yes, the disintegration of the Soviet Union had a devastating impact on the traditional left-wing parties in the West. Wedded to some form of state socialism, these parties were forced on the defensive and in many instances became marginalized in public life. However no sooner were these parties forced to adopt a survival strategy before their crisis of identity spread to parties of the right. The case of Italy was paradigmatic in this respect. There the demise of the powerful Italian Communist Party was followed by that of the Christian Democratic Party, which, having ruled Italy for decades as the bastion of anti-communism, now found itself with no *raison d'être*.

With the benefit of hindsight, it seems that the end of the Cold War created the condition where politics in all its forms – left or right – was increasingly perceived as pointless. The end of the Cold War coincided with the erosion of the master-narratives of modernity. These were what Judt referred to as 'the great nineteenth-century theories of history, with their models of progress and change, of revolution and transformation, that had fuelled the political projects and social movements that tore Europe apart in the first half of the century'. Judt added that 'after 1989 there was no overarching ideological project of Left or Right on offer in Europe'.[33] At the time this process of de-politicization was misinterpreted as the retreat of the left. But soon it became clear that the hegemony of the right was far from durable. Soon the Reagan-Thatcher era was succeeded by that of Blair and Clinton.

The absence of any 'overarching' ideological project and the general tendency towards the de-politicization of public life was most coherently expressed through the different Third Way projects in the 1990s. What was significant about the doctrine of the Third Way, such as that promoted by New Labour, was its self-conscious attempt to transcend adversarial politics. What political theorist Chantal Mouffe has characterized as 'politics without adversary' represented the constitution of a form of technocratic politics where social conflict would be mediated through the deliberations of an oligarchy of policy-makers and experts.[34]

The New Labour project under Tony Blair systematically expressed the apolitical logic of the Third Way. As Weltman argued:

> New Labour's Third Way project does not involve simply taking up a position at another point on the spatially configured left-right scale. Rather, it is about largely rejecting the very idea of a political scene organized on an adversarial – left versus right basis. It puts forward a distinct line on recent political change, one drawing on a notion of modernization.[35]

Numerous parties in Europe embraced this anti-adversarial perspective and, as Mudde explained, encouraged the transformation of their societies 'into "depoliticized democracies", in which administration has replaced politics'.[36] This apolitical and technocratic turn was most vividly captured by the displacement of government by the technical and process-driven practice of governance.

The de-politicization of public life in the West had been anticipated for a long time. Though the end-of-ideology discussions in the 1950s and 1960s captured a trend of development, its arguments were based as much on hope as on an accurate assessment of development. The narrowing of political and ideological differences and the cultural turn in the 1970s reinforced the trend towards the contraction of the terrain of the political. The final act in this drama, the erosion of left-wing radical culture provided an opportunity for liberal and centrist movements to avoid their own problem of identity by rendering political issues into technical ones. But it is important to understand that this technocratic turn would not have succeeded without the acquiescence of all the main political parties and movements.

In effect, the tensions and conflicts immanent in capitalist societies ceased – at least temporarily – to be fought on the battlefield of the political. This development was most vividly expressed through a phrase that Margaret Thatcher hurled at her detractors: TINA – there is no alternative. By the 1990s very few people needed to be reminded that TINA had acquired a life of its own and appeared as a fact of life. As Perry Anderson, one of Britain's leading leftist intellectuals argued in 2000, 'for the first time since the Reformation there are no longer any significant oppositions – that is, systematic rival outlooks'.[37]

Its exponents have celebrated the triumph of TINA as an affirmation of capitalism. To its critics it appears as the outcome of the omnipotent forces of neo-liberalism and globalization. Yet, if one takes a long historical view of this development, it is more accurate to interpret the credibility of the dictum TINA as an expression of the exhaustion of the political movements across the old ideological divide. In the current analysis of social science, TINA is far too simplistically represented as the arrogant slogan of the forces of neo-liberalism. Indeed the fetish of neo-liberalism has reached the point where it is literally represented as an ideology to end all ideologies. 'Whatever limitations persist to its practice, neo-liberalism as a set of principles rules undivided across the globe: the most successful ideology in world history', argued Anderson.[38]

Yet as a political concept, neo-liberalism lacks both analytical content and empirical validation. Represented as a uniquely successful ideology that more or less dominates the world, it serves as an all-purpose explanation for literally every event. The phrase 'the forces of neo-liberalism' is regularly chanted to assign blame and responsibility for an unhappy occurrence. The chant communicates an impending act of malevolence by a power akin to the irresistible forces of nature. Yet this is an ideology without a doctrine and with virtually no self-identified supporters. Indeed, at a time when so many themes associated with anti-capitalism – corrupt bankers, greedy companies, capitalist exploitation, manipulative advertisers, bankrupt culture of consumption – resonate with popular culture, it is difficult to find any enthusiastic intellectual support for neo-liberalism.

Despite the relative absence of adversarial politics, twenty-first century society has more than its share of bitter conflicts and disputes. As most readers intuitively sense, the past decades have not been free of conflict and tension. What has occurred is that de-politicization of the domain of public life usually associated with politics has led to the politicization of other domains of social experience – particularly that of morality and culture. The politicization of culture represents the latest phase in the history of claims-making about modern social problems. Before the outbreak of the Great War, tensions were often expressed in a cultural form; in the interwar era and after, such conflicts were translated into the language of ideology, only to reconstitute themselves as cultural in the late twentieth century.

Politicization of culture

Of course, politics has always been implicated in culture and cultural differences frequently gain definition through the language of political conflict. Historically this relationship acquired an institutional expression through the conventions that regulated the interaction between the religious and secular. However, since modern times and the hegemony of secular institutions, the relationship between culture and politics has become fluid and often unclear. Liberal societies with their assumption of the autonomy of the political expressly attempt to differentiate it from the domain of the moral. Such sentiments serve as the premise of pluralism and in contemporary times are most clearly expressed through the celebration of the value of non-judgementalism.[39]

Since culture provides the medium through which people gain meaning, it is not surprising that it serves as resource that is constantly mobilized by people and parties in public life. Liberals have often found it difficult to deal with culture, since their outlook is seen by many as lacking moral depth and appeal. This problem has been recognized by liberal political thinkers who have sought to resolve this problem through the cultivation of a civic culture.[40] But calls for the creation of a 'democratic' or 'civic' culture overlook the fact that culture cannot be created instrumentally; it evolves through the historical experience of a community. As Jurgen Habermas warned, 'There is no administrative production of meaning'. Indeed the very attempt to mobilize cultural practices for the construction of a civic ethos invariably threatens to empty them of meaning.[41]

Habermas's important study of the *Legitimation Crisis* provides a compelling account of the way that the rationalization of public life contradicts the cultural norms and values associated with tradition. 'While organizational rationality spreads, cultural traditions important for legitimation are undermined and weakened', he warned.[42] The focus of Habermas's study was the legitimation deficit suffered by liberal capitalism when what he called 'the interpretive systems that guarantee identity lose their social integrative power'.[43] The weakening of 'interpretive systems' has a powerful influence on social behaviour. When what Habermas described as the 'consensual foundation of normative structures' is damaged, that which was previously a focus for unity can be become a locus for conflict. In the years leading up to World War One the reaction to organizational rationality provoked a cultural revolt, which, as we noted indirectly, nurtured a sensibility that regarded the war as an opportunity for recovering meaning.

In the post-Second World War decades, Cold War conflicts attracted the public's attention to the point that the emergence of important cultural tensions was rarely commented upon. But by the 1960s the casual use of the term 'counter-culture' indicated that these tensions had acquired great significance in public life, at least in the United States. However, at the time, the counter-culture tended to be understood in generational terms and the tensions it provoked were represented as merely the latest version of intergenerational conflict. In reality what was at stake was not simply the so-called generation gap. As Kolko wrote in his 1968 study *The Politics of War*, there was a 'vital cultural dynamic involved in generating this cultural realignment'. According to Kolko, this 'realignment in America's public culture' represented 'allegiances to different formulations and sources of moral authority'. He claimed that these contrasting sentiments were expressed through the 'institutionalization and politicization of two fundamentally different cultural systems'. Kolko pointed out that the battleground for the conduct of this conflict was now the pre-political domain of private life. And he warned that this conflict was not susceptible to the usual formulae of compromise because 'each side of the cultural divide operate[s] with a different conception of the sacred [and] the mere existence of the one represents a certain desecration of the other'.[44]

Although Kolko's analysis was based on the experience of the United States, a similar pattern was at work throughout Western Europe – albeit in a more muted form. Culture has always been an unsettled background and, as the early twentieth-century reaction to liberalism indicated, it could lead to the most unexpected of consequences. Historically the cultural revolt against liberalism tended to assume a romantic and conservative form. Such reactions represented a defensive response to what were perceived as attacks on traditional norms and values by liberal technocratic modernizers wedded to the authority of science and expertise. Typically such reactions had as their target the uprooted, cosmopolitan intellectual. Anti-intellectual sentiments represented a defensive reaction to a group that succeeded in claiming authority on the basis of their monopoly of (anti-traditional) knowledge.

By the 1960s and 1970s intellectuals and their allies in the media and education were frequently characterized by their conservative critics as the 'new class'. Jeanne Kirkpatrick advanced the classical conservative account of this group in an essay that explored how the new class succeeded in gaining 'the control of the symbolic environment and the relationship between the ideal and the real'. She concluded that what was important about this class is not its socio-economic position but 'its relation to culture: to the meanings that constitute a culture and to the symbols through which those meanings are expressed'.[45]

From the perspective offered by Kirkpatrick, some of the most significant battles on the home front during the Cold War in the United States can be interpreted as the first skirmishes in what would come to be known in the 1990s as the Culture Wars. Accordingly McCarthyism can be seen as a belated attempt to discredit the moral authority of the intellectual by equating its noncon-formist ethos with disloyalty. 'McCarthy served then and now as a symbol of the demands that intellectuals support the values and beliefs of society, revere what the society defines as sacred, and respect whomever the society defines as authorities and whatever it defines as authoritative', wrote Kirkpatrick.[46] This was a battle which, despite the highly polarized atmosphere of the Cold War, the intellectuals eventually won. She claims that the legacy of the campaign against McCarthy was to strengthen the jurisdiction of this group over matters of culture.

The virulent conflict over the question of who possessed the moral authority in the 1950s has set the pattern for the culture war to this day. The affirmation of traditional values as sacred is directly challenged by those who uphold the superior insights of science and expertise. In this contestation of cultural authority, the conflict is frequently conducted in an intolerant language that designates opponents as not just wrong but morally inferior – so frequently traditionalists and conservatives are depicted as either stupid or as suffering from a psychological deficit. As one study of the intellectual devaluation of conservatism explains, 'the imputation of intelligence and of its associated characteristics of enlightenment, broad-mindedness, knowledge and sophisti-cation to some ideologies and not to others is itself therefore a powerful tool of ideological advocacy'.[47] One outcome of this depiction of conservatism as an intellectually inferior creed is that it has provoked the bitter anti-intellectual reaction of the right.

As against the claims of their liberal opponents, conservatives sought to strengthen their appeal through engaging with people's quest for meaning and identity. Conservatives criticized what they perceived as the one-sided emphasis of liberal democracies on material and economic issues and for their indifference to the problems confronting people in the private sphere. This critique was eloquently spelled out by Irving Kristol in a 1973 essay titled

'Capitalism, Socialism and Nihilism'. Although the essay is a polemic against the counter-culture, it is principally directed against bourgeois liberalism. It criticises liberalism for avoiding the issue of morality and for failing to provide spiritual meaning for its citizens. In effect, he claims that 'liberal civilization' had 'spiritually expropriated the masses of its citizenry'.[48]

One reason why the conservative reaction against liberalism gained momentum in the late 1960s and 70s was because the escalation of the cultural attacks on traditional conventions and values fostered a sense of insecurity among a significant section of Western – particularly American – society. Modernizers and technocrats regarded traditional conventions and taken-for-granted assumptions as old-fashioned and an obstacle to be overcome. According to a fascinating study by Alvin Gouldner, a central role in this anti-traditionalist turn was played by a new class of intellectuals and knowledge workers. The exercise of the monopoly that this group had over education and expertise unleashed forces that worked towards the de-authorization of traditional and cultural authority. Gouldner contends that this development was facilitated by the decline of paternal authority within the family. The twin forces of women's emancipation and the expansion of education in the context of growing prosperity weakened paternal authority, which in turn damaged the capacity of the prevailing system of socialization to communicate the legacy and the values of the past. As Gouldner explained, material prosperity meant that the 'autonomy strivings of children are now more difficult to repress' and 'rebellion against paternal authority can become more overt'. He added that 'There is, correspondingly, increased difficulty experienced by paternal authority in imposing and reproducing its social values and political ideologies in their children'.[49]

One of the most fascinating features of Gouldner's analysis are his insights regarding the role of disrupted socialization to the intensification of cultural conflict. He claimed that schools and universities provided the 'institutional basis for the *mass* production of the New Class'. In these institutions teachers claim to represent society as a whole and in that capacity are 'not defined as having an *obligation* to reproduce parental values in their children'. The expansion of education works towards the insulation of parental cultural influence from their children. Gouldner wrote that:

The new structurally differentiated educational system is increasingly insulated from the family system, becoming an important source of values among students divergent from those of their families. The socialization of the young by their families is now mediated by a *semi*-autonomous group of teachers.[50]

As a result of this development, 'public educational systems' become a 'major *cosmopolitanizing* influence on its students, with a corresponding distancing from *localistic* interests and values'. Gouldner asserted that 'parental, particularly paternal, authority is increasingly vulnerable and is thus less able to insist that children respect societal or political authority outside the home'.[51]

One of the ways in which children become culturally distanced from the values of their parents is through their 'linguistic conversion' to a form of speech that reflects the values of the new class. What Gouldner characterized as the 'culture of critical speech' of the new classes 'de-authorizes all speech grounded in traditional societal authority, while it authorizes itself, the elaborated speech variant of the culture of critical discourse, as the standard of *all* "serious" speech'.[52] Although published in 1979, Gouldner's analysis anticipates the institutionalization of speech codes and the policing of language in the decades to follow. It also provides important insights into the vitriol that often surrounds disputes about words, the conservative reaction to what is described as political correctness and the counter-calls for the censoring of 'offensive' speech.

Gouldner's analysis of the new class constitutes an attempt to interpret the cultural tensions of late twentieth-century society as an expression of its contestation of authority against the old class. His claim that the new class has integrated counter-cultural values and those associated with the cultural critique of capitalism such as environmentalism has considerable force. From this standpoint the ideology of the new class can be seen as a synthesis of the anti-instrumental romantic revolt against rationalism as well the affirmation of professional and expert authority. Although formally the claims of professional expert authority contradict those of the anti-rationalist revolt, they have converged and mutually reinforced one another in contesting the norms and values of the old class.

Although sympathetic to the goals of what he calls the new class, Gouldner recognizes that it represents a force that is at times unrestrained in its ambition. He wrote that 'the culture of discourse of the New Class seeks to *control* everything, its topic and itself, believing that such domination is the only road to truth'. And he concluded that 'it's a universal class in embryo, but badly flawed'.[53] One flaw in Gouldner's prescient analysis is its tendency to represent the cultural conflict that crystallized in the 1970s through the language of class and subjective intent. Whatever its subsequent outcome, the conflict over norms and values was driven by contradictory motives and forces that had evolved over the previous seven or eight decades.

For example, although the principal target of the counter-culture was the modernist values associated with capitalist rationality and consumerism, its hedonistic and individualistic ethos represented a fundamental challenge to tradition. Thus, inadvertently, the radical challenge to modernity by the counter-culture led to a conflict with those who challenged modernity from a conservative perspective. To complicate matters, for different reasons both traditionalist conservatives and counter-cultural crusaders were hostile to and criticized the conventions and institutions of the liberal mainstream.

Moreover the displacement of anti-capitalism by an anti-consumerist and anti-materialist cultural outlook drew sections of the left towards an anti-modernist outlook. The convergence of the left with anti-modernist sentiments represented a departure from the practices of the past, when such attitudes tended to be confined to conservatives and the romantic right. In the long term, the cumulative outcome of this convergence of strange bedfellows was to strengthen anti-modernist ideas and hostility to the outlook of the Enlightenment. At times the vehement denunciation of Enlightenment values by the nihilistic wing of the New Left resembled the anti-modernist polemic of the nineteenth-century conservative reaction to them.

In the early 1970s tensions over culture and morality became mediated through party political competition. Kirkpatrick claimed that in the 1972 American elections the 'politics of cultural polarization' became significant. For the first time the 'issues that pre-empted voter attention were not the bread-and-butter questions that structured the electorate since the New Deal', she wrote.[54] The election, which was won by the Republican candidate Richard Nixon in a landslide victory, created the impression that conservative cultural causes were in the ascendancy. Events would prove that the attempt by conservative campaigners to politicize cultural issues was fundamentally a defensive response and had a character of a backlash to forces that were steadily increasing their influence.

The introduction of cultural conflict into American politics occurred some time before it gained importance in other societies. But even in the 1970s it was evident that conflicts over culture would play an increasingly significant role in other societies. In Britain the tension between modernizers and traditionalists always lurked in the background. Samuel Beer's study of this conflict, *Britain Against Itself*, has as its main theme the decline of civic culture and of deference. Beer is aware that in this battle between modernity and tradition, the latter has prevailed, and he sensed that the result of this technocratic turn would be the erosion of the British way of life.[55]

In the literature on the Culture Wars the conflict was generally perceived as a split between orthodox and progressive views of morality.[56] Divisions over issues that are considered moral dominate the Culture Wars, particularly in the United States. But the conflict is by no means confined to disputes about the family, sex, abortion or the role of religion. These are key issues for social conservatives and for movements that are hostile to the influence of traditional values in the private sphere. But the wider cultural critique of capitalism is far more directed at issues that transcend the private or pre-political sphere. It targets consumerism, materialism, the work ethic, technocratic ethos and numerous Enlightenment values such as individual autonomy, rationality and progress.

In the 1980s the traditional moral and cultural critique of capitalist materialism began to intersect over a variety of questions, principally environmentalism and health. Nevertheless it is important to distinguish between the trajectory and constituency of the different trends in the conflict of culture. For example, one study of cultural conflict in Europe during and after the Cold War concludes that while America was relatively successful in winning the culture war during the Cold War, it was defeated in the subsequent 'battle against anti-Americanism with all its negative connotation about American culture'.[57] Anti-Americanism, which enjoys significant validation in Europe within popular and elite culture, should be interpreted as a reflection of antimodernist and anti-consumerist sentiments.

The politicization of culture is directly connected to the exhaustion of ideological alternatives. Culture and politics exist in a dynamic relation to one another and developments in one sphere influence those of another. So, for example, the culture of limits of the 1970s fostered a climate of fatalism, which had a corrosive influence on the political imagination. At the same time the sensibility of limits was itself an outcome of the inability of pre-existing ideologies to formulate alternatives that resonated with the times. Thus the loss of belief in the efficacy of the state and of government existed alongside the belief that the problems facing humanity could not be fixed by politics. By the early 1980s it was evident that the emotional energies that were hitherto invested in political ideals were increasingly channelled into moral and cultural issues. At the time, Lasch pointed out that the questions posed by classical political ideologies had given way to debates posed by cultural conflict.[58]

Since the early 1980s the trends identified by Lasch have, if anything, intensified and today issues such multiculturalism, immigration, sexuality as well as lifestyle matters dominate public debate.

Culture Wars

Back in 1914 the cultural rejection of modernity was not only confined to relatively small groups within society but also coexisted with a relatively active and thriving political sphere. That is why the analogy that the authors of the previously discussed study *Risk, Threat and Security* make with the situation with 1914 Britain is misplaced. The politicization of culture in contemporary Britain has little in common with the cultural insecurities faced by the Establishment in the years leading up to the outbreak of World War One.

Concern and anxiety about the sense of purpose of British society have been raised on many occasions throughout history, but representing today's crisis of elite confidence as a present-day version of past problems is ultimately misleading. It is true that in 1914 Britain was afflicted by a powerful social crisis. In the years leading up to the Great War there was an unprecedented degree of class polarization and conflict. In the early years of the twentieth century, the British elites became defensive about the way in which their Empire was run. After the Boer War there was a palpable sense of loss of moral authority. Dozens of publications held forth on the subject of England's decline. Nevertheless, when the Great War came, the government of the day embraced it with relish. It regarded the war as an opportunity to demonstrate its moral virtues and consolidate its authority at home and abroad. Its call to arms enjoyed widespread public support; people from all social backgrounds volunteered to fight a war that they believed in. Subsequent disenchantment with the outcome of the war should not obscure the close relationship that the government enjoyed with its public. One study of national confidence and character in England concluded that despite the 'trauma of self-doubts' that followed the Great War, a common sense of shared history continued to give meaning and security.[59] For better or worse, most of the time those in authority could act authoritatively and with meaning; it was a very different situation to that which exists today, where officialdom lacks any substantial connection with the public.

In the twenty-first century, not only is Britain an island without a story; it is also a place that discourages debate about what kind of stories should be told. 'The deep guarantee of real strength is our knowledge of who we are', argues *Risk, Threat and Security*. Very true. But when, as today, the very meaning of what it means to be British has become a subject of cultural contestation, that understanding is far from evident – a point that this study recognizes. The authors rightly argue that the strength of any society is based on its belief in shared values and its sense of purpose. They note that 'the confidence and loyalty of the people are the wellspring from which flows the power with which all threats to defence and security are ultimately met'. They argue that, in Britain, people have become estranged from the nation's institutions, and that what binds them together is far too flimsy to constitute a 'dynamic community'. Of course, fears about a 'loss of confidence' in British society have been raised many times over the past century. So one key question that is implicitly raised by the authors is: what's new today?

One obvious, significant development is that in the post-9/11 world is a manifest loss of a sense and moral purpose in British society, which has intensified the sense of threat to the nation's security. According to Prins and Salisbury, 'the country's lack of self-confidence is in stark contrast to the implacability of its Islamist enemy, within and without'.[60] This acknowledgment of cultural insecurities in the face of the so-called War on Terror serves as testimony to the absence of clarity about what values, if any, bind people together. Although in this instance such concerns have as their focus national security, cultural conflicts also directly express themselves through anxieties about individual identity and the troubles of everyday live.

These insecurities are expressions of a world where the conventions and practices of the post-Second World War civic culture have lost their force. Beer noted this trend in the early 1980s and concluded: 'it is no exaggeration to speak of the decline of the civic culture as a "collapse".[61] The unravelling of the normative foundation for public life has created a condition where instead of serving as an instrument for the achievement of unity, values become a source of conflict.

The politicization of culture contains the potential for expressing conflicts and problems in a form that is difficult to resolve. Cultural norms and values define communities, their way of life and their members' identity. These sentiments are internalized and become constitutive elements of who we are. Since the 1960s cultural attitudes have become increasingly privatized and experienced in a very personal manner. One reason for this shift has been the growing influence of individualization and the celebration of self-expression and individual identity. The other force encouraging a shift in this direction has been the expansion of cultural conflict into the private sphere. As noted previously, de-politicization of public life has coincided with the politicization of the private sphere. Conflict over the family, sexuality and the conduct of intimate relationship has rendered cultural conflicts a dramatically personal character. The phrase 'personal is political' expressed the shift towards the contestation of values prevailing in the private sphere. Conflict in the private and pre-political sphere resembles that which pertains to wider society in one very important respect. In both spheres the absence of consensus about fundamental norms and values creates the foundation for conflicts and divisions. Moreover, the privatized manner in which these conflicts are experienced means that in some cases they can acquire an intensely personal and emotional character.

One reason why it is difficult to capture the dynamic of the culture war is that this conflict rarely assumes an explicit and systematic character. Numerous studies insist claims about the polarization of culture are exaggerated and some even go so far as to deny its very existence.[62] Conservative denunciations of political correctness have been continually met with angry denial and the assertion that such charges represent the desperate attempt by backward-looking fundamentalists to justify their prejudices. The reluctance to openly discuss conflicts over culture is understandable given the difficulties it poses to attempts to forge consensus. Officials and policy-makers tend to fear the open contestation of cultural values because of its divisive and potentially explosive character. Daniel Bell, for one, was convinced that divisive moral questions had to be de-politicized because these 'cultural and symbolic issues' are 'by their nature, non-negotiable and can only invite public conflict'.[63]

Patrick Buchanan's famous Culture War speech at the 1992 Republican Party Conference indicated that Bell's view was shared even by those who were sympathetic to the speaker's view. This right-wing conservative political figure faced a tirade of hostile criticism for what was described as his extreme rhetoric at the conference. Buchanan's rhetorical call to arms was reminiscent of the language of religious wars in the past. Buchanan insisted that differences over values were far more significant than arguments over economic resources regarding 'who gets what':

It is about who we are. It is about what we believe. It is about what we stand for as Americans. There is a religious war going on in our country for the soul of America. It is a cultural war, as critical to the kind of nation we will one day be as the Cold War itself.[64]

Buchanan's denunciation of what he perceived as a threat to the American way of life highlighted the claim that this was war and not simply the usual rivalries that exist between parties that inhabit a shared moral universe. He later expanded on this point by contrasting the conflict faced by 1990s America with those of the interwar depression. Citing Roosevelt, who said that 'our common difficulties' concern 'thank God only material things', Buchanan noted that in contrast 'our national quarrel goes much deeper'.[65]

What was noteworthy about Buchanan was not simply the content of his speech but that he articulated it in public at a major party conference and in front of television cameras. For unlike the wars fought between armies or by rival ideologies such as the Cold War, the conflict that Buchanan drew attention to is essentially a silent one. Since his speech, there has been a greater willingness to acknowledge the fact that party political conflict, particularly in the United States, is frequently focused on values rather than simply traditional economic issues. Moreover, it is widely recognized that differences over cultural values are subject to a polarizing imperative that is far more powerful than disputes over other matters. That is also why, in European societies, there is often a hesitation to openly engage with cultural insecurities over multiculturalism, immigration and national identity.

In contrast to the United States, where despite the widely acknowledged war of values there are frequent attempts to uphold and assert the American Way of Life, in Western Europe there is a tendency to avoid public expressions of national pride. For example, a report authored by Michael Hand and Jo Pearce of the London-based Institute of Education argued that 'patriotism should not be taught in school'. The report, based on a survey of 300 teachers, concluded that patriotism should only be taught as a 'controversial issue'. Hand and Pearce went on to claim that Britain, with its 'morally ambiguous' history, should no longer be made into an object of school pupils' affection.[66] Hand and Pearce's indictment of patriotism offers a paradigmatic illustration of what Gouldner described as the culture of critical discourse. Their study is not simply a critique of British national identity but also of loyalty to the tradition it embraces. They rhetorically asked, 'are countries really appropriate objects of love?', and called for implicit cultural hostility towards 'national histories' which are all apparently 'morally ambiguous'. Their advice is that 'loving things can be bad for us', especially when the 'things we love are morally corrupt'. The message they communicated is that we should morally condemn any attempt to construct a British 'way of life'.

Three-quarters of the teachers surveyed by Hand and Pearce apparently agreed with the outlook of a patriotic-free education, and said they felt they had an obligation to alert their pupils to the hazards of patriotic feelings. Although the authors subsequently complained about the 'press hysteria' evoked by their research, it is evident that they believed that their sentiment resonated with the times. They boasted that 'there are signs that the wave of patriotic rhetoric has now begun to break on the shores of public indifference'. After listing a number of failed official initiatives designed to boost British national identity, the reader was left in no doubt that the authors were convinced that they occupied the moral high ground[67]

The failed projects promoting British national identity to which Hand and Pearce drew attention represented half-hearted attempts to respond to the challenges raised in the course of the so-called War on Terror, a war that was eventually rebranded as the Long War. The humiliating failure to produce a 'statement of British values' by the government of Gordon Brown indicated that the meaning of what it means to be British could no longer be taken for granted. It also showed the risks of drawing public attention to the troublesome conflict that tends usually to be waged behind the scenes. Yet the exigency of responding to the intellectual and moral challenges posed by the Long War forced governments to respond to a conflict that they would have preferred to ignore. Since its outbreak numerous officials have made statements about the necessity of upholding a democratic way of life and about the need to defend the values associated with it. As events would indicate, the very attempt to spell out a way of life showed that by the early twenty-first century Western societies lacked a language through which it could be expressed.

From a way of life to lifestyle

The cultural attachments that motivated people to support their government's war aims in 1914 were focused on the way of life associated with the nation. A century later, the term 'way of life' still retains usage and politicians continue to speak about the 'American way of life' or the British way of life'. After the terrorist bombing in London in July 2005, the then Prime Minister Tony Blair declared:

> It's important, however, that those engaged in terrorism realize that our determination to defend our values and our way of life is greater than their determination to cause death and destruction to innocent people in a desire to impose extremism on the world.[68]

However, experience demonstrates that unlike in 1914, when political leaders promoting their 'wars of cultures' had a story to tell, their twenty-first century counterparts are struggling to explain the meaning of their way of life. The rhetorical character of the statement 'our values and our way of life' was exposed a few years later when the government's plans to launch a British Day had to be quietly abandoned.

The attempt to construct a British Day was a direct response to the tragic bombing in London in July 2005. When he announced this initiative, the then Chancellor Gordon Brown stated:

> We have to face uncomfortable facts that while the British response to July 7th was remarkable, they were British citizens, British born apparently integrated into our communities, who were prepared to maim and kill fellow British citizens irrespective of their religion. We have to be clearer now about how diverse cultures which inevitably contain differences can find the essential common purpose also without which no society can flourish.[69]

However, after more than two years of reflection, the government realized that it lacked the moral and intellectual resources necessary for the elaboration of a 'common purpose'. Indeed, the very attempt to celebrate Britishness only revealed an absence of clarity of what it was that ought to be commemorated.

Since September 2001, insecurities regarding the state of consensus about a way of life have been exacerbated by the realization that threats to security sometimes emanate from within. The phenomenon of 'home-grown terrorism' has forced Western societies to conclude that the domestic front cannot be taken for granted. However, the tendency to locate the fault line of the conflict between values as one that separates tolerant democrats from fundamentalist jihadists simply externalizes the problem. The intense hatred with which cultural warriors claiming to be liberal secularists denounce religious fundamentalists is matched by the invectives that sections of the Religious Right hurl at their opponents. 'Religious fundamentalism is a social cancer', argues a blogger on *The Daily Kos*.[70] In turn, 'wicked liberals' are castigated for their numerous sins. The rhetoric of hate may be more bitter and explicit in the US than in other Western societies but the tensions that underpin it is evident throughout Europe. Competing claims about national identity, social cohesion, multiculturalism, immigration, family life and marriage play a significant role in the European public sphere. The conflict about group identity and the lifestyles through which it is expressed is rarely suspended in the interest of a wider form of national unity. In the immediate aftermath of 9/11, numerous commentators argued that it would lead to a ceasefire in the culture war. One reporter for the *New York Times* wrote that one consequence of the terrorist attacks was the 'apparent ceasefire in the cultural skirmishing that had previously pitted right against left and Washington against Hollywood'. As evidence of this thesis he cited Robert J. Thompson, a professor of media and popular culture at Syracuse University, who asserted that 'the culture wars have been redefined by this'. Thompson went on to assert that this development 'has been one of the most overlooked and under-discussed consequences of Sept. 11'.[71] This ceasefire proved to be a very short affair.

Almost fifteen years after 9/11 it is evident that there has been a steady escalation of cultural conflicts in Western societies. One of the most memorable expression of the intensity of this politicization of lifestyle occurred in April 2008 when, during the course of the American Presidential campaign, Barack Obama gave his 'Bittergate' speech. This was the name given to the controversy caused by Obama's remarks at a fundraising event in San Francisco. Obama was talking about his difficulty in winning over white working-class voters in the Pennsylvania primary, when he said: '[It's] not surprising they get bitter, they cling to guns or religion or antipathy to people who aren't like them or anti-immigrant sentiment or anti-trade sentiment as a way to explain their frustrations.' This casual and knowing putdown of small-town folk sent a very clear message about the cultural fault line that divides America today. He is blue (Democrat and liberal), they are red (Republican and traditionalist); he is enlightened, they are bitter.

From a sociological perspective, Obama's Bittergate remarks can be interpreted as an example of what Max Weber called the 'stylisation of life'. Through the embrace of styles people set themselves apart, reinforce their status and draw a moral contrast between their styles of life and those of others. As Pierre

Bourdieu in his magisterial sociological essay, *Distinction*, noted, 'aesthetic intolerance can be terribly violent'. He explained that 'aversion to different life-styles is perhaps one of the strongest barriers between classes'. Struggles over the 'art of living' serve to draw lines between behaviour and attitudes considered legitimate and those deserving moral condemnation.[72]

What underpinned Obama's contemptuous description of the small-town folk of the Rust Belt is the conviction that they inhabit a different moral universe from that of enlightened America. Differences in lifestyle have become politi-cized to the point that what you eat, how you bring up children, have sex, regard religion and relate to wider culture have acquired a politicized and moralistic dimension. Most of the time the segmentation of society along lifestyle has little disruptive effect, but when politicized it expresses the form assumed by the crisis of valuation in the twenty-first century.

Notes

1   Furet (1999) p.vii.
2   Fukuyama (1992) pp.90–1.
3   Fukuyama (1992) p.215.
4   Fukuyama (1992) p.160.
5   Marwick (1998) p.37.
6   Crozier, M., Huntington, S., Watanuki, J. (1975) p.7.
7   See Inglehart (1977).
8   Fukuyama (1992) p.214.
9   Fukuyama (1992) p.215.
10   Fukuyama (1992) p.215.
11   For the text of this speech, see http://www.reaganfoundation.org/bw_detail.aspx?p=LMB4Y GHF2&h1=0&h2=0&sw=&lm=berlinwall&args_a=cms&args_b=74&argsb=N&tx=1770
12   See http://www.britannica.com/blogs/2011/02/reagan%E2%80%99s-%E2%80%9Cevil-empire%E2%80%9D-speech/
13   McGirr (2011).
14   Text of speech is available on https://www.mtholyoke.edu/acad/intrel/bush/cheneyiraq. htm
15   Phillips-Fein (2011) p.740.
16   Laidi (1998) p.172.
17   *Financial Times*; 7 January 1991.
18   Bracher (1984) p.194.
19   Laidi (1998) p.16.
20   McNeill (1990) p.161.
21   See Pharr, Putnam and Dalton (2000) p.9.
22   See Leonard, Small and Rose (2005) p.11.

23 Prins and Salisbury (2008) p.4.

24 Prins and Salisbury (2008) p.3.

25 Prins and Salisbury (2008) p.3.

26 Muller (2013) p.237.

27 Fukuyama (1992) p.xl.

28 See Boas and Gans-Morse (2009).

29 Oliver Hartwich 'Neoliberalism: The Genesis of a Political Swearword', Published by The Centre for Independent Studies, 21 May 2009, http://www.cis.org.au/publications/occasional-papers/article/938-neoliberalism-the-genesis-of-a-political-swearword

30 Friedman (2002) p.xiii.

31 Friedman (2002) p.6.

32 Packer (2003) p.11.

33 Judt (2007) p.7.

34 Mouffe (1998).

35 Weltman (2003) p.244.

36 Mudde (2004) p.546.

37 Anderson (2000) p.17.

38 Anderson (2000) p.17.

39 For a discussion of the concept of non-judgementalism, see Furedi (2011) pp.80–3.

40 See for example Fukuyama (1992) p.215.

41 Habermas (1976) p.70.

42 Habermas (1976) p.47.

43 Habermas (1976) p.4.

44 Kolko (1968) pp. 118, 128, 131.

45 Kirkpatrick (1979) p.33.

46 Kirkpatrick (1979) p.42.

47 Proudman (2005) p.202.

48 Kristol (1973) p.11.

49 Gouldner (1979) p.2.

50 Gouldner (1979) p.3.

51 Gouldner (1979) p.14.

52 Gouldner (1979) p.29

53 Gouldner (1979) p.89.

54 Kirkpatrick (1979) p.43.

55 Beer (1982).

56 See Hunter (1991). See also Taviss Thomson (2010).

57 Gienow-Hecht (2010) p.419.

58 Lasch (1984) p.196.

59 Soffer (1987) p.103.

60 Prins and Salisbury (2008) p.4.

61 Beer (1982) p.119.

62 See for example Fiorina (2006).

63 Bell (1985) p.62.

64   The speech is available on http://www.learner.org/courses/amerhistory/resource_archive/
     resource.php?unitChoice=21&ThemeNum=1&resourceType=2&resourceID=10155

65   http://buchanan.org/blog/the-cultural-war-for-the-soul-of-america-149

66   Cited in 'Patriotism "should not be taught in schools"', *Daily Telegraph*, 1 February 2008.

67   Hand and Pearce (2009) p.465.

68   Tony Blair MP. "PM's statement on London explosions" —

69   'Brown Speech Promotes Britishness', *BBC News*; 14 January 2006.

70   http://www.dailykos.com/story/2006/11/06/267218/-Religious-fundamentalism-is-a-
     social-cancer-part-4-Lying-for-power#

71   Thompson is cited by Rick Lyman in 'At Least for the Moment, a Cooling Off in the
     Culture Wars', *New York Times*; 13 November 2001.

72   See Bourdieu (2010) p.49

9

Conclusion: The war without ending

When in 1946, Sigmund Neumann characterized the years between 1914 and the end of World War Two as 'another Thirty Years' War', he stressed the point that what mattered were not 'artificial partitions' and that 'declarations of war and cessations of hostilities are not the real demarcations of an era'. He argued that what was important about the 'great drama' was the 'inner coherence and steady development of basic, common issues from World War I through the interwar period to World War II'. His approach showed the logic immanent in the unresolved tensions at the heart of modern conflict, but his verdict that the peace treaties concluded at the end of World War Two represented the conclusion of the drama proved to be premature.[1]

A year after Neumann used the appellation Thirty Years' War to describe the epoch of 1914–1945, the American historian Charles Beard informed his colleague Harry Elmer Barnes that the foreign policy of the Presidents of his country should be described as 'perpetual war for perpetual peace'.[2]

This phrase has been interpreted by many as referring to wars that are pursued for unlimited and unrealizable objectives. Not surprisingly, some have used the term 'perpetual war' to portray the so-called 'War against Terrorism' that erupted after the destruction of the World Trade Center in September 2011.[3] However, there is also a different way of decoding the idea of 'perpetual war for perpetual peace', which is that of 'perpetual war in search of meaning'. The shift from the geopolitical to the cultural motif of war does not in the least absolve the promoters of military conflicts from their responsibility for the destructive outcomes of their actions. However, when the Great War broke out in 1914, those who looked for answers to their existential problems on the battlefields of Europe could be forgiven for their illusions. Tragically, despite ample evidence that wars evade rather than confront the quest for meaning, a century later there is still a tendency to look to them to provide answers to the questions that society struggles with during the normal course of everyday life.

Not long after the destruction of the World Trade Center, the former American Secretary for Education, William Bennett published a fascinating testimony that seamlessly made a conceptual leap from the Cold War to the Culture War and then landed in the middle of the Long War. His book, titled *Why We Fight: Moral Clarity And The War On Terrorism*, is as open as it is naïve about its hope in gaining meaning and a sense of belonging through the War on Terror. He declared:

> And what a wonderful, heart swelling surprise *that* was, especially to those of us, veterans of the 'culture war' of the last three or four decades, who had kept an alarmed watch over the hardening of divisions among us and the downward course of our country's cultural indicators [...] There were moments during those years when even the basic, taken for grated unity of the US, in anything more than a rhetorical sense, was beginning to seem in doubt. But the events of September 11, and the amazing response to them, had killed all such doubts.[4]

Here a 'veteran' of the decades-long culture wars paused to revel in the 'wonderful, heart swelling surprise' that, confronted with a brutal act of terror, the nation is united after all. Bennett had little doubt that an unexpected unity of his nation was gained through the war. The question posed in his book's title – *Why We Fight* – invited the answer: because of the moral clarity gained through it.

It is evident that Bennett, along with many of his colleagues, regarded the War on Terror as an opportunity to relive the Cold War and experience the sense of national unity created in a global environment where the choice between good and evil was straightforward and self-evident to all. That at the turn of the twenty-first century, war appeared as the source of clarity that evaded society during normal times indicates that the temptations which proved irresistible to so many in 1914 still fascinate the imagination of some a century later.

Critics of American foreign policy have frequently asserted that Washington has consciously embraced this war to help forge 'a dominant, unifying idea that would enable it to reassert and legitimize its leadership of global security'.[5] From this standpoint the War on Terror constitutes the continuation of the Cold War and the terrorist plays a role that is the 'functional equivalent' of the nuclear weapons of the 1950s.[6] It is possible and even likely that members of the political and military elites regarded 9/11 as an opportunity to put right some the problems afflicting their society. But even if this claim has any basis in fact, it is difficult to argue that it has provided 'a unifying idea' that may attribute to it. The hope invested in the gaining of moral clarity through the conduct of this war has proved illusory. A decade after the publication of *Why We Fight*, it is painfully evident that instead of clarity, confusion prevails about even the most elementary dimensions of this war.

The American government has been singularly unsuccessful in mobilizing a powerful base of support for the War on Terror. The absence of any genuine enthusiasm for the War on Terror in the US is not simply symptomatic of war-weariness, it also shows up the lack of meaning the conflict has for the general public. There is not even any consensus on the facts about what happened on 9/11. A significant section of the American public even questions who bears responsibility for the atrocity. In August 2006, a survey of 1,010 adults found that 36 per cent of the American public suspected that federal officials assisted the 9/11 attacks, or took no action to stop them, so that the US could justify going to war in the Middle East. According to this Scripps Howard/Ohio University poll, a significant number of respondents refuse to believe the official version of events.[7] That more than a third of the American public buys into various conspiracy theories about 9/11 illustrates the crisis of meaning afflicting the West in the post-9/11 world.

Wars often possess the virtue of providing society with an unusual degree of clarity about the issues at stake. A war can tempt society with irresistibly simple choices between them and us, enemy and friend, right and wrong, triumph and defeat or survival and annihilation. It was all too easy during the Cold War. Every schoolboy in the West knew that They – the Evil Empire was hell-bent on destroying Us – that is, our democratic way of life. That was then, when it was clear who was our friend and who was our enemy.

What's remarkable about the post-9/11 era is that none of these polarized couplets can be articulated with conviction. How can society make sense of a series of global conflicts when governments even appear to lack a language with which to interpret it? A few weeks after the destruction of the World Trade Center President Bush asked a question that has proved to be unanswerable: 'Why do they hate us?' One reason why the American government has failed to answer this question is because the couplet 'they' and 'us' lacks the clarity provided by a meaningful moral contrast. A satisfactory reply to Bush's question demands clarity – who are 'they'? And after years of linguistic confusion, Western governments appear to have made no headway to resolving this quandary.

Historical experience shows that when the meaning of 'they' and 'us' is self-evident there is no need to pose morally naive questions about 'why do they hate us'. Roman emperors confronted with invading hordes of Vandals did not need to ask why they hated Pax Romana. German soldiers facing up to their enemies in the fields of Flanders in 1915 knew that they were fighting for the 'soul' of their nation. Neither President Roosevelt nor Churchill felt it necessary to ask why their way of life was detested by the Nazis. Nor was this the type of question that Western leaders directed at the Kremlin during the Cold War. In all of these cases the battle lines were reasonably clear and so were the interests at stake.

Since 9/11 it has proven increasingly difficult to grasp and characterize the interests and principles – geopolitical or otherwise – at stake in a variety of global conflicts and wars. It is far from evident what purpose is served by the wars in Afghanistan and Iraq. These are interventions that frequently appear to have an arbitrary, even random quality to them. One day officials in Whitehall are praising Libya and British universities award Gadaffi's son with a Ph.D. degree. A few days later NATO's airplanes are striking targets at Tripoli to teach this despot a lesson. Clarity is not a term that can be applied to the conduct of these foreign adventures – which make little sense from a geopolitical point of view. There is no equivalent of a Truman doctrine or even a Carter doctrine today. Ronald Reagan was the last American president who advocated a foreign policy doctrine that could be characterized as coherent. Although periodically Bush's War on Terror has been flattered with the term doctrine, this was a make-it-up-as-you-go-along set of responses that was detached from any coherent expression of national interest.

The main achievement of the Western – principally Anglo-American – global response to 9/11 has been to unravel the existing balance of power in the Middle East and in the region surrounding Afghanistan. This demise of the old order has not been paralleled with the ascendancy of a stable alternative. In such circumstances it is difficult to claim that these interventions have served the interests of their initiators. Moreover, the incoherent status of such foreign policy has, if anything, undermined domestic consensus for it. These wars have little populist appeal and do little to bind people together. These are military conflicts that are detached from people's lives, which is why we are confronted with a very interesting situation where there is neither enthusiasm nor war-weariness. Unlike in 1914, very few people have illusions in the possibility of discovering a sense of community or gaining meaning through the post-9/11 conflicts.

Anything But Clarity

Unlike the wars that followed one another since 1914, the current conflict even lacks a name. The failure of language is most powerfully symbolized by the continuing reference to 9/11. Why rely on two numbers to serve as the representation of a historic moment? No one refers to the attack on Pearl Harbor on 7 December 1941 as 7/12, nor was the war against Japan coded in such euphemistic terms. The principal reason for communicating a significant violent episode as 9/11 or as 7/7 is to avoid having to explicitly account for and give meaning to these events. This preference for numbers rather than words exposes a sense of insecurity about what lessons to communicate to the public.

The absence of a language with which to account for some of the most important events of the twenty-first century ensures that the use of shallow rhetoric acquired an unprecedented significance in the post-9/11 era. Take the significance that *New York Times* columnist Roger Cohen attached to the use of a new language adopted by the Obama presidency to account for the successful elimination of Osama Bin Laden in 2011. Cohen noted that American foreign policy successes such as the killing of Bin Laden are linked to the new language that President Obama adopted towards the Islamic world. 'This is a triumphant day for a young American president who changed policy, retiring his predecessor's horrible misnomer, the Global War On Terror, in order to focus, laser-like, on the terrorists determined to do the United States and its allies harm.'[8]

So what is Obama's laser-like linguistic alternative to Bush's 'horrible misnomer'? A memorandum sent to the Pentagon's staff members in March 2009 stated that 'this administration prefers to avoid using the term "Long War" or "Global War on Terror" [GWOT]'. It added: 'please use "Overseas Contingency Operation"'. Whatever the merits of this designation, it is not its claim to clarity. Indeed, if anything OCO is even more mystifying to normal human beings than GWOT. For all its faults, the term Global War on Terror is actually comprehensible to someone with a basic grasp of the English language. That's more than can be said for OCO. The term Contingency Operation self-consciously evades clarity about itself.

Throughout the past decade, correcting official language and inventing new phrases has been a flourishing enterprise. In his first speech as head of MI5 in November 2007, Jonathan Evans pleaded with newspaper editors to avoid words that help the enemy. He asserted that we must 'pay close attention to our use of language' and avoid words that encourage the association of terrorism with

Islam, since that would undermine the government's ability to win the hearts and minds of Britain's Muslim communities.[9] Soon after this statement, reports were circulated indicating that officials were 'rethinking' their approach and 'abandoning what they admit has been offensive and inappropriate language'. The acknowledgement that UK officials expressed themselves in a language that was offensive and inappropriate betrayed a palpable sense of disorientation in Whitehall. Reassurances were issued to the effect that the phrase 'war on terror' will no longer be heard from ministers and the threat will not be described as a 'Muslim Problem'.[10]

It is difficult to possess moral clarity when the act of communication falters. It is all too apparent that the principal task of the current narrative of war is to avoid using the wrong words. That is why officials have continually corrected and altered the language they use to describe a war without name. It is important to recall that even before the Obama presidency Washington was painfully aware of its linguistic deficit. During Bush's second term, the then Defense Secretary Donald Rumsfeld advocated replacing GWOT with the term GSAVE or 'global struggle against violent extremism'. At the time Bush rejected this Rumsfeldian formulation, but not because he was not open to adopting new phraseology. Bush was even prepared to concede the fact that he got his lines mixed up. 'We actually misnamed the war on terror', conceded President Bush in August 2004. Without a hint of irony he added that 'it ought to be the struggle against ideological extremists who do not believe in free societies who happen to use terror as a weapon to try to shake the conscience of the free world'.[11] For obvious reasons this incoherent phrase was not adopted as the new designation for the post-9/11 conflict.

In the very attempt to rectify the 'misnaming' of a war, Bush exposed the poverty of the intellectual resources with which the battle against terror is fought. It is difficult to avoid the conclusion that the confusion lies not just with the occasional malapropism but the entire script. The constant display of verbal acrobatics is testimony to the poverty of ideas that underpin strategic thinking about the post-9/11 era. But of course the problems confronting public relations officials are not so much linguistic as ideological and political. As one report on the state of British public diplomacy noted, public opinion remains detached and switched off from a war fought in its name. The report noted that:

Responses to the threat of nuclear war or Russian invasion had much broader and less questioning support than do responses to the threat of terrorist attack, which are coloured by deep popular scepticism about pre-emptive wars and about the principle of regime change for 'terrorism-sponsoring' states.[12]

For all its rhetorical quality, the slogan 'a war to end all wars' captured the imagination of millions as they suffered and waited for the termination of what seemed at the time the endless Great War. In the twenty-first century the war neither inspires or has much meaning. Unlike the millions of people who were shocked by the length of World War One, we no longer regard the claim that the current Long War will go on forever as unreasonable. There was only a muted response to the announcement of the US military in April 2006 that the War on Terror would now be branded as the Long War since it was likely to continue for decades to come.[13] Since this change in terminology, policy-makers have frequently asserted the assumption that this is a war without an end. One leading American military policy expert argued in July 2013 that 'U.S. policymakers should view the al Qa'ida threat as a decades-long struggle like the Cold War'.[14] Policy-makers throughout the West frequently echo similar claims. In February 2010, Charles Farr, the head of the UK's Office for Security and Counter-Terrorism, stated that the threat of terrorism would continue for decades and would last at least as long as the Cold War.[15]

The characterization of a conflict that has no agreed-upon name as an unending one lends it an abstract, if not fantasy-like quality. The superficial and contrived character of official statements about the war tends to reinforce the belief that there is some kind of hidden agenda behind its conduct. Yet it is very difficult to detect any Western geopolitical interests that are served by the seemingly arbitrary interventions in Iraq, Afghanistan, Pakistan, Libya, Syria and countless other places. Absurdly, the current pointless drift into regional wars conveys echoes of the confusing pattern of events that led to the unexpected cataclysmic conflict of 1914–1918. Writing of the current disturbing chain of events in Egypt, Syria, Iraq and Iran, one commentator in *The Times* warned that 'history is taking a dangerous turn' and asserted that the 'guns of August, usually held to describe Europe's slide to war in 1914, are now rumbling in Egypt'.[16]

Of course, it is likely that individuals and political interests including governments embraced the war as an opportunity to revitalize a sense of national purpose. But whatever the motives behind the waging of the Long War, its outcome has been to intensify rather than resolve the domestic tensions that preceded it.

The Long War posited as endless by policy-makers says more about the outlook of the official mind than it does about the military conflict waged on the ground. The threat assessment on which the thesis of an endless war is based relies on the procedure of equating the normal threats and insecurities of human existence with an existential crisis. Such assessments are not based on a hard-nosed calculation of geopolitical realities; they are the outcome of a loss of political imagination. The survivor outlook that emerged in the 1970s has over the decades turned into a rigid risk-averse sensibility that perceives routine global problems as threats to existence. Such perceptions are reinforced by a crisis of valuation that deprives society from endowing its experiences with meaning. With his customary rhetorical flourish, the French sociologist Jean Baudrillard wrote of a 'triumphant globalisation battling against itself'.[17]

Historical comparison with the Cold War ought to explode the fallacy that the Long War represents a continuity with the past. But that does not inhibit officials from plundering the past and claiming moral authority for the Long War by drawing on the experience of World War Two or the Cold War. Radical critics of the Long War demonstrate a similar ahistorical imagination. The American historian Peter Meyers contends that the post-9/11 wars follow the 'cultural logic' of the Cold War and are driven by the US President's 'aspiration to an omnipotence'. According to this analysis, the current policy of Washington represents the continuation of the Reaganite project of reigniting the Cold War and mobilizing support through preying on the insecurity of the public. From this perspective it is the domestic political culture institutionalized during the Cold War that provides both the precedent and the logical imperative for the conflict today.[18]

In his attempt to explore the relationship between the domestic environment and the global conflict, Meyers's focus is set firmly in the past. He rightly recognizes that war – or the intimation of war – has been a regular feature of modern times, but instead of isolating the distinct phases of this experience, opts to highlight what he sees as its continuity. He posits the Long War as an extension of the way the Cold War shaped 'political life through the management of citizens' emotions'.[19] This ahistorical approach is expressed through a tendency to rediscover the present in the past. Such an analysis necessarily relies on forced abstractions, which lead to statements such as, then and now, 'we face unlimited war based on the possibility that the enemy could strike anywhere and anytime'.[20]

Attempts to represent the Long War as the twenty-first-century equivalent of the Cold War overlook the fundamental difference between these two episodes. An unprecedented level of support and consensus in the Western world underpinned the Cold War. It could not entirely eliminate domestic tension and conflict but it possessed sufficient ideological influence to provide the conditions for domestic stability. Nor could there be any doubt about the issues at stake in this conflict. Nor is there any ambiguity about the fact that the Cold War finished off the Soviet Union and the official communist movement. Although the Cold War overlapped with the conflicts that crystallized into the Culture War, East-West tensions served to legitimate Western governments for a considerable period of time. The moral clarity provided by this episode stands in sharp contrast to the confusion and incoherence of the Long War.

The absence of clarity about the Long War is not surprising. If Bennett himself had worked through the logic of his own analysis, he would have been forced to confront the uncomfortable truth that a war cannot provide an answer to questions raised by a culturally divided society. In his *Why We Fight*, Bennett recognized that America is a divided society. The problem, he wrote, is 'not that Americans are unpatriotic' but that 'those who *are* unpatriotic are, culturally, the most influential among us'.[21] Whether Bennett's cultural opponents are unpatriotic or not is a moot point. What matters is that these divisions reveal an absence of clarity about what it means to be American. Similar conclusions could be drawn from the case of Britain or France and many other Western nations where the contestation of cultural authority has diminished the capacity of these societies to elaborate a sense of national purpose.

In the absence of possessing a sense of national purpose, the leaders of Western societies are at a loss to know what kind of stories to tell about the war. Bennett's concern about the influence of an unpatriotic cultural elite actually deflects attention from what must be, for him, the uncomfortable truth, which is that in the twenty-first century, patriotism itself appears to lack substance and meaning. Phillip Hammond, in his study *Media, War and Postmodernity*, shows that contrary to the polemics of radical critics regarding the allegedly opportunist flag-waving of the Anglo-American military, governments are inhibited from openly displaying symbols of patriotism. As Hammond noted, 'worries about appearing too militaristic' mean that there is little flag-waving over the war. So 'the "multi-faith" service held at St Paul's Cathedral in London after the Iraq campaign was declared officially finished could not find any appropriate words with which to celebrate "victory"'.[22] Instead, the service projected a powerful sense of defensiveness and ambiguity about Britain's role in the war.

'An inability to celebrate victory or to portray soldiers as soldiers is symptomatic of the elite's lack of confidence', says Hammond. In the years since 9/11,
such defensiveness has become more and more entrenched; perhaps its gravest
symptom is the absence of any coherent language to explain what the 'war on
terror' actually means.

If war is a continuation of politics by another name, what does the current
unending conflict say about tensions and rivalries in twenty-first-century
society? The war, like conflicts in domestic life, lacks emotional commitment
and passions and a capacity to inspire and motivate. The occasional outburst of
jingoism or patriotism comes across as a contrived display of bad faith. It is as if
everyone involved in the war effort is going through the motions of pretending
that this is a war that really matters. Hesitancy towards the display of patriotism
is not surprising, since self-assertive patriots are conspicuously absent from
public life. The lack of emotional investment in the war is more than matched
by the listless and unimaginative character of protest against it. The American
television serial *Homeland* captures the mood of estrangement from the war. In
this serial, the line between loyalty and disloyalty to the nation is blurred. There
is rarely an attempt to associate the conflict with a cause. In this morally ambivalent television drama there are no heroes, only badly flawed characters who
are victims of circumstances beyond their control. In this programme, the very
term *Homeland* is rendered problematic by the appearance of people who are
far from certain where they belong and far from certain where to go home to.

During the First World War, the phase of disillusionment was preceded by
a period when people's illusions developed to the point where at least some
regarded the war as a crusade. The sense of disillusionment was all the more
palpable because there were powerful illusions to lose. After 9/11 there were
few illusions to lose, and almost from the outset the war failed to inspire the
public imagination. After the Great War, disillusionment led to an outburst of
artistic creativity and political experimentation. In the current war, lethargy
and fatalism appear to be the main outcome of disillusionment. It is as if the
aimlessness of public life intersects with the pointlessness of the Long War.
The acts of nihilistic terror by isolated 'home-grown' bombers indicates that a
confused, purposeless outlook affects all sides of the Long War

War without illusions

One of the accomplishment of the Great War was that it shattered the belief that after such a conflict there could be a return to the Golden Years of peace that preceded it. As Neumann reminded his readers in 1946, 'there is no simple return to prewar normalcy, as people still might have believed after World War One'. He warned that 'there is no way back to the age of innocence' and that 'there is no nineteenth-century answer to a twentieth-century query'.[23] There was clearly no nineteenth-century answer to the questions haunting the twentieth century and therefore those queries continue to confront society today.

It is difficult to genuinely leave our illusions behind. After the termination of the Great War, many Europeans reacted to the jingoistic nationalist propaganda of their governments with cynicism and rejected it. However, in the interwar era nationalism became far more politicized than in the past and acquired an unprecedented virulence and force. By the 1930s, most commentators of a liberal or democratic persuasion in the Anglo-American world feared that this perilous force could destroy civilization.[24] The experience of World War Two confirmed these fears and since that time nationalism in the West has lost much of its credibility. In the twenty-first century, nationalism is often represented as an anti-modern pathology. Even the status of national sovereignty is questioned by a significant body of opinion-makers, who prefer transnational or what they call cosmopolitan democracy. So nationalism and the open display of patriotism is frequently treated as an embarrassment to be avoided. The declining status of nationalism in the West has been paralleled by the erosion of the normative foundation of national identity. Since the Cold War there have been constant debates about the theme of 'What does it mean to be British' – or American or French. Western societies are so concerned about the problem of 'social cohesion' and national identity that there is little appetite for the promotion of patriotism. Increasingly the metaphor of national disintegration is applied to the analysis of domestic conflicts. So a strike of lorry drivers in France in 1992 was described by *Le Monde* a case of 'social balkanisation'. At the same time a US publication wrote about the 'Lebanonisation of America'.[25] The authors of a recent report on Britain's security demands that 'our common understanding to the United Kingdom must be restored'.[26] But what does allegiance mean in the twenty-first century when society finds it so difficult to communicate a positive account of national attachments?

As we noted in Chapter 1, after the culmination of the Great War words like loyalty, heroism and honour lost some of their force. Such sentiments were provoked by a sense of betrayal and the realization that there was little that appeared honourable about the mechanically driven destruction in the trenches. D. H. Lawrence's description of a group of soldiers shooting at one another in Italy in 1914 self-consciously seeks to demystify the war of its heroic pretensions:

> What work was there to do? Only mechanically to adjust the guns and fire the shot. What was there to feel? Only the unnatural suspense and suppression of serving a machine which, for ought we knew, was killing our fellow men, whilst we stood there, blind, without knowledge or participation, subordinate to the cold machine. This was the glamour and the glory of the war: blue sky overhead and living green country all around, but we, amid it all, a part in some iron insensate will, our flesh and blood, our soul and intelligence shed away, and all that remained of us a cold, metallic adherence to an iron machine. There was neither ferocity nor joy nor exhilaration nor even quick fear: only a mechanical, expressionless movement.[27]

Today, in an age of air-to-air missiles and drones, the mechanization of warfare has surpassed anything that could be imagined in 1918.

It was only towards the end of the twentieth century that the cultural values associated with Western society in 1914 lost most of their force. Despite the best efforts of cynics and sceptics, the ideals of heroism, loyalty and honour inspired millions until well into 1960s. However, the promotion of the Loyalty Oath in the US in the 1950s indicated that this was a value that could not be taken for granted. In the 1960s the growing phenomenon of the 'drop-out' showed that many were prepared to reject a way of life. But the cultural devaluation of the values of loyalty, heroism and honour only succeeded in gaining influence over the mainstream in the late 1970s.

Back in 1914 the ideals of fighting for a cause and even risking death attracted millions of young people to their nation's cause. A century later it is unthinkable that a significant section of society could find meaning in war. As Christopher Coker explained in his *Waging War Without Warriors?*, wars have become detached from the values that influence everyday life. Wars like that of 9/11 are not so much a cause but a policy conducted for pragmatic reasons.[28] In contrast to the celebration of heroic death by romantic intellectuals in 1914, today the loss of life in combat is regarded as a 'futile waste' with little meaning.

Instead of the glorification of heroism, the ethos of safety has also become institutionalized within the military. British Army commanders now have to draw up risk assessments for every aspect of their soldiers' training. General Sir Michael Rose, former head of the SAS, has spoken out about the destructive impact of risk-aversion and the ethos of safety on the morale of the military. He has denounced the 'moral cowardice' that has encouraged what he describes as the 'most catastrophic collapse' of military ethos in recent history.[29]

From the standpoint of the contemporary cultural imagination it is unthinkable that the Great War could have any positive meaning. The very attempt to retain any empathy for the values of loyalty, patriotism or sacrifice is dismissed as a symptom of a mindless celebration of militarism. Warning against commemorating the centenary of the Great War through the prism of patriotic nostalgia, one journalist wrote:

> The scale of what we were prepared to do to one another was a shock and it inspired poets and artists to appalled eloquence, which, by the way, subsequently added to the aura of the doomed generation and, to some degree, distracted from the barbarity. Can an event that prods Owen, Sassoon, Graves, Remarque, Gurney and Nash into great art be completely bad? Their answer would have been yes. So the temptation to wallow in the sacrifice and heroism should be resisted, if only to keep straight in our minds what war on a continental scale would mean for us.[30]

In fact, at a time when the virtues of sacrifice and heroism have become objects of derision, the warning against the temptation to wallow in them is a pointless rhetorical gesture. No sooner were plans for commemorating World War One announced in the UK than officials warned against turning the event into one that was too triumphalist or patriotic.[31]

There can be little left of the illusion that insight into the problem of existence can be found in war when the values associated with heroism and sacrifice run so much against the grain of society. But while the military ethos has become marginal to twenty-first-century Western society, the quest for purpose and meaning continues to generate conflicts no less than in 1914. The crisis of self-belief and authority, which were important drivers of conflict during the years leading up to the Great War, persist to this day.

A way of life and the question of democracy

During the summer of 1914 the propaganda machines pouring out statements about their country's destiny knew what values their nations stood for.
Matters are radically different today. Since the turn of the twenty-first century
the leaders of all the major Western societies have been preoccupied with the
challenge of spelling out the values that define their society. Often statements
about such values are communicated in a manner that conveys defensiveness
and insecurity. Such sentiments are informed by the realization that contemporary societies are divided culturally and segmented into different lifestyles.
The former British Prime Minister Tony Blair was sensitive to the need to
project a clear set of values to succeed in the battle of ideas. 'When it comes to
our essential values, the belief in democracy, the rule of law, tolerance, equal
treatment for all, respect for this country and its shared heritage – then that is
where we come together, it is what gives us what we hold in common; it is what
gives us the right to call ourselves British' said Blair in December 2006.[32] He
added that 'no distinctive culture or religion supersedes our duty to be part of an
integrated United Kingdom'. That he had to write a statement to remind British
citizens of their duty to be loyal to the nation suggests that, in fact, what he
called 'our essential values' lack the moral depth to genuinely move and inspire.

As we noted earlier, the liberal values associated with democracy were one of
the main ideational casualties of World War One. Waldemar Gurian's statement
that 'liberalism has become obsolete in a period of masses' appeared as common
sense to the political and cultural elites of the West during the Great War.[33] The
rhetoric of a war fighting for democracy was always contradicted by the deeply
held conviction that the masses were far too irrational and unpredictable
to take popular consent really seriously. Support for the ideal of democracy
declined rapidly during the interwar years as Western societies opted for either
explicitly authoritarian or technocratic solutions. That everyone has to speak
the language of democracy in the twenty-first century is a consequence of the
destructive historical experience of World War Two, which led to the discrediting of an explicitly anti-democratic ethos. But fear of authoritarian rule is not
a sufficient foundation for a democratic culture to flourish. Democracy needs to
be upheld as a value in its own right, otherwise it will serve instrumental needs
and lack inspirational content.

As the institutionalization of insulated democracy in the post-World War
Two era indicates, suspicion of the masses and a rejection of popular sovereignty

persist to this date. Since 1945 the steady advance of the juridification of political life and the displacement of parliamentary decision-making by technocratic intervention serves as proof of the low esteem with which popular consent is held. For well over a century the ruling elites of all societies have understood that no government can aspire to legitimacy unless its authority is seen to be based on some form of popular consent. Resigned to having to provide some role for public opinion, governments have sought to insulate the key institutions of the state from its pressure and influence.

The paradox of universal rhetorical avowal of democracy coupled with the impulse to confine its influence was implicitly recognized even by Francis Fukuyama in his famous celebratory essay on the demise of the Cold War. Pointing to the erosion of explicitly authoritarian alternatives, he remarked that there is no ideology 'with pretensions to universality that is in the position to challenge liberal democracy' and, he added, 'no universal principle of legitimacy other than the sovereignty of the people'. Fukuyama acknowledged that democracy constitutes the only foundation for authority and concluded that 'even non-democrats will have to speak the language of democracy in order to justify their deviation from the single universal standard'.[34]

Fukuyama himself was not totally confident about the inner strength of the idea of democracy. Despite writing at the end of the Cold War, after the collapse of the Soviet Union, Fukuyama's argument is principally founded on the self-evident erosion of the appeal of other ideologies. He wrote:

> Of the different types of regimes that have emerged in the course of human history, from monarchies and aristocracies, to religious theocracies, to the fascist and communist dictatorships of this century, the only form of government that has survived intact to the end of the twentieth century has been liberal democracy.[35]

Consequently there is no ideology 'with pretensions to universality that is in the position to challenge liberal democracy' and, he added, 'no universal principle of legitimacy other than the sovereignty of the people'. And today, 'we have trouble imagining a world that is radically better than our own, or a future that is not essentially democratic or capitalist'. In other words, 'we cannot picture to ourselves a world that is *essentially* different from the present one, and at the same time better'. This loss of imagination is expressed by Fukuyama in the following terms: 'we arrive at this conclusion exhausted, as it were, from the pursuit of alternatives we felt *had* to be better than liberal democracy'.[36]

The alternatives that emerged from the ideological battles spawned during the Great War have lost their appeal. But just because they lost the battle of ideas does not mean that liberal democracy had triumphed. One important point overlooked in Fukuyama's analysis is that democracy's belief in the sovereignty of people as the 'universal principle of legitimacy' had itself become a casualty of the century-long war.

When instinctively anti-democratic people speak a language that they internally abhor, it is evident that this exercise in rhetoric lacks conviction. It is as if they are saying that we talk the talk because the other alternative narratives have been discredited. However, that everyone feels compelled to speak the language of democracy does not mean that narratives that fundamentally contradict its spirit are absent from public life. It is worth noting that in the current cultural conflicts there is little genuine support for the ideal of popular sovereignty. As I noted elsewhere, attitudes towards ordinary people are often condescending and infused with suspicion towards populism.[37] In the United States, one section regards the people as the 'silent majority' who need to be protected from the liberal elites while the other side regards them as prejudiced religious bigots whose ideas can not be taken seriously. In the EU, expressions of populist discontent are regularly treated as the pathology of the mob. Often when EU officials and their intellectual advocates discuss populism they treat it as the equivalent of an old-style fascist movement.

So when political leaders attempt uphold their society's way of life by appealing to the value of democracy, they are skating on thin ice. Democracy remains an ideal in search of conceptual clarification, intellectual validation and meaning. The evasion of this challenge in the early part of the twentieth century is at least historically excusable. But after the bitter experience of a century of conflicts, tackling the question of how to ensure that popular consent serves as the foundation for authority remains the question of our time.

The road ahead

Our story, which began in 1914, emphasized time and again the central role of the crisis of self-belief of the Western elites. This crisis was integral to the chain of events that led to August 1914 and, in turn, the Great War served to intensify it. Since the interwar decades the crisis of ruling-class belief has become hardened to the point that there is very little left of an ethos through which its authority can be articulated. Yet, if an elite is to be more than a collection of individuals who are arbitrarily propelled into a position of power, it needs to possess an *esprit de corps* – a common ethos and outlook – through which it can understand its role, express its interest, legitimate its values and inspire the public. There can be no *esprit de corps* unless there is clarity about such principles. The absence of an ethos that can bind the political elite together and provide it with a narrative to engage with citizens is a far more pervasive problem today than it was in 1914.

As I write this conclusion on 3 September 2013, the war drums are again beating, even if in a rather deflated manner. This time the target is Syria. But the call to arms lacks conviction. The political elites of the Western world are divided and are even uninhibited about demonstrating their confusion in public. The most remarkable feature of this episode is that the public is entirely switched off and is totally indifferent to the performance of fear that accompanies the war propaganda. It is evident that the political elites lack the intellectual and moral resources necessary for conducting a serious conversation with the people.

In 1914 the crisis of bourgeois self-belief was one of the key influences that created the conditions for the chain of events that led to the Great War. In the twenty-first century it is not merely one but the principal influence on the conduct of political life. Unlike the social and class conflicts of the early part of the twentieth century or the ideological struggles that paralleled it, the Culture Wars of today have as their source the internal crisis of the political elites. As we noted, the cultural tensions expressed in response to the process of rationalization are integral to the evolution of capitalist society. Such strains were expressed periodically through reactions against commerce, materialism, consumerism or modernity. With the demise of ideologies these tensions have acquire an unprecedented intensity and a more pervasive form.

The Culture Wars and the bitter conflict between competing lifestyles should be interpreted, as Bourdieu argued, as 'symbolic struggles' within the dominant classes.[38] These interminable disputes are fuelled by competing claims about the constitution of legitimacy and authority.[39] Bourdieu noted that these conflicts represent a battle of ideas that aim to 'impose the definition of the legitimate stakes and weapons of social struggles; in other words, to define the legitimate principle of domination, between economic, educational or social capital'.[40]

What's important about these symbolic struggles over the constitution of legitimate lifestyles is that they intensify the fragmentation and incoherence of social life. Periodically such struggles intrude into global affairs and increasingly disputes between nations are communicated through the language of cultural differences. Such disputes are not confined to the perennial conflict between fundamentalist and modern or religious and secular. Nations and governments are criticized for their policies on the environment, women, gay rights and a variety of other cultural issues. It is likely that such issues will provide an increasingly important medium through which international disputes will be expressed.

Today the tendency for conflicts to assume a cultural form is widely recognized. Twenty years ago, Samuel Huntington predicted that in the future the dominant source of global conflict would become cultural. He concluded that 'the clash of civilization will dominate global politics'.[41] Huntington was right to point out the significance of culture as medium for the expression of conflict. But his assertion that such conflicts will assume the form of civilizational clashes was misguided. Aside from the dubious status of civilizational narratives, it is evident that the defining feature of the contemporary world is divisions within society itself. When Huntington claimed that 'civilizational identities will replace all other identities', he overlooked the fact that such identities are constantly contested within a civilization itself.[42] Societies that are divided about the values that constitute a way of life are unlikely to unify around wider civilizational values. Instead of representing global conflicts as civilizational clashes, it makes more sense to see them as, in part, the externalized manifestation of cultural tension immanent within capitalist society. As I noted elsewhere, the phenomenon of home-grown terrorism and the estrangement of a significant section of the Muslim population from the society they inhabit points to the domestic source of some of the wider global conflicts.[43]

The tension between different claims to legitimacy – which lies at the roots of the Culture Wars – is not an inevitable outcome of modern life. The legitimation of public life requires that the question of popular sovereignty and of democratic accountability is taken seriously. For well over a century it has been recognized that the legitimacy of government is founded on the consent of the public. At the same time, this question has been avoided by political elites who lacked the confidence in their ability to motivate and inspire citizens. The absence of such confidence often disposed ruling elites to embrace anti-democratic sentiments and at least for a time during the interwar era it appeared that democracy was in peril. In response to the catastrophic events surrounding World War Two, democracy was rehabilitated and briefly it seemed possible that as an ideal it would be revitalized. Tragically this opportunity was lost and during the

Cold War little was done to develop and promote the ethos of democracy and popular sovereignty.

Since Plato's time, political theorists and philosophers have been more worried about containing the threat posed by the *demos* than in developing ideas, institutions and practices through which a genuine democratic life could flourish. There are of course honourable exceptions to this trend, but during most of the twentieth century they were conspicuous by their absence. As long as this question continues to be avoided, the Long War will never end.

Until the ideals of popular democracy are reconstituted, the road ahead will be strewn with the casualties of the symbolic struggles of the dominant classes. Most often the Culture Wars will not have direct physical and material consequences. Their main accomplishment is to exacerbate the fragmentation of social experience through the consolidation of segmented lifestyles. However, though such conflicts rarely lead to military ones, they do exact a high price. They also distract societies from confronting the challenges they face and at times tempt them to go down paths that lead to violent conflict and war. That is our future unless we re-politicize the ideal of democracy and public life and consign cultural and lifestyle issues to its margins.

Notes

1   Neumann (1946) p.7.
2   See http://mises.org/daily/2783 for a discussion of this conversation.
3   See for example Gore Vidal's book *Perpetual War for Perpetual Peace: How We Got to Be So Hated*, published in 2002.
4   Bennett (2003) p.145.
5   Buzan (2006) p.1101.
6   Meyers (2008) p.109.
7   See 'A third of US public believe 9/11 conspiracy theory', Scripps Howard News Service: 2 August 2006
8   http://www.nytimes.com/2011/05/03/opinion/03iht-edcohen03.html?_r=1 .
9   'Speech: counter-terrorism and public trust. Text of the address by Jonathan Evans, Director-General of MI5, to the Society of Editors conference in Manchester', *The Times Online*; 5 November 2007.
10 See Richard Norton-Taylor 'Counter-terrorism officials rethink stance on Muslims', *Guardian*; 20 November 2007 for a report of this story.
11 Online NewsHour, 'Campaign Snapshots', 6 August 2004, http://regimechangeiniran. com/2006/07/senator-santorum-delivers-spee/http://www.pbs.org/newshour/bb/ politics/july-dec04/snapshot_8-6.html

12 Leonard, M., Small, A., with Rose, M. (2005) *British Public Diplomacy In The 'Age of Schism'*, London: The Foreign Policy Centre, p.11.

13 See James Westhead, 'Planning the US "Long War on terror"', 10 April 2006.

14 *Seth G. Jones is Associate Director of the International Security and Defense Policy Center at the RAND Corporation*, 'Re-Examining the Al Qa'ida Threat to the United States Testimony presented before the House Foreign Affairs Committee, Subcommittee on Terrorism, Nonproliferation, and Trade on July 18, 2013, http://www.rand.org/content/dam/rand/pubs/testimonies/CT300/CT396-1/RAND_CT396-1.pdf .

15 'War on Terror' to last as long as Cold War', *Daily Telegraph*; 9 February 2010.

16 Roger Boyes, 'The Middle East Crisis is as ominous as 1914', *The Times*, 21 August 2013.

17 Baudrillard (2003) p.11.

18 Meyers (2008) p.174.

19 Meyers (2008) p.108.

20 Meyers (2008) p.163.

21 Bennett (2003) p.153.

22 Hammond (2007) p.77.

23 Neumann (1946).

24 See discussion in Furedi (1994) pp.41–3.

25 *Le Monde* article is cited in *Guardian;* 10 July 1992.

26 Prins and Salisbury (2008) p.4.

27 D. H. Lawrence 'A War of Machines', reproduced in *Observer;* 9 November 2008.

28 Coker (2002).

29 'J'Accuse! Top General lambasts "moral cowardice" of government and military chiefs', *Daily Mail*, 12 April 2007.

30 See Henry Porter, 'The Great War: we are as blind to our times as the innocent lovelorn boy was in 1913', *Observer*, 3 August 2013.

31 Rowena Mason, 'WWI commemorations must not turn into "anti-German festival", Eric Pickles warns', *Daily Telegraph;* 10 June 2013.

32 http://www.telegraph.co.uk/news/uknews/1536408/Adopt-our-values-or-stay-away-says-Blair.html .

33 Gurian (1946) p.7.

34 Fukuyama (1992) p.45.

35 Fukuyama (1992) p.45.

36 Fukuyama (1992) p.46.

37 Furedi (2005).

38 Bourdieu (2010) p.251.

39 For a wider discussion of the problem of authority, see Furedi (2013).

40 Bourdieu (2010) p.251.

41 Huntington's original article is republished in Rose (2013) p.3.

42 Huntington in Rose (2013) p.26.

43 See the discussion in Chapter 7 of Furedi (2007).

Bibliography

Adler, L. K. and Paterson, T. G. (1970) ' Red Fascism: The Merger of Nazi Germany and Soviet Russia in the American Image of Totalitarianism, 1930's–1950's', *The American Historical Review*, vol. 75, no. 4, pp. 1046–64.

Altbach, P. (1979) 'From revolution to Apathy – American student activism in the 1970s', *Higher Education*, vol. 8, issue 6, pp. 609–26.

Amendola, G. (1961) ' "The economic miracle" and the democratic alternative', *Foreign Bulletin of the Italian Communist Party*, nos. 8–9, August–September, pp. 46–7.

Anderson, P. (2000) 'Renewals', *New Left Review*, 2/1.

Arendt, H. (2006) *Between Past and Future*, Faber & Faber: London.

Aron, R. (1957) *The Opium of the Intellectuals*, Secker & Warburg: London.

—(1978) *Politics and History*, The Free Press: New York.

Bachrach, P. (1967) *The Theory of Democratic Elitism: A Critique*, Little, Brown & Co.: Boston.

Baehr, P. and Richter, M. (2004) 'Introduction', Baehr, P. and Richter, M. (eds) (2004) *Dictatorship In History And Theory*, Cambridge University Press: Cambridge.

Barry, B. (2001) *Culture and Equality; An Egalitarian Critique of Multiculturalism*, Polity Press: Cambridge.

Barzun, J. (2000) *From Dawn to Decadence: 1500 To The Present: 500 years of Western Cultural Life*, HarperCollins Publishers: London.

Bastow, S. and Martin, J. (2003) *Third Way Discourse: European Ideologies In The Twentieth Century*, Edinburgh University Press: Edinburgh.

Baudrillard, J. (2003) *The Spirit Of Terrorism, And Other Essays*, Verso Books: London.

Becker, C. L. (1941) *New Liberties For Old*, Yale University Press: New Haven.

Beckett, A. (2010) *When The Lights Went Out: What Really Happened to Britain in the Seventies*, Faber & Faber: London.

Benda, J. (1959) *The Betrayal of the Intellectuals*, Beacon Press: Boston.

Beer, S. (1982) *Britain Against Itself: The Political Contradictions Of Collectivism*, W. W. Norton & Company: New York.

Bell, D. (1972) 'The Cultural Contradictions of Capitalism', *Journal of Aesthetic Education*, vol. 6, no. 1/2, pp. 11–38.

—(1976) *The Cultural Contradictions of Capitalism*, Heinemann: London.

—(1980) *Sociological Journeys: Essays 1960-1980*. Heinemann: London.

—(1985) 'The Revolt Against Modernity', *Public Interest*, 81.

—(2000) *The End of Ideology; On the Exhaustion of Political Ideas in the Fifties*, Harvard University Press: Cambridge, MA.

Bennett, W. J. (2003) *Why We Fight: Moral Clarity and the War on Terrorism*, Regnery Publishing: Washington, DC.

Berger, S. (1979) 'Politics and Antipolitics in Western Europe in the Seventies', *Daedalus*, vol. 108, no. 1, pp. 27–50.

Berman, S. (2006) *The Primacy of Politics: social democracy and the making of Europe's twentieth century*, Cambridge University Press: Cambridge.

Birch, A. H. (1984) 'Overload, Ungovernability and Delegitimation:The Theories and the British Case', *The British Journal of Political Science*, vol. 14, no. 2, pp. 135–60.

Bird, C. (1999) *The Myth of Liberal Individualism*, Cambridge University Press: Cambridge.

Bloom, A. (1987) *The Closing of the American Mind: How Higher education Has Failed Democracy and Impoverished the Souls of Students*, Simon and Schuster: New York.

Boas, T. and Gans-Morse, J. (2009) 'Neoliberalism: From New Liberal Philosophy to Anti-Liberal Slogan', *Studies in Comparative International Development*, vol. 44, no. 2.

Bonefeld, W. (2012) 'Freedom and the Strong State: On German Ordoliberalism', *New Political Economy*, vol. 17, issue 5, pp. 633–56.

Booker, C. (1980) *The Seventies; Portrait Of a Decade*, Allen Lane: London.

Borch, C. (2012) *The Politics of Crowds: An Alternative History of Sociology*, Cambridge University Press: Cambridge.

Bourdieu, P. (2010) *Distinction: A Social Critique Of The Judgment Of Taste*, Routledge: London.

Bracher, K. D. (1984) *The Age Of Ideologies; A History of Political Thought in the Twentieth Century*, Weidenfeld and Nicolson: London.

Bracken, P. (2002) *Trauma: Culture, Meaning and Philosophy*, Whurr Publishers: London.

Braunthal, G. (1978) *Socialist labor and politics in Weimar Germany*, Archon Books: Hamden.

Brick, H. (1986) *Daniel Bell and the Decline of Intellectual Radicalism*, The University of Wisconsin Press: Madison.

Brinkley, A. (1998) *Liberalism and its Discontents*, Harvard University Press: Cambridge, MA.

—(2011) 'Conservatism as a Growing Field of Scholarship', *The Journal of American History*, vol. 98, no. 3, pp. 748–51.

Brittan, S. (1975) 'The Economic Contradictions of Democracy', *British Journal of Political Science*, vol. 5, no. 2, pp. 129–59.

Brown, N. O. (1959) *Life Against Death: The Psychoanalytical Meaning of History*, Wesleyan University Press: Middletown, CN.

Bruce-Briggs, B. (ed.) (1979) *The New Class?*, McGraw-Hill Books: New York.

Burgin, A. (2012) *The Great Persuasion: Reinventing Free Markets since the Depression*, Harvard University Press: Cambridge, MA.

Burnham, J. (1941) *The Managerial Revolution*, Putnam: London.

Buzan, B. (2006) 'Will the "global war on terrorism" be the new Cold War?', *International Affairs*, vol. 82, no. 6, pp. 1101–18.

Caldwell, P. (1997) *Popular Sovereignty and the Crisis of German Constitutional Law*, Duke University Press: Durham.

Carr, E. H. (1944) *Conditions of Peace*, Macmillan: London.

Carrillo, S. (1977) *Eurocommunism and the state*, Lawrence and Wishart: London.

Carsten, F. I. (1988) *Revolution in Central Europe, 1918–1919*, Wildwood House: Aldershot.

Ceadal, M. (1994) 'Attitudes to War: pacifism and Collective Security' in Johnson, P. (1994) (ed.) *Twentieth-Century Britain: Economic, Social And Cultural Change*, Longman: London.

Christofferson, M. S. (2004) *French Intellectuals Against The Left: The Antitotalitarian Moment of the 1970s*, Berghahn Books: New York.

Cohen, G. A. (1983) 'Forces and Relations of Production' in Matthews, B. (ed.) (1983) *Marx 100 years on*, Lawrence and Wishart: London.

Cohen, L. (2004) *A Consumers' Republic: The Politics of Mass Consumption in Postwar America*, Vintage Books: New York.

Coker, C. (2002) *Waging War Without Warriors?: The Changing Culture of Military Conflict*, Lynne Rienner: Boulder, Co.

Collier, P. and Horowitz, D. (2006) *Destructive Generation: second thoughts about the sixties*, Encounter Books: San Francisco.

Copland, D. (1953) 'Authority and Control in a Free Society', *Studies: An Irish Quarterly Review*, vol. 42, no. 167, pp. 275–92.

Crozier, M. (1975) 'Western Europe' in Crozier, M., Huntington, S. and Watanuki, J. (1975) *The Crisis of Democracy; Report on the Governability of Democracies to the Trilateral Commission*, New York University Press: New York.

Crozier, M., Huntington, S. and Watanuki, J. (1975) *The Crisis of Democracy; Report on the Governability of Democracies to the Trilateral Commission*, New York University Press: New York.

Dahl, R. (1956) *A Preface to Democratic Theory*, Chicago University Press: Chicago.

Davies, C. (1975) *Permissive Britain*, Pitman Publishing: London.

Dewey, J.(1931) *Individualism: Old And New*, George Allen & Unwin Ltd: London.

Dickstein, M. (1993) 'After the Cold War; Culture as Politics, Politics as Culture', *Social Research*, vol. 60, no. 3, pp. 531–44.

Dittberner, J. L. (1979) *The End Of Ideology and American Social Thought: 1930–1960*, UMI Research Press: Ann Arbor, MI.

Douglas, E. T. (1945) *The Annals of the American Academy of Political and Social Science*, vol. 240, pp. 7–10.

Durkheim, E. (2002) *Suicide: A Study in Sociology*, Routledge: London.

Eisenstadt, S. N. (1971) 'Generational Conflict and Intellectual Antinomianism', *Annals of the American Academy of Political and Social Science*, vol. 395, pp. 68–79.

Eksteins, M. (1989) *Rites of Spring: The Great War and the Birth of the Modern Age*, Houghton Mifflin: Boston.

Elliott, W. (1926) 'Mussolini, Prophet of the Pragmatic Era in Politics', *Political Science Quarterly*, vol. 41, no. 2, pp. 161–92.

Engerman, D. C. (2010) 'Ideology and Origins of the Cold War 1917–62' in Leffler, M. and Westad, O. A. (eds) (2010) *The Cambridge History Of The Cold War*, Cambridge University Press: Cambridge.

Favretto, I. (2003) *The Long Search for a Third Way: The British Labour Party and the Italian Left since 1945*: Palgrave Macmillan: Houndmills, Basingstoke.

Fay, S. B. (1947) 'The Idea of Progress', *The American Historical Review*, vol. 52, no. 2, pp. 231–46.

Feenberg, A. (2003) *Questioning Technology*, Routledge: London.

Fiorina, M. P. (2006) *Culture War? The Myth of a Polarized America*, Pearson Longman: New York.

Fournier, M. (2013) *Emile Durkheim; A Biography*, Polity: Cambridge.

Freeden, M. (2006) 'Ideology and political theory', *Journal of Political Ideologies*, 11:1, 3–22.

Freeman, M. and Marshall, K. (1978) *Who Needs The Labour Party?*, Junius Publications: London.

Frezza, D. (2007) *The Leader and the Crowd: Democracy In American Public Discourse, 1880–1941*, University of Georgia Press: Athens, GE.

Friedman, M. (2002) *Capitalism And Freedom*, The University of Chicago Press: Chicago and London.

Fryer, P. (1984) *Staying Power: The History of Black People in Britain*, Pluto Press: London.

Fukuyama, F. (1989) 'The End of History'? *The National Interest*, Summer.

—(1992) *The End of History And the Last Man*, The Free Press: New York.

Furedi, F. (1986) *The Soviet Union Demystified*, Junius Publications: London.

—(1994) *The New Ideology of Imperialism*, Pluto Press: London.

—(1998) *The Silent War: Imperialism and the Changing Perception of Race*, Pluto Press: London.

—(2004) *Therapy Culture: Cultivating Vulnerability In An Anxious Age*, Routledge: London.

—(2011) *On Tolerance: In Defence of Moral Independence*, Continuum Press: London.

—(2013) *Authority: A Sociological Introduction*, Cambridge University Press: Cambridge.

Furet, F. (1999) *The Passing Of An Illusion: The Idea Of Communism In The Twentieth Century*, The University of Chicago Press: Chicago.

Fussell, P. (1975) *The Great War and Modern Memory*, Oxford University Press: Oxford.

Galbraith, J. K. (1977) *The Affluent Society*, Andre Deutsch: London.

Geoghegan, V. (1996) 'Has socialism a future?' *Journal of Political Ideologies*, vol. 1, Issue 3.

Gienow-Hecht, J. (2010) 'Culture and the Cold War in Europe' in Leffler and Westad (2010).

Ginsberg, M. (1964 [originally 1921]) *The Psychology of Society*, Methuen: London.

Gollancz, V. (1946) *Our Threatened Values*, Victor Gollancz Ltd: London.

Gouldner, A. (1973) *The Coming Crisis Of Western Sociology*, Heinemann: London.

Gouldner, A. W. (1979) *The Future of Intellectuals and the Rise of the New Class*, The Macmillan Press: London.

Gurian, W. (1946) 'After World War II', *The Review of Politics*, vol. 8, no. 1, pp. 3–11.

Habermas, J. (1976) *Legitimation Crisis*, Heinemann: London.

Hall, S., Pearson, G., Samuel, R. and Taylor, C. (1957) 'Editorial', in *Universities & Left Review*, vol. 1, no. 1, Spring, no pagination.

Hallock, S. (2012) *The World in the 20th Century*, Pearson Education: London.

Hallowell, J. H. (1946) *The Decline of Liberalism As An Ideology*, Kegan Paul, Trench, Trubner & Co. Ltd: London.

Hammond, D. and Hammond, C. (2008) 'Means and Ends in Post-War Liberalism', Paper given at *Second Annual Conference on the History of Recent Economics Technical University of Lisbon*, 5–7 June 2008.

Hancock, W. K. (1950) *Wealth of Colonies*, Cambridge University Press: Cambridge.

Hand, M. and Pearce, J. (2009), 'Patriotism in British Schools: Principles, practices and press hysteria', *Educational Philosophy and Theory*, vol. 41, pp. 453–65.

Hayek, F. A. (1949) in de Huszar, G. B. (ed.) (1960) *The Intellectuals: A Controversial Portrait*, The Free Press: Glencoe, IL.

—(1986 [originally published 1944]) *The Road To Serfdom*, Routledge & Kegan Paul: London

Hayes, C. (1940) 'The Novelty of Totalitarianism in the History of Western Civilization', *Proceedings of the American Philosophical Society*, vol. 82, no. 1, pp. 91–102.

Heale, M. J. (2005) 'The Sixties as History: A review of the Political Historiography', *Reviews in American History*, vol. 33, no. 1, pp. 133–52.

Herf, J. (1981) 'Modernism: Some Ideological Origins of the Primacy of Politics in the Third Reich', *Theory and Society*, vol. 10, no. 6, pp. 805–32.

Hewison, R. (1981) *In Anger; British Culture in the Cold War 1945–60*, Oxford University Press: New York.

Hobsbawm, E. (2004) *The Age of Extremes: The Short Twentieth Century, 1914–1991*, Abacus Books: London.

Hopkins, H. (1963) *New Look: A Social History Of The Forties And Fifties In Britain*, Secker & Warburg: London.

Horne, J. (2010a) 'Introduction', Horne, J. (ed.) (2010) *A Companion To World War I*, Blackwell Publishing: Oxford.

Horowitz, D. A. (2003) *America's Political Class Under Fire: The Twentieth Century's Great Culture War*, Routledge: London.

—(2005) *The Anxieties of Affluence: Critiques of American Consumer Culture, 1939–1979*, University of Massachusetts Press: Amherst.

Hughes, H. S. (1951) 'The End of Political Ideology', *Measure*, no. 2, pp. 153–4.

Hunter, J. D. (1991) *Culture Wars; The Struggle To Define America*, Basic Books: New York.

Huntington, S. (1975) 'The United States', in Crozier, M., Huntington, S. and Watanuki, J. (1975) *The Crisis of Democracy; Report on the Governability of Democracies to the Trilateral Commission*, New York University Press: New York.

Huntington, S. P. (1996) *The Clash of Civilizations and the Remaking of World Order*, Simon & Schuster: New York.

de Huszar, G. B. (ed.) (1960) *The Intellectuals: A Controversial Portrait*, The Free Press: Glencoe, Ill.

Hynes, S. (1991) *The War Imagined: The First World War and English Culture*, Atheneum: New York.

Inglehart, R. (1977) *The Silent Revolution: Changing Values and Political Styles Among Western Publics*, Princeton University Press: Princeton.

—(1981) 'Post-Materialism in an Environment of Insecurity', *The American Political Science Review*, vol. 75, no. 4, pp. 880–900.

—(2008) 'Changing Values among Western Publics from 1970 to 2006', *West European Politics*, vol. 31, nos. 1–2, pp. 130–46.

Judt, T. (2007) *Postwar: A History Of Europe Since 1945*, Random House: London.

Kaegi, W. (1968) 'Freedom and Power In History', in Krieger, L. and Stern, F. (1968) *The Responsibility of Power*, Macmillan: London.

Kahan, A. S. (2001) *Aristocratic Liberalism: The Social and Political Thought of Jacob Burckhart, John Stuart Mill and Alexis de Tocqueville*, Transaction Publishers: New Brunswick, NJ.

Kahan, A. S. (2010) *Mind vs Money: The War between Intellectuals and Capitalism*, Transaction Publishers: New Brunswick.

Katznelson, I. (2013) *Fear Itself*, Liveright Publishing Corporation: New York.

Kazin, M. (1995) *The Populist Persuasion: An American History*, Cornell University Press: Ithaca, NY.

Koestler, A. (1983) *The Yogi and the Commissar and Other Essays*, Hutchinson: London.

Kohn. H. (1929) *A History of Nationalism in the East*, George Routledge & Sons Ltd: London.

—(1932) *Nationalismand Imperialism in the Hither East*, George Routledge & Sons: London.

—(1964) 'Political Theory and the History of Ideas', *Journal of the History of Ideas*, vol. 25, no. 2, pp. 303–7.

—(1966) *Political Ideologies of the Twentieth Century*, Harper & Row: New York.

Kolko, G. (1968) *The Politics of War: The World and United States Foreign Policy 1943–1945*, Vintage Books: New York.

—(1994) *Century Of War: Politics, Conflict and Society Since 1914*, The New Press: New York.

Kramer, A. (2007) *Dynamics of Destruction: Culture and Mass Killing in the First World War*, Oxford University Press: Oxford.

Kramer, H. (2000) *The Twilight of the Intellectuals: Culture And Politics In The Era Of The Cold War*, Ivan R. Dee: Chicago.

Krieger, L. (1977) 'The Idea of Authority in the West', *The American Historical Review*, vol. 82, no. 2. pp. 249–70.

Krieger, L and Stern, F. (1968) *The Responsibility of Power*, Macmillan: London.

Kristol, I. (1972) *On The Democractic Idea In America*, Harper & Row: New York.

—(1973) 'Capitalism, Socialism and Nihilism', *Public Interest*, issue 31.

—(1979) 'Adversarial Culture and Intellectuals', *Encounter*, October.

Laidi, Z. (1998) *A World Without Meaning: The Crisis Of Meaning In International Politics*, Routledge: London.

Lasch, C. (1969) *The Agony of the American Left*, W. W. Norton & Company: New York.

—(1984) *The Minimal Self; Psychic Survival in Troubled Times*, W. W. Norton & Company: New York.

—(1991) *The True And Only Heaven*, W. W. Norton & Company: New York.

Laski, H. (1919) *Authority in The Modern State* Yale University Press: Yale.

Lassiter, M. D. (2011) 'Political History beyond the Red-Blue Divide', *The Journal of American History*, vol. 98, no. 3.

Lasswell, H. D. (1935) 'The Person: Subject and Object of Propaganda', *Annals of the American Academy of Political and Social Science*, vol. 179, pp. 187–93.

Leffler, M. and Westad, O. A. (eds) (2010) *The Cambridge History Of The Cold War, Vol. 1 Origins*, Cambridge University Press: Cambridge.

— (eds) (2010a) *The Cambridge History of the Cold War, Vol. 3: Endings 1975–1991*, Cambridge University Press: Cambridge.

Lemke. T. (2001) 'The birth of bio-politics': Michel Foucault's lecture at the Collège de France on neo-liberal governmentality, *Economy and Society*, vol. 30, no. 2, pp. 190–207.

Leonard, M., Small, A. and Rose, M. (2005) *British Public Diplomacy in the 'Age of Schisms'*, The Foreign Policy Centre: London.

Lipset, S. M. (1964) *Political Man*, Mercury Books: London.

Lipset, S. M. and Dobson, R. B. (1972) 'The Intellectual as Critic and Rebel: with special reference to the United States and the Soviet Union', *Daedalus*, vol. 101, no. 3, pp. 137–98.

Loewenstein, K. (1935) 'Autocracy Versus Democracy in Contemporary Europe', *The American Political Science Review*, vol. 29, no. 4, pp. 571–93.

—(1937) 'Militant Democracy and Fundamental Rights, part 1', *The American Political Science Review*, vol. 31, no. 3, pp. 417–32.

—(1937a) 'Militant Democracy and Fundamental Rights, part 2', *The American Political Science Review*, vol. 31, no. 4, pp. 638–58.

Maier, C. S. (1977) 'The Politics of Productivity: Foundations of American International Economic Policy after World War II', *International Organisation*, vol. 31, no. 4, pp. 607–13.

—(1981) 'The two postwar eras and the conditions for stability in twentieth-century Western Europe', *American Historical Review*, vol. 86, no. 2, pp. 327–52.

—(2000) 'Consigning the Twentieth Century to History: Alternative Narratives for the Modern Era', *The American Historical Review*, vol. 105, no. 3, pp. 807–31.

Malia, M. E. (1972) 'The Intellectuals: Adversaries or Clerisy?', *Daedalus*; vol. 101, no. 3, pp. 206–16.

Mann, T. (2005) *The Magic Mountain*, Everyman: New York.

Mannheim, K. (1943) *Diagnosis Of Our Time: Wartime Essays of a Sociologist*, Routledge & Kegan Paul Ltd: London.

Marwick, A. (1998) *The Sixties: Cultural Revolution in Britain, France, Italy and the United States, c.1958–1974*, Oxford University Press: Oxford.

Matthews, B. (1930) *The Clash of Colour; A Study In The Problem Of Race*, Edinburgh House Press: London.

May, H. F. (1992) *The End of American Innocence: A Study of the First Years of our Time, 1912–1917*, Knopf: New York.

Mayall, J. (1990) *Nationalism and International Society*, Cambridge University Press: Cambridge.

Mayer, A. (1967) 'The Primacy of Domestic Politics' in Krieger, L. and Stern, F. (eds) (1967) *The Responsibility of Power: Historical Essays In Honor Of Hajo Holborn*, Doubleday: Garden City, NY.

—(1969) 'Internal Causes and Purposes of War in Europe, 1870–1956: A Research Assignment', *The Journal of Modern History*, vol. 41, no. 3, pp. 291–303.

Mazower, M. (1999) *Dark Continent: Europe's Twentieth Century*, Penguin Books: London.

McAuliffe, M. S. (1978) *Crisis on the Left: Cold War Politics and the American Liberals, 1947–1954*, The University of Massachusetts Press: Amherst.

McGirr, L. (2011) *The Origins of the New American Right*, Princeton University Press: Princeton.

McNeill, W. (1970) 'World History', in Ballard, M. (ed.) (1970) *New Movements in the Study and Teaching of History*, Temple Smith: London.

—(1990) 'Winds of Change', *Foreign Affairs*, Fall, pp. 159–67.

McNight, D. (2005) *Beyond Right And Left: New Politics And The Culture Wars*, Allen & Unwin: Crows Nest.

Meyers, P. A. (2008) *Civic War and the Corruption of the Citizen*, University of Chicago Press: Chicago.

Milbrath, L. W. (1965) *Political Participation*, Rand McNally: Chicago.

Mills, C. W. (1959) *The Causes of World War Three*, Secker & Warburg: London.

—(1959a) *The Sociological Imagination*, Oxford University Press: New York.

Milward, A. S. (1984) *The Reconstruction Of Western Europe 1945–51*, Methuen & Co. Ltd: London.

Mommsen, H. (1981) 'Totalitarian Dictatorship versus Comparative Theory of Fascism', in Menze, E. A. (ed.) (1981) *Totalitarianism Reconsidered*, Kennikat Press: Port Washington: New York.

Mommsen, W. (1984) *Max Weber and German Politics, 1890–1920*, University of Chicago: Chicago.

Money, L. C. (1925) *The Peril of the White*, W. Collins and Sons: London.

Moore, B. (1967) 'The Society Nobody Wants: A Look Beyond Marxism and Liberalism', in Wolff, K. H. and Moore, B. (1967) *The Critical Spirit: Essays in Honor of Herbert Marcuse*, Beacon Press: Boston.

Morgan, D. and Evans, M. (1993) *The Battle for Britain: Citizenship and Ideology in the Second World War*, Routledge: London.

Morris-Jones, W. H. (1954) 'In Defense of Apathy', *Political Studies*, vol. 2, pp. 25–37.

Mouffe, C. (1998) 'The radical centre; a politics without adversary', *Soundings*, issue 9, pp. 11–23.

Mudde, C. (2004) 'The Populist Zeitgeist', *Government and Opposition*, vol. 39, issue 4.

Müller, J.-W. (2009) 'The triumph of what (if anything)? Rethinking political ideologies and political institutions in twentieth-century Europe', *Journal of Political Ideologies*, vol. 14, no. 2, pp. 211–26.

—(2010a) 'The Cold War and the Intellectual History of the Late Twentieth Century', in Leffler, M. P. and Westad, O. A. (2010) (eds) *The Cambridge History of the Cold War, Vol. 3: Endings 1975–1991*, Cambridge University Press: Cambridge.

—(2011) 'European Intellectual History as Contemporary History', *Journal of Contemporary History*, vol. 46, no. 3, pp. 574–90.

—(2012) 'Beyond Militant Democracy', *New Left Review*, 73.

—(2013) *Contesting Democracy: Political Ideas In Twentitieth Century Europe*, Yale University Press: New Haven.

Nelson, E. (1989) *The British Counter-Culture, 1996–73*, Macmillan: Houndsmills.

Neumann, S. (1946) *The Future in Perspective*, Putnam's Sons: New York.

—(1949) 'The International Civil War', *World Politics*, vol. 1, no. 3 pp. 333–50.

Nisbet, R. (1985) 'The Conservative Renaissance In Perspective', *The Public Interest*, no. 81, pp. 134–5.

Nordau, M. (1913) *Degeneration*, William Heinemann: London.

Offe, C. (1980) 'The separation of Form and Content in Liberal Democractic Politics', *Studies in Political Economy*, vol. 3, pp. 5–16.

Oldham, J. H. (1924) *Christianity and Race Problem*, Student Christian Movement: London.

Oliver, K. (1999) 'Post-Industrial Society and the Psychology of the American Far Right, 1950–74', *Journal of Contemporary History*, vol. 34, no. 4, pp. 601–18.

Overy, R. (2009) *The Morbid Age: Britain Between the Wars*, Allen Lane: London.

Packer, G. (2003) 'Introduction: Living Up to It', in Packer, G. (2003) (ed.) *The Fight is for Democracy: Winning the War of Ideas in America and the World*, HarperCollins: New York.

Palmer, P. A. (1967) 'The Concept of Public Opinion in Political Theory', in McIlwain, C. H. (1967) *Essays In History And Political Theory; In Honor Of Charles Howard McIlwain*, Russell & Russell ; New York.

Parsons, T. (1963a) 'Christianity and modern industrial society', in Tiryakian, E. A. (1963) (ed.) *Sociological Theory, Values, and Social-Cultural Change*, The Free Press: New York.

Parsons, T. (1964) 'Democracy and Social Structure in Pre-Nazi Germany', in Parsons, T. (1964) *Essays In Sociological Theory*, The Free Press: Glencoe.

Parsons, W. (1982) 'Politics Without Promises: the Crisis of "Overload" and Governability', *Parliamentary Affairs*, vol. 35, no. 4, pp. 421–35.

Pells, R. H. (1985) *The Liberal Mind in a Conservative Age: American Intellectuals in the 1940s and 1950s*, Harper & Row: New York.

Pennell, C. (2012) *A Kingdom United: Popular Responses to the Outbreak of the First World War in Britain and Ireland*, Oxford University Press: Oxford.

Pfaff, W. (1993) *The Wrath of Nations*, Simon and Schuster: New York.

Pharr, S. J. and Putnam, R. D. (eds) (2000) *What's Troubling the Trilateral Democracies?*, Princeton University Press: Princeton.

Pharr, S. J., Putnam, R. D. and Dalton, R. J. (2000) 'A Quarter-Century of Declining Confidence', *Journal of Democracy*, vol. 11, no. 2, pp. 5–25.

Phillips-Fein, K. (2011) 'Conservatism: A State of the Field', *The Journal of American History*, vol. 98, no. 3, pp. 723–43.

Piccone, P. (1999) '21st Century Politics', *Telos*, Fall, no. 117, pp. 185–90.

Pietila, K. (2011) *Reason of Sociology: George Simmel and Beyond*, Sage: London.

Plumb, J. H. (1986) *The Death of the Past*, Macmillan: London.

Podhoretz, N. (1979) 'The Adversary Culture And The New Class', Bruce-Briggs, B. (1979) (ed.) *The New Class?*, McGraw-Hill Books: New York.

Prins, G. and Salisbury, R. (2008) *Risk, Threat and Security; The case of the United Kingdom*, RUSI: London.

Proudman, M. F. (2005) ' "The stupid party": Intellectual repute as a category of ideological analysis', *Journal of Political Ideologies*, vol. 10, no. 2, pp. 199–217.

Putnam, R. D., Pharr, S. J. and Dalton, R. J. 'Introduction: What's Troubling the Trilateral Democracies?' in Pharr, S. J. and Putnam, R. D. (eds) (2000) *What's Troubling the Trilateral Democracies?*, Princeton University Press: Princeton.

Raico, R. (1997) 'Keynes and the Reds', *The Free* Market, vol. 15, no. 4, available http://mises.org/freemarket_detail.aspx?control=136http://mises.org/freemarket_detail.aspx?control=136

Rich, P. (1989) 'Imperial Decline and the resurgence of British national identity', in Kushner, T. and Lunn, K. (eds) (1989) *Traditions of Intolerance*, Manchester University Press: Manchester.

Richards, F. (1987) 'The Myth of State Capitalism', *Confrontation*, no. 2, pp. 87–114.

Riesman, D. (1954) *Individualism Reconsidered*, Free Press: Glencoe.

Rizzi, B. (1985) *The Bureaucratisation of the World*, The Free Press: New York.

Roberts, M. (1941) *The Recovery of the West*, Faber & Faber Limited: London.

Robin, R. (2001) *The Making of the Cold War Enemy; Culture and Politics in the Military-Intellectual Complex*, Princeton University Press: Princeton.

Ropke, W. (1958) *A Humane Economy; The Social Framework of the Free Market*, Oswald Wolff Ltd: London.

Rose, G. (ed.) (2003) *The Clash of Civilizations?: The Debate: Twentieth Anniversary Edition*, Foreign Affairs: New York.

Ross, E. A. (1945)'The Post-War Intellectual Climate', *American Sociological Review*, vol. 10, no. 5, pp. 648–50.

Roszak, T. (1970) *The Making Of A Counter Culture: Reflections on the Technocratic Society*, Faber & Faber: London.

Salvati, B. (1972) 'The rebirth of Italian trade unionism 1943–54' in Woolf, S. (ed.) (1972) *The Rebirth of Italy 1943–50*, Humanitas Press: New York.

Sartori, G. (1975) 'Will Democracy Kill Democracy? Decision-Making by Majorities and by Committees', *Government and Opposition*, vol. 10, no. 2, pp. 131–58.

Sartre, J. P. *The Reprieve*, Vintage Books: New York.

Sassoon, D. (2000) 'Socialism in the twentieth century: an historical reflection', *Journal of Political Ideologies*, vol. 5, no. 1, pp. 17–34.

Schefold, B. (1980) 'The General Theory for a totalitarian state? a note on Keynes's preface to the German edition of 1936', *Cambridge Journal of Economics*, vol. 4, no. 2, pp. 175–6.

Schlesinger, A. M. (1949) *The Vital Center*, Houghton Mifflin: Boston.

Schmitt, C. (1988) The Crisis of Parliamentary Democracy. The MIT Press: Cambridge, MA.

Schumpeter, J. A. (1976) *Capitalism, Socialism and Democracy*, George Allen & Unwin: London.

Scott-Smith, G. (2002) 'The Congress for Cultural Freedom, the End of Ideology and the 1955 Milan Conference: "Defining the Parameters of Discourse"', *Journal of Contemporary History*, vol. 37, no. 3. pp. 437–55.

Shannon, C. (2001) *A World Made Safe for Differences: Cold War Intellectuals and the Politics of Identity*, Rowman & Littlefield Publishers: Lanham, MD.

Shepard, W. J. (1935) 'Democracy in Transition', *The American Political Science Review*, vol. 29, no. 1, pp. 1–20.

Shils, E. (1955) 'The End of Ideology?', *Encounter*, November.

—(1972) *The Intellectuals and the Powers and Other Essays*, The University of Chicago Press: Chicago.

Shonfield, A. (1965) *Modern Capitalism; the changing balance of public and private power*, Oxford University Press: Oxford.

Simmel, G. (1990) *The Philosophy of Money*, Routledge: London.

Singh, N. P. (1998) 'Culture/Wars: Recoding Empire in an Age of Democracy', *American Quarterly*, 50, 3.

Soffer, R. (1987) 'Nation, Duty, Character and Confidence: History at Oxford, 1850–1914', *The Historical Journal*, vol. 30, no. 1, pp. 77–104.

Sontag, R. (1971) *A Broken World: 1919–1939*, Harper & Row: New York.

Spengler, O. (1926) *Decline of the West*, George Allen & Unwin: London.

Stanley, B. (1990) *The Bible and the Flag*, Appolos: Leicester.

Stern, F. (1974) *The Politics of Cultural Despair*, University of California Press: Berkeley.

Sternhell, Z. (2008) 'How To Think About Fascism and Its Ideology', *Constellations*, vol. 15, issue 3, pp. 280–90.

Stewart, W. K. (1928) 'The Mentors Of Mussolini', *The American Political Science Review*, vol. 22, no. 4.

Strachey, J. (1934) *The Coming Struggle For Power*, Victor Gollancz Ltd: London.

Suri, J. (2009) 'The Rise and Fall of an International Counter-Culture', *The American Historical Review*, vol. 114, no. 1.

Symonds, R. (1991) *Oxford and Empire: The last lost cause?*, Clarendon Press: Oxford.

Talshir, G. (1998) 'Modular ideology: the Implications of Green theory for a reconceptualization of "ideology"', *Journal of Political Ideologies*, vol. 3, no. 2, pp. 169–93.

Taviss Thomson, I. (2010) *Culture Wars and Enduring American Dilemmas*, University of Michigan Press: Ann Arbor.

Taylor, A. J. P. (1966) *From Sarajevo To Potsdam*, Thames and Hudson: London.

Thornton, A. P. (1959) *The Imperial Idea And Its Enemies: A Study in British Power*, Macmillan: London.

Tinbergen, J. (1965) 'Convergence of Economic Systems in East and West', *Research on the International Economics of Disarmament and Arms Control*, Oslo Conference August, pp. 29–31.

Tonnies, F. (1955) *Community and Association*, Routledge & Kegan Paul Ltd: London.

Trilling, L. (1964) *The Liberal Imagination: Essays On Literature And Society*, Mercury Books: London.

—(1965) *Beyond Culture*, Viking Press: New York.

Tucker, S. and Roberts, M. R. (eds) (2005) *The Encyclopedia of World War I: A Political, Social, and Military History*, ABC Clio Ltd: Oxford.

Turner, C. H. (1923) *Public Opinion and World Peace*, ILCA: Washington, DC.

Valery, P. (1927) *Variety*, Harcourt Brace: New York.

Walker, J. L. (1966) 'A Critique of the Elitist Theory of Democracy', *The American Political Science Review*, vol. 60, no. 2, pp. 285–95.

Wallas, G. (1929) *Human Nature In Politics*, Constable & Co.: London

Webb, S. and Webb, B. (1937) *Soviet Communism, a new civilization?*, Longmans: London.

Weber, M. (1915) 'Religious rejections of the world and their directions' in Gerth, H. H. and Wright Mills, C. W. (eds) (1958) *From Max Weber: Essays in Sociology*, Galaxy Books: New York.

—(1919) 'Politics as a Vocation' in Gerth, H. H. and Mills, C. W. (eds) (1958) *From Max Weber: Essays in Sociology*, Galaxy Books: New York.

Weltman, D. (2003) 'From Political Landscape to Political Timescape; The Third Way and the ideological imagining of political change and continuity', *Time and Society*, vol. 12, no. 2/3.

Westad, O. A. (2010) 'The Cold War and the international history of the twentieth century', in Leffler, M. and Westad, O. A. (eds) (2010) The Cambridge History of the Cold War, Cambridge University Press, Cambridge.

Whitfield, S. J. (1996) *The Culture of The Cold War*, The Johns Hopkins University Press: Baltimore.

Wiener, P. (1945) *Martin Luther. Hitler's Spiritual Ancestor*, Hutchinson: London

Wilkin, R. N. (1945) 'The Science of Peace', *Journal of the American Judicature Society*, vol. 29, pp. 115–24.

Willets, D. (1992) *Modern Conservatism*, Penguin Books: London.

Willoughby, W. W. (1930) *The Ethical Basis of Political Authority*, The Macmillan Company: New York.

Wilson, F. (1937) 'The Prelude to Authority', *The American Political Science Review*, vol. 31, no. 1.

—(1955) 'Public Opinion and the Middle Class', *The Review of Politics*, vol. 17, no. 4.

Winner, L. (1977) *Autonomous Technology: Technics-out-of-Control as a Theme in Political Thought*, The MIT Press: Cambridge, MA.

Winter, J. and Prost, A. (2005) *The Great War In History: Debates And Controversies, 1914 to the Present*, Cambridge University Press: Cambridge.

Wirth, L. (1936) 'Preface' to Mannheim, K. (1960) *Ideology and Utopia*, Routledge & Kegan Paul: London.

Wolin, R. (2010) *French Intellectuals, the Cultural Revolution, and the Legacy of the 1960s*, Princeton University Press: Princeton.

Wolpert, J. F. (1950) 'Towards A Sociology Of Authority' in Gouldner, A. (ed.) (1950) *Studies In Leadership: Leadership and Democratic Action*, Harper & Brothers: New York.

Zieger, Robert (2004) ' "Uncle Sam wants You…to Go Shopping": A Consumer Society Responds to National Crisis, 1957–2001', *Canadian Review of American Studies*, vol. 34, no. 1.

Zweig, S. (1953) *The World of Yesterday*, Cassell: London.

Index